Struggle and Survival
on Wall Street

Struggle and Survival on Wall Street

THE ECONOMICS OF COMPETITION AMONG SECURITIES FIRMS

John O. Matthews

New York   Oxford
OXFORD UNIVERSITY PRESS
1994

Oxford University Press

Oxford—New York   Toronto
Delhi   Bombay   Calcutta   Madras   Karachi
Kuala Lumpur   Singapore   Hong Kong   Tokyo
Nairobi   Dar es Salaam   Cape Town
Melbourne   Auckland   Madrid

and associated companies in
Berlin   Ibadan

Published by Oxford University Press, Inc.
200 Madison Avenue, New York, New York 10016

Oxford is a registered trademark of Oxford University Press

Library of Congress Cataloging-in-Publication Data
Matthews, John O.
Struggle and survival on Wall Street : the economics of
competition among securities firms / John O. Matthews.
p.   cm.   Includes bibliographical references and index.
ISBN 0-19-505063-0
1. Securities industry—United States.   I. Title.
HG4910.M353 1994   332.64'273—dc20   93-98

Page v constitutes a continuation of the copyright page.

9 8 7 6 5 4 3 2 1

Printed in the United States of America
on acid-free paper

Grateful acknowledgment is made to the following for permission to reprint previously published material.

Elsevier Science Publishers: *Journal of Financial Economics* and *Journal of Banking and Finance*

Greenwich Associates

Institutional Investor

McGraw-Hill, Inc.: Reprinted from May 18, 1981, issue of *Securities Week* by special permission, copyright © 1981 by McGraw-Hill, Inc.; Reprinted from August 8, 1977, issue of *Business Week* by special permission, copyright © 1977 by McGraw-Hill, Inc.; Reprinted from June 10, 1991, issue of *Business Week* by special permission, copyright © 1991 by McGraw-Hill, Inc.

The MIT Press

National Association of Securities Dealers, Inc.: Reprinted with permission from the *1992 Fact Book & Company Directory.* © 1992 National Association of Securities Dealers, Inc. All rights reserved

The New York Times. Copyright © 1985 by the New York Times Company

The Rand Journal of Economics. Copyright 1977. Reprinted with permission of Rand

The Securities Industry Association

Turner Broadcasting System. © 1991 Cable News Network, Inc. All rights reserved

Preface

This book is about one of the most important industries in the United States: the broker-dealer industry. Broker-dealers, or securities firms, provide access to stock and bond markets for investors and issuers. The effectiveness with which these markets allocate capital to competing uses determines the overall growth and efficiency of the economy itself.

This industry, compared with other financial service industries, has been underanalyzed by economists, perhaps because there are few data available about the industry. Relatively few securities firms are publicly owned, and several of the most important firms went public only in the 1980s.

It is worthwhile examining this complex and relatively esoteric industry for at least three reasons. First, U.S. securities firms are clearly world leaders in this global industry because they are more innovative and dynamic than any other country's securities firms. They therefore present an excellent case study of how firms adapt to rapidly changing conditions. Second, the industry is a regulated industry with the U.S. Securities and Exchange Commission as its principal regulator. One of the fundamental recommendations of this book is that the regulators continue to provide a framework that allows these firms to adapt and compete effectively in domestic and international markets. Third, the positive performance of the broker-dealer industry relative to that of the banking and savings and loan industries in the 1980s may provide some insights into the past and lessons for the future for the financial services industries.

This book is an industry study within the industrial organization field of economics, and is accessible to a wide variety of readers who have an interest in the securities industry. Although the book assumes some basic knowledge of economics, extensive training is not assumed. The book will be of interest to economists who specialize in industrialization organization, finance, financial institutions, money and banking, and regulated industries. In addition, securities and other financial industry professionals, regulators, students of financial services, members of the securities bar, corporate financial officers, and sophisticated investors will find this book useful.

This book is the extension of a research topic suggested to me by Erwin Blackstone. He, together with Andrew Buck and the late David Meinster, all of Temple University, supported my early work on this project with advice, encouragement, and criticism.

Most of the understanding I have of the industry I owe to the men and women of the SEC's Directorate of Economic and Policy Analysis, with whom I worked from 1977 to 1984. I would particularly like to thank Jeffry Davis, Hugh Haworth, Charles Bryson, William Dale, Vance Anthony, Ulysses Lupien, Terry Chuppe, William Atkinson, Lois Lightfoot, Peter Martin, and Carolyn Gordon for their help and encouragement. I would also like to salute their strong commitment to bring critical economic analysis to bear on the issues facing the Commission.

I would also like to express special thanks to Gene Finn, former chief economist at the SEC and currently chief economist at the National Association of Securities Dealers, for his continuing efforts to teach me about the industry.

My appreciation is also expressed to my colleagues at Villanova University who have supported this effort, including Charles Zech, Wilfred Dellva, John Leonard, Cathy Rusinko, and Alvin Clay. Very special thanks go to Eleanor Dulin for her cheerful cooperation through the typing of ever-changing drafts.

John Kolmer of the First Boston Corporation, George Piper of G. W. Piper and Co., Joseph Rizzello of the Philadelphia Stock Exchange, and James Shapiro of the New York Stock Exchange all were very generous in providing me with insights into the industry.

Gene Finn, Vance Anthony, and John Leonard went the extra mile by reading early drafts of the manuscript and contributing valuable criticisms. I also am indebted to Jeffry Davis; William Dale; Hans Stoll and John Siegfried, both of Vanderbilt University; and William Freund of Pace University for useful comments on specific chapters.

My thanks also go to Mary A. McLaughlin for her support and encouragement during the writing of the book.

I owe an enormous debt of gratitude to Herbert Addison of Oxford University Press, who took an early interest in the study and provided encouragement as I tried to keep up with a rapidly changing industry, and to Irene Pavitt, whose high standards and tight editing were important in making this book what it is.

Any errors, of course, are my responsibility.

Villanova, Pa.   J.O.M.
February 1993

Contents

I

Introduction
to the Securities Industry

1

Introduction

More than 51 million Americans are direct owners of corporate shares and stock mutual funds. In addition to these direct owners, in 1985 more than 150 million more people owned stock indirectly through such assets as life insurance policies, pension plans, and bank trust accounts.

The buying and selling of stocks and bonds are, for the most part, conducted through the securities industry. In this country, securities firms have provided intermediation services for investors for over 200 years, of which the last 20 years have seen more change than the previous 180 years. First, deregulation has obligated securities firms to operate in highly competitive markets in which only the most efficient and innovative can prosper. Second, technical advances have lowered data-processing and communications costs, opened new markets, and facilitated instantaneous, worldwide links among the world's financial capitals, including New York, London, and Tokyo. And third, financial markets have become more volatile, and so the environment in which these firms operate is more risky. How the industry has changed in order to deal with this increasing risk is a major theme of this book.

The securities industry operates within a complex regulatory framework, with the U.S. Securities and Exchange Commission (SEC) as its principal regulator. The objective of this study is to compare the industry's changing economic environment with the existing regulatory structure.

The activities of securities firms that deal with the public are our main concern. The other significant players in a more broadly defined securities industry, such as the securities exchanges, exchange specialists, floor brokers on the exchanges, and other brokers and dealers who do not deal with the public, are included in this study only as supporting players. Rather, the focus of this book is the 5,400 securities firms that have registered with the SEC as brokers doing a public business. Such firms are usually called *broker-dealers* and range from large worldwide firms like Merrill Lynch, Salomon Brothers, and Morgan Stanley to the small one-person mutual fund sales office.

To cope with the increasing riskiness of the industry, firms rely on several approaches: They use the new financial instruments developed on the options and futures exchanges to hedge some of this risk, and they use new products and new lines of business that provide a more diversified revenue stream. In this new environment, innovation is one of the most important forms of competition among the largest firms—that is, the national full-line firms and the large investment bankers. The regional firms generally followed the lead of these larger firms in adopting innovative products and services. These new products and services developed in the 1970s and 1980s led to the creation of multibillion-dollar markets in mortgage- and asset-backed securities, high-yield (or junk) bonds, and derivative securities. To those firms that were early entrants, these new products have proved highly profitable.

DESIGN OF THE STUDY

An industrial organization analysis of an industry systematically determines both how the industry operates and how government policies affect the industry. We will consider the following elements:

Structure   (1) number and size of sellers, (2) barriers to entry, (3) cost and technology considerations of production, (4) extent of integration and diversification of firms, (5) size and nature of buyers, and (6) structure of demand for industry products.

Behavior   (1) pricing policies, (2) advertising and marketing approaches, (3) innovation and diversification practices, and (4) strategies followed by firms and groups of firms.

Performance   (1) size of profits, (2) risk levels of industry firms, (3) firm stability, and (4) dynamic and allocational efficiency.

The structure, conduct, and performance approach was developed by Mason (1939, 1949) and his colleagues and students, such as Bain (1959). Traditional industrial organization theory assumes a causal flow from structure to conduct to performance, although there also can be strong feedback effects. Firms that are frequent innovators can capture a larger share of the market and alter the industry's concentration. In addition, because structure, conduct, and performance are constantly interacting with one another, they cannot be truly separated analytically. For example, conditions of entry are part of structure, but the behavior of incumbent firms can affect entry.

Our analysis will also incorporate those insights into industry structure developed by Baumol, Panzar, and Willig in their book *Contestable Markets and the Theory of Industry Structure* (1982). The theory of contestable markets is a generalization of the theory of perfect competition. It attempts to extend the theory of perfect competition to a world characterized by firms with multiple lines of business. The theory focuses on cost structures, principally multiproduct cost structures, to identify the properties of those costs that influence industry structure, cost-minimizing configurations, and market performance.

Baumol, Panzar, and Willig emphasize that industries with only a few firms can be very competitive if there is a threat of entry by other firms. Those markets in which there are a few firms but in which others will enter if prices exceed costs are called *contestable markets*. Both exit and entry are emphasized. That is, firms will be reluctant to enter an industry if it is very costly to exit. If entry or exit is difficult, a market is not contestable, and the strategic behavior of firms becomes relevant to analysis. If entry and exit are easy, a market is contestable and can have the properties of a competitive market. That is, price equals marginal cost, and so strategic behavior is irrelevant (Carlton and Perloff 1990, p. 5).

The securities industry has multiple lines of business. In some of these lines, entry and exit are easy, but in others, entry and exit are difficult, and so an analysis of strategy is relevant.

THE NEW ECONOMICS OF ORGANIZATION

Williamson (1990) argues that the unit of analysis with which Bain worked, characterized by the structure–conduct–performance paradigm, is the "industry or competing group of firms." Williamson believes that although this composite level of aggregation is useful for describing the economic context in which competition takes place, it incompletely considers the organizational/institutional structures in which economic activity takes place. The "new economics of organization" offers a more general framework, asking (more fundamentally) why we have firms and what factors are responsible for limiting a firm's size. This approach recognizes that firms incur costs in transacting business, such as the cost of writing and enforcing contracts. Transactions cost analysis is therefore important to explaining the final configuration or shape of a firm or an industry—that is, what products or services the firm produces internally and what it purchases from outside sources.

Understanding the environmental and human factors that affect transaction costs across markets and within firms is also part of this analysis. Key environmental factors are the uncertainty that decision makers face and the number and size distributions of firms in an industry. Key human factors are bounded rationality and opportunism.

Bounded rationality refers to the fact that human beings have a limited ability to process information and make decisions. In addition, the world is complex and uncertain, and not all contingencies can be anticipated in advance. It may be too difficult or too costly to negotiate contracts that deal with all possible contingencies, and so firms may produce goods and services internally, even though it would be cost effective to rely on markets or outside providers.

Bargaining problems arise when the number of firms is small and individuals behave opportunistically. In this situation, firms may not want long-term contracts for fear of being victimized in the future. If a firm's suppliers have it "over a barrel," the best thing for the firm to do is to start producing on its own. A firm is thus more likely to rely on outside markets when there is little uncertainty and there are many firms (competition) and limited opportunities for opportunistic behavior (Carlton and Perloff 1990, p. 5; Martin 1988, p. 231). As we will show, the multiproduct nature of the typical securities firm is related to the extreme uncertainty of the business and the potential for opportunistic behavior in this industry.

STRATEGIC CHOICE

Jacquemin's (1987) view of the "new" industrial organization focuses on the debate between the proponents of a "natural" adaptation of industry to environmental conditions and those whose analysis focuses on the "strategy" and manipulation of the environment by the industry's firms.

According to the first view, a market structure naturally emerges in which the corresponding monetary value of a representative firm's inputs is lower than the monetary value of those inputs required for any other possible allocation of outputs. The resulting firm configuration minimizes both production and transactions costs along the lines of the Baumol, Panzar, and Willig approach.

The second view stresses the role of economic agents in modifying their environment instead of being subject to predetermined conditions. In this view, economic agents can manipulate their environment and can determine market conditions to some extent. Therefore, the configuration of industry and organizational forms is as much the outcome of deliberate strategies as of initial conditions and predetermined rules of the game. Jacquemin observes that these two approaches are not necessarily contradictory. In this study, I will show that the innovation and diversification strategies pursued by firms have altered the structure of the industry. But I also believe that the underlying economic structure offers incentives to certain firms to develop and implement these innovation and diversification strategies.

A BRIEF LOOK AT STRUCTURAL CHANGE BETWEEN 1960 AND 1980

The industry enjoyed one of its great bull markets in the 1960s as shares traded on the New York Stock Exchange (NYSE) increased from 1.3 billion shares in 1961 to 3.3 billion in 1968. The total value of shares traded increased from $52.7 billion in 1961 to $145 billion in 1968. The market turned down abruptly in 1969 as the NYSE composite index declined by about 37 percent between May 14, 1969, and May 25, 1970 (Lorie and Hamilton 1973, p. 9). With paper losses estimated at $300 billion, many investors left the market, and many broker-dealers failed.[1] Some broker-dealers decided at the time that they would follow these investors by providing a wider range of financial services, which meant expanding the boundaries of their industry.

In the 1960s, the institutional investors[2] emerged as the dominant factor in the securities markets. In 1961, individual investors were responsible for 66.7 percent of the volume and 61.3 percent of the value of public volume on the NYSE. By 1969, individual volume was down to 44.1 percent, and value was down to 38.1 percent. This "institutionalization" of the market was due to increased investment in mutual funds and pension plans. Portfolios also turned over more rapidly as institutions began to manage them more actively.

Despite the greater institutional trading activity, the NYSE enforced a fixed commission rate schedule for member firms that prohibited discounts for large orders. The commissions on a 10,000-share order were ten times those on a 1,000-share order, although execution costs did not rise by a factor of ten. An extensive system of sub-rosa rebates to institutions thus was devised to circumvent the NYSE's fixed-rate schedule.

At the SEC's urging, on December 5, 1968, the NYSE instituted volume discounts on transactions of over 1,000 shares. Subsequent commission rate changes were made until by 1975 all commissions were determined by negotiation. From 1975 on, the broker-dealers' drive to diversify and innovate was intensified by the relative reduction in the importance of revenues from securities brokerage: They were 61 percent of revenues in 1965, 50 percent by 1975, and only 17 percent in 1991.

Merrill Lynch, Salomon Brothers, First Boston, Morgan Stanley, and Drexel Burnham Lambert aggressively extended the boundaries of their industry. Through products such as cash management accounts, mortgage- and asset-backed securities, high-yield bonds, derivative securities, swaps and repurchase agreements, and new trading strategies like program trading, these firms changed not only the securities business but the commercial banking business as well.

The changing environment also demonstrated that securities firms are rather fragile organizations. The demise of such traditional names as Drexel Burnham Lambert, Lehman Brothers, and E. F. Hutton can be traced to each firm's failure to adapt its organization to the new demands of a dynamically competitive environment.

REGULATION

The riskier economic environment and the importance of innovations and diversifications for securities firms call for a new regulatory approach. The central focus of federal securities regulation has been to provide investors with sufficient material information to make informed investment decisions, to prohibit fraud in connection with the sale of securities, and to provide a safe and sound securities industry environment. The broad regulatory charge of protecting investors and maintaining fair and orderly markets grew out of the stock market crash of 1929 and the fraud, securities price manipulation, and other practices that took place before the crash.

In the current, more volatile environment for securities firms, regulators must be more responsive to the needs of the regulated firms. Important new financial instruments have helped securities firms manage the increasing risks they face, and the regulators should facilitate the development of these instruments.

Securities firms in the United States face tougher competition from foreign securities firms than they have at any time in the history of the industry. Regulators should also be sensitive to the needs of U.S. firms in engaging foreign competitors and not overly constrain them in competing internationally.

The securities industry has not been subject to the turmoil that has affected the savings and loan and banking industries. The failure of numerous savings and loan institutions has depleted the federal insurance fund and required Congress to construct a $200 billion bailout plan for the industry. Bank failures have reached levels not seen in this country since the Great Depression, but the problems in these industries were not anticipated or well managed by the industries' regulators.

The SEC's regulatory framework relies on the industry itself to play an active role in regulating member firms. This "self-regulation," with oversight by the SEC, has proved effective in preventing widespread failures among broker-dealers, even in the current environment. Perhaps there are lessons for other government regulators in the experience of the securities industry.

This book recommends that the SEC improve its economic capabilities in order to provide a supportive regulatory environment for economic change in the securities industry. Improved economic capability will also make the SEC more able to manage unanticipated problems in the industry.

AN OVERVIEW OF THE BOOK

Part I introduces the securities industry. Chapter 2 discusses the significant economic events for the industry that took place in the 1980s and the development of the markets for junk bonds, program trading, and derivative securities. Chapter 3 presents an overview of the current industry and shows how its income and balance sheets changed between 1972 and 1992.

Part II describes the legislative and regulatory framework within which the industry operates. Chapter 4 outlines the securities legislation of the 1930s and major changes in that legislation since then. Chapter 5 enumerates the SEC's rules specifying the capital that broker-dealers are required to hold in order to ensure the safety and soundness of the industry. Chapter 6 discusses how conflicts of interest are managed through market arrangements and regulation.

Part III begins the industrial organization analysis with an examination of the economic structure of the broker-dealer industry. Chapter 7 looks at the demand for services by individuals and institutions; Chapter 8 reviews costs and entry barriers; and Chapter 9 traces the history of mergers and discusses two studies of economies of scale and scope for broker-dealers.

Part IV focuses on conduct. Chapter 10 analyzes securities brokerage pricing for individuals and institutions and considers ''soft dollar'' payments for research. Chapter 11 examines the increasingly important market-making and proprietary trading lines of business, and Chapter 12 discusses the prestigious and highly profitable investment-banking line of business. Chapter 13 develops an innovation model to explain the importance of innovation competition in the operation of this industry. Chapter 14 argues that sound diversification choices are necessary for the survival of broker-dealers, and Chapter 15 reviews the history of three firms—Merrill Lynch, Salomon Brothers, and Morgan Stanley—to show how successful firms adapt, change, make mistakes, and yet continue to grow and prosper.

Part V concludes this study with a brief look at international competition and an evaluation of industry performance and policy. Chapter 16 describes the highly competitive global securities market, in which U.S. firms have been very successful participants. Chapter 17 judges how well the industry performs its economic functions. Finally, Chapter 18 discusses the public policy implications and recommendations that flow from the study.

NOTES

1. In 1969, fifty-two NYSE member firms were liquidated or merged.
2. Institutional investors are bank trust departments, pension-benefit plans, investment companies (including mutual funds), insurance companies, investment advisory complexes, foundations, and educational endowments.

2

Accelerating Change, 1980–1992

In the 1980s, the pace of change in the securities industry accelerated. Securities markets throughout the world became more closely linked. Economic disturbances were more rapidly transmitted from one national economy to another, and securities markets became more volatile. Investors looked outside their own countries for the best investment alternatives as communications and transactions costs fell. New financial theories provided the basis for new financial products, allowing investors to better structure and manage the risk of the portfolios they held. With their large portfolios and sophisticated analytical capabilities, institutions were better able than individuals were to deal with the changing environment. Individuals sensibly responded to these changes by switching from individual stock ownership to mutual fund ownership.

For broker-dealers, the 1980s were characterized by years of extremely high profits, high salaries, and a great deal of publicity and notoriety. Newspapers were filled with stories of young investment bankers earning hundreds of thousands to even millions of dollars a year. The king of the hill in compensation was Drexel Burnham Lambert's Michael Milken with his on-paper compensation of $550 million in 1987. Major movies like *Wall Street, Working Girl,* and *Bonfire of the Vanities* took the audience into the offices and trading rooms of fictitious Wall Street firms.

New product lines such as junk bonds, mortgage- and asset-backed securities, interest rate and currency swaps, and program trading became important elements in the mix of services provided by firms. The private placement market expanded and entered new territory.

Broker-dealers were major players in the booming takeover market of the 1980s: Initially, they acted as deal managers for both the acquiring and the acquired firms; then, they helped provide financing for acquirers through the junk bond market; and later in the 1980s, they became both the financiers and the principals for a number of deals, by offering bridge loans to the acquirers. In the late 1980s, the broker-dealers became the acquirers themselves through their merchant-banking subsidiaries.

With the globalization of the securities markets, major U.S. broker-dealers decided that they needed a stronger presence in foreign financial capitals like London and Tokyo, and so they beefed up their staffs in these cities in order to benefit from financial deregulation in both London and Tokyo. In the 1980s, an enormous amount of foreign capital was invested in U.S. markets; indeed, the U.S. government relied on the strong demand for government bonds by Asian and European investors to pay for its $200 billion budget deficits.

Table 2-1 shows a time line of economic events and new products developed by the securities firms and the exchanges from 1971 to 1986. The cause-and-effect relationship is immediately apparent. These new products have enabled investors to cope with this changing environment, and since change is inevitable, so too is innovation—and innovation competition.

Table 2-1. Economic Events $^{(+)}$ and Financial Innovations $^{(o)}$

1971	$^+$United States suspends gold convertibility
1972	$^+$Inflation rate at 3.3% for year
	^{o}First money market mutual funds
	^{o}Foreign currency futures
1973	$^+$Floating exchange rates mark suspension of gold standard
	$^+$Oil prices quadruple to $12
	^{o}Chicago Board Options Exchange established
	^{o}Black–Scholes options model published in JPE
1974	$^+$Dow hits low of 570
	$^+$Commodity Futures Trading Commission created
	$^+$Inflation rate at 11% for year
	$^+$Franklin National Bank failure
1975	$^+$Fixed commission rates eliminated
	$^+$Japanese yen at 292 to the dollar
	^{o}Ginnie Mae futures
1976	$^+$Gold drops to $101 an ounce
	^{o}Ninety-day Treasury Bill futures
1977	$^+$Foreign broker-dealers permitted to obtain NYSE membership
	^{o}Long-term Treasury Bond futures
	^{o}Merrill Lynch introduces Cash Management Account
1979	$^+$Inflation rate reaches 11.3% for year
	$^+$Second oil shock strikes United States during Iranian crisis
	$^+$Federal Reserve tightens money supply
1980	$^+$Price of gold peaks at $875 an ounce
	$^+$Federal Reserve discount rate rises to 13%
	$^+$Inflation rate at 13.5% for year
	^{o}Home purchase revenue bonds
1981	$^+$Interest rates peak at 21.5%
	$^+$Price of oil peaks at $39 a barrel
	^{o}Foreign currency swap
	^{o}Bonds with detachable warrants offered
	^{o}First offering of an original-issue discount convertible
	^{o}First debt-for-equity swap
	^{o}Portfolio insurance invented
	^{o}Futures on Eurodollars
	^{o}Futures on bank CDs
1982	$^+$Latin American debt crisis—Mexico undergoes peso devaluation
	$^+$Shelf registration starts

⁺Unemployment rate at 9.7% for year
⁺First 100-million share day on NYSE
°Stock index futures tied to Value Line, S&P's 500, and NYSE
°Options on Treasury bond futures
°Options on common stock index
°Retail CDs zero coupon
°Tigers
°Second mortgage passthrough securities
°Zero coupon Eurobond issue
°Financial futures–linked Eurobonds
°Zero coupon money multiplier notes
°Extendable notes with rates adjusted at holder's putable option
°Federal Home Loan Mortgage Corporation offers zero coupon bond
°Treasury note futures

1983 °Wings
°Dates
°Cats
°CMO
°Libor-based floating rate notes
°Swap equity of American company for foreign debt
°Stilts
°S&P's 100 index futures

1984 ⁺Run on Continental Illinois bank, nation's eighth largest
°Dutch auction rate preferred stock
°Fannie Mae zero coupon
°Fannie Mae thirty-five-year zero coupon subordinated cap debenture
°Synthetic bonds
°Eurobond discount mortgage-backed bonds
°Zero coupons by mortgages
°STAR

1985 °Colts
°Stripped floating rate notes with a cap
°CARS
°Zero coupon sterling issue
°New hybrid bond–dual series discount bonds
°Flexible Credit Account
°Floating rate securities—capped, Mini/Max, mismatched, partly paid
°Nondollar FRNS
°Shoguns
°Sushi
°Yen-denominated Yankees
°ECU-denominated securities
°Dual currency yen bonds
°Down Under bonds
°Variable duration notes
°Collateralized securities—multifamily passthrough, leaseback
°Commercial mortgage passthroughs
°Cross-collateralized pooled financing
°Pooled nonrecourse commercial mortgage
°Daily adjustable tax-exempt securities
°Municipal option put securities
°Periodically adjustable rate trust securities
°UPDATES

(continued)

Table 2-1. Economic Events $^{(+)}$ and Financial Innovations $^{(o)}$ (continued)

	°Options on Eurodollar futures
	°Options on Treasury note futures
	°Japanese government yen bond futures
	°ECU warrants
	°European-style options
	°Range forward contract
	°U.S. dollar index
	°Options on cash five-year Treasury notes
1986	+Dow hits all-time high of 1910
	+Federal funds rate at 6.8%
	+Budget deficit surges to $230.2 billion
	+Unemployment rate for year at 7%
	+Inflation for year at 1.9%
	+West German deutsche mark drops to 2.07 to the dollar
	+Japanese yen drops to 154 to the dollar
	+Price of oil dips to $10 a barrel
	+U.S. broker-dealers join London and Tokyo exchanges
	°SYDS
	°Remarketed preferreds
	°Euro MTNS
	°Real-estate master limited partnership
	°Extendable bonds—step up or put coupon bonds
	°Universal Commercial Paper
	°Oil-indexed bonds
	°Municipal Receipts

Sources: Forbes, September 22, 1986, pp. 150–53, NYSE *Fact Book* (1992).

CHANGING ECONOMIC CONDITIONS

From the end of World War II until 1973, the world's international monetary system was based on a system of fixed exchange rates. However, by the early 1970s, dramatic differences in inflation rates among the industrialized countries created significant problems for currency conversion. The move to floating exchange rates occurred because there was no viable alternative mechanism to accommodate the monetary changes in the international economy taking place in the late 1960s and early 1970s.

After very low inflation in the United States, in the 1950s and the early 1960s, the country experienced increasing inflation in the late 1960s and 1970s. The first OPEC (Organization of Petroleum Exporting Countries) oil price shock in 1973 added to the upward spiral of prices. Average yearly inflation increased from 2.6 percent and 2.7 percent in the 1950s and 1960s to 7.1 percent in the 1970s. Another oil shock in 1979 was followed by a U.S. inflation rate of 18 percent in 1980. In late 1979, the U.S. Federal Reserve engineered a monetary tightening that drove interest rates to 21.5 percent and was an important cause of the most severe U.S. recession since the Great Depression. In the early 1980s, high worldwide interest rates and the declining demand for imports in the United States hurt many less developed countries. Despite strong economic growth in these countries in the 1970s, the double whammy of high interest rates and declining exports weakened their economies and pushed some of them to nearly defaulting on large loans from U.S. and European banks.

In the first year of the Reagan administration, the largest tax cut and spending package in this country's history was enacted. Personal income taxes were cut 25 percent (over three years), and corporate tax rates were lowered from 48 to 42 percent. In addition, a host of incentives for investment and for research and development by corporations were enacted by Congress. Military spending was increased, and the United States entered an era of record budget deficits. Budget deficits, which averaged $57.9 billion between 1977 and 1981, averaged $192.6 billion between 1982 and 1989.

In 1982, the Federal Reserve reversed its tight monetary policy and allowed the money supply to grow more rapidly. This looser monetary policy, together with the fiscal stimulus provided by the tax cuts and increased military spending, pushed the economy to sustained economic growth in the 1980s. The economy also benefited from cheaper oil, as the price of a barrel fell from $35 in 1980 to just over $12 in June 1990. In turn, the lower oil prices helped restrain inflation.

After trading in the 700-to-1000 range for the Dow Jones Industrial Average (DJIA) in the 1970s to early 1980s, in August 1982 the stock market began one of its strongest bull markets ever. From around 840 in August 1982, the DJIA peaked at 2746 in August 1987. On October 2, 1987, it was at 2640. Following the market's free-fall on October 19, the DJIA dropped to 1708 by midday on October 20, a decline of 37 percent from its August high.

The rapidly changing economic, tax, and regulatory environment, combined with advances in finance theory and improvements in communications and computing capabilities, provided fertile ground for innovations. Miller (1986) argues that many of the innovations developed in response to these changes had already existed for years in one form or another before they sprang into prominence. They were lying like seeds beneath the snow, waiting for some change in the environment to bring them to life. And broker-dealers were ideally positioned to create that life.

JUNK BONDS

Of all the products that became important in the 1980s, none were more controversial than junk bonds, or, as their proponents prefer, high-yield corporates. Junk bonds were used by medium- and small-size firms to raise capital for new business investments and by large companies to finance leveraged buyouts. These smaller issuers could not obtain the investment-grade bond ratings that the larger, more established corporations received. Therefore, the smaller corporations issued bonds that paid higher interest rates than did investment-grade bonds. The advantage to the issuer was that the junk bonds resulted in lower interest costs than did money borrowed from banks, the other major source of nonequity capital for these firms.

The bond agreements for junk bonds often did not have as many restrictive covenants as did the traditional bond instrument. The covenants are intended to protect bondholders in times of financial distress and restrict a company's actions in certain

Table 2-2. High-Yield Bonds, 1982–1991

	Total Dollar Value of High-Yield Bonds Issued ($ Billion)
1982	2.5
1983	7.4
1984	14.0
1985	14.2
1986	31.9
1987	28.1
1988	27.7
1989	25.3
1990	1.4
1991	10.0

Source: Securities Industry Association, *Fact Book* (1992), p. 12.

areas (e.g., the payment of dividends, maximum debt to total capitalization, executive compensation). Junk bonds are also designed for use in highly leveraged and risky circumstances, with more flexibility to facilitate recapitalizations and workouts (Jarrell 1987, p. 58).

By 1990, however, junk bonds had fallen out of favor, as shown in Table 2-2, although, they started to make a comeback in 1991 and 1992.

The decline in the junk bonds' popularity can be traced to several factors. In response to problems in the savings and loan industry, federal regulators now require that thrifts reduce their holding of junk bonds, so that by 1993, they will hold none. In addition, Wigmore (1990) found that there was a substantial decline in the credit quality of junk bonds that were issued in 1986 to 1988, compared with those issued in 1983 to 1985. He argues that this decline in credit quality reflected that over 75 percent of junk bonds issued from 1986 to 1988 were issued to finance merger-related transactions at prices and capitalization ratios entailing interest coverage ratios well below one.

FINANCIAL FUTURES AND OPTIONS

One of the most important developments in the 1970s and 1980s was the introduction of exchange-traded financial futures and options products. In 1972, the Chicago Mercantile Exchange began the exchange trading of foreign currency futures contracts. In 1973, organized trading of options on common stock was initiated by the newly formed Chicago Board Options Exchange (CBOE) (Schwartz and Whitcomb 1988, pp. 149–51). Until this time, options were traded only in the over-the-counter (OTC) market. Exchange trading was also established for stock index futures, which are financial futures contracts in which the underlying asset is a group of stocks included in one of the major stock price indexes such as Standard & Poor's (S&P) 500 Composite Price Index. By 1985, interest rate futures, interest rate options, exchange rate options, and commodity options had been introduced.

Stock index futures dramatically changed the way that equity investments are managed by large investors. Despite their need to hedge, institutions generally shied away from the listed options markets, which primarily serve retail investors. The premiums were too high, and there were limits on the size of a position. To serve the needs of the institutions, therefore, financial engineers developed in the 1980s a technique known as *portfolio insurance,* which replicated options using stock index futures.

NEW APPROACHES TO MANAGING RISK

Managing Stock Market Risk with Stock Index Futures

Stock returns are uncertain because stock prices and dividends vary over time.[1] This volatility comes from two sources: (1) economic events specific to individual firms (firm-specific risk) and (2) economic events that affect every firm in the economy (market risk). Investors can more easily manage the first type of risk than the second. Firm-specific risk can be managed by holding a diversified portfolio of stocks, but diversification across stocks cannot reduce market risk. An increase in interest rates, for example, would cause all stock prices to fall, and so the change in one firm's stock price could not offset the change in another firm's stock price.

Stock index futures provide a tool for managing market risk. These futures contracts differ from traditional commodity futures contracts in that there is no claim on an underlying deliverable asset. Instead, the claim is on the value of the contract, and the settlement is in cash. Stock index futures are therefore referred to as *cash settlement contracts.* Stock index futures also allow investors who hold stock portfolios to hedge market risk. If the stock market falls, investors must make a profit from falling futures prices in order to offset the loss on their portfolio. Since sellers of futures make a profit when futures prices fall, investors can hedge by selling futures. The value of a portfolio hedged with financial futures is thus less variable than is an unhedged portfolio. The volatility of returns on a hedged portfolio, measured by its variance, is 91 percent lower than the volatility of returns on the unhedged portfolio (Morris, 1989b, p. 159).

Managing Interest Rate Risk with Interest Rate Futures

Increased interest rate volatility in the 1970s and 1980s led to greater volatility in the returns on bonds and other fixed-income assets. Consequently, broker-dealers with fixed-income assets and liabilities on their balance sheets are now exposed to much greater risks from bond market capital gains and losses.[2] When interest rates rise, securities dealers suffer losses like those of other bondholders because the value of the bonds they hold invariably falls. Securities dealers can also suffer losses when interest rates fall, because they often commit themselves to delivering bonds at a future date for a fixed price when they do not have the bonds in inventory or the funds to purchase them immediately. If interest rates fall before dealers purchase the bonds, the dealers will suffer a loss because the price they must pay for the bonds they have to deliver will be higher than expected when the initial commitment was made.

New instruments—such as interest rate futures, options on interest rate futures, and interest rate swaps—have been invented to allow investors in fixed-income assets to manage, by means of hedging, interest rate risk at a relatively low cost. Fixed-income investors can hedge the interest rate risk of an asset, such as a Treasury bond, by buying hedging assets whose values change in the direction opposite to that of the value of the Treasury bond when interest rates change. The interest rate riskiness of a hedged Treasury bond is lower than the interest rate riskiness of the unhedged bond because the change in the value of the hedging asset due to a change in interest rates offsets at least some of the changes in the value of the bond. Hedging reduces price volatility because it offsets increases, as well as decreases, in the price of Treasury bonds. Although hedging can reduce risk, it generally cannot eliminate it. So, as a practical matter, hedging permits investors to manage, but not eliminate, risk.

PROGRAM TRADING

Program trading is the generic name given to various trading strategies made possible by financial futures indexes. It is sometimes defined as the simultaneous purchase or sale of a group of stocks. The New York Stock Exchange defined it as the purchase or sale of at least fifteen stocks with the value of the trade exceeding $1 million. Program trading accounted for approximately 9.9 percent of total NYSE volume in 1989 (NYSE *Fact Book* 1990, p. 21).

Program trading of U.S. stocks also takes place abroad. The volume in foreign markets as a proportion of all program trading has varied from 10 to 30 percent. After the imposition of new restrictions on program trading in October 1989, foreign activity rose to the upper end of this range, with London as the most popular trading center.

The major program-trading strategies are stock index arbitrage, index fund arbitrage, and portfolio insurance (Duffee, Kupiec, and White 1990).

Stock Index Arbitrage

Corporations, pension funds, endowments, and broker-dealers all use stock index arbitrage. The objective of this strategy is to generate short-term returns at least 1 or 2 percentage points above the U.S. Treasury bill rate, but sometimes they can earn significantly more.

The idea behind arbitrage is to buy and sell similar commodities, taking advantage of price disparities and locking in a risk-free rate of return. Usually the arbitrage is between the Standard & Poor's 500-stock index and a futures contract based on that index. The price of the futures contract is equal to the index on its expiration date. Generally, before expiration, futures sell at slightly above the value of the index. But when, for example, stock prices begin to climb, the futures prices will rise above the index, and then stock index arbitrage comes into play.

Suppose that the S&P 500 index is at 280 and that the future on that index is selling at 283 and expires in three months. Traders buy the stocks in the index and sell index futures short, usually in packages of at least $10 million. At this point the traders are hedged, and their profits—the spread between the prices of the future and the basket of stocks—are locked in. In addition, they are collecting dividends on the stocks they hold. If the index falls to 270 by expiration, the futures will also fall to 270, 3 points more than the decline in stock prices. So, the short position in futures will yield a net return of 3 points. If the stocks instead climb to 290, the price of the futures also will rise to 290, 3 points lower than the increase in the stock index. The long position in stocks thus yields a net profit of 3 points. There is nothing sacred about expiration dates. Traders can cash in earlier and earn a higher rate of return than if they wait. Whenever the futures get close to the cash price, traders have an opportunity to sell their stocks and buy back futures.

Index Fund Arbitrage

Institutions that own ''index'' funds—portfolios that duplicate the S&P 500—try to increase their returns by exploiting the disparities between futures and cash markets. If the price of the futures drops below the underlying value, the index fund can lighten its basket of stocks, replacing them with cheaper futures. When the futures again trade above the cash prices, index fund managers sell the futures and buy back the stock.

Portfolio Insurance

Institutions use portfolio insurance to protect against losses. Portfolio insurance covered about $60 billion in 1987 and covers considerably more institutional assets today.

If the market begins to decline, portfolio insurers begin to sell futures short. Losses in the portfolio are offset by gains in the value of the short positions. The more the market falls, the more futures will be sold. If the trend reverses, the portfolio insurers start to buy back futures. Portfolio insurers sell into weakness and buy into strength. Rather than countering the trend of the market, their trading accentuates trends, making for higher highs and lower lows. Advocates of the strategy argue that without the ability to hedge with futures, institutions would sell the stock outright.

DERIVATIVE SECURITIES

Derivative securities represent an important new line of business for securities firms. Derivatives allow investors to participate in several different markets at once, without the burden of going through exchanges and incurring transaction costs. They are essentially custom-made options and futures and may involve anything from international stocks and bonds to currencies, and oil, gold, and other commodities (*Wall Street Journal,* November 30, 1990, p. C-1).

These investments are referred to as *synthetic,* since the investor does not own a security at all. The derivative represents a private agreement between a broker and a customer, involving perhaps hundreds of millions of dollars and promises to pay months or years down the road, no matter what happens in the markets.

Derivatives are based on the market's ability to pass off an inventory of risks to dozens of different parties, converting market risk to credit risk in the process. The worry is that some day, some of the parties in this complex web of obligations will fail, leaving the other players holding the bag. However, there are often three or four parties linked behind each product, and they bridge different tax and regulatory systems across countries.

In addition to hedging, derivatives also offer investors a way to venture into unfamiliar foreign markets at a lower cost—and often a lower risk—than by using the conventional route. Some derivatives are listed on exchanges, such as the highly popular put warrants on the Nikkei 225 index of Japanese stocks. But for the most part, they are traded in unregulated markets among brokers, banks, and large institutional investors.

Bankers Trust of New York has been a major innovator in this area. The bank is credited with developing customized ways to hedge the performance of foreign stock markets. Several years ago, it all but owned the business of making and marketing sophisticated stock-related derivatives. Bankers Trust, like other banks, is excluded by regulation from parts of the securities business in the United States, although that has not prevented it from moving aggressively into handling stock-related derivatives in offshore markets (*Wall Street Journal,* December 9, 1990, p. C-1).

THE IMPACT OF PROGRAM TRADING AND DERIVATIVES ON BROKER-DEALERS' TRADING ACTIVITIES

Program-trading strategies and derivatives securities are the product of a relatively new group of people on Wall Street. This new breed, referred to as *quants* or *rocket scientists,* apply advanced mathematics and finance theories to the securities markets. Quants have been around for more than a decade, but they are having more of an impact now that the profitability of other lines of business has fallen off. By devising new products for clients to hedge portfolios, the quants not only generate sales income for their firms, but also create new trading volume (*Business Week,* June 10, 1991, pp. 80–86).

Broker-dealers are also using quantitative techniques to make big money in their trading business. But by engaging more than ever in "proprietary" trading—that is, trading for the firm's own account—broker-dealers are risking more of their own capital than they have in the past. Proprietary trading usually involves some form of arbitrage. How much proprietary trading the firms do is not publicly known, but Morgan Stanley's chairman stated that about 20 percent of its trading revenues come from proprietary trading. Proprietary trading is so profitable at some firms that some traders earn more than the firm's CEO does. It was reported that Salomon employee Lawrence E. Hilibrand, a thirty-one-year-old Massachusetts Institute of Technology economist, earned a bonus of $23 million for his work in computer-assisted bond arbitrage.

Proprietary trading does mean more risk for broker-dealers. At any one time, Salomon's bond arbitrage operation uses an average of five different strategies, each of which involves $1 billion worth of securities, say former traders. Even though a portion may be hedged, Salomon may still stand to lose $50 million or so per position. *Business Week* (June 10, 1991, p. 82) reported that proprietary trading was probably responsible for the $90 million hit that Salomon Brothers took in the last quarter of 1990.

Even with risk-hedging features, some derivatives may still be quite risky. For example, brokers are issuing specialized over-the-counter derivatives with life spans of up to five years when no futures market exists. These derivatives require taking much longer positions, and they also trade infrequently, so they are difficult to price and hedge.

A striking illustration of the potential risks associated with large positions in derivatives is the case of the failed Bank of New England (BNE) (*Wall Street Journal,* June 18, 1991, p. 1-A). Reporting of BNE's collapse focused on the bank's bad real-estate loans. Everyone knew that the bank had $30 billion in assets on the balance sheet, but only a small group of regulators and analysts knew that the bank had $36 billion in off-balance-sheet activity. These were big bets on the future course of currencies and interest rates with derivative securities.

Although banks are major players in the derivative markets, many of their trades do not show up on their balance sheets because the transactions do not fit into ordinary categories of assets and liabilities, such as deposits and loans. Regulators call these hybrid transactions *off-balance-sheet* activities. BNE was a large player in derivative markets in the United States and also traded frequently with Tokyo, Frankfurt, and London banks.

Because many derivatives involve long-term agreements, a high credit rating is the only assurance that banks (and broker-dealers) have that their trading partners will be around when the contracts come due years later. But today, the perception of a bank's creditworthiness can change overnight, and banks can disappear quickly. The *Wall Street Journal* detailed the difficulties that BNE officials had in unwinding the $30 billion in currency and interest rate contracts as nervous bankers around the world slammed their doors on the troubled bank after the news became public that the bank was in serious trouble. With BNE wounded, confidence in its ability to make good on its trades wilted, and BNE officials soon found it difficult to buy or sell currency in the high foreign-currency market to meet its obligations. Fortunately, the bank was able to bypass the banking system and turn to the Chicago Mercantile Exchange's International Monetary Market and enlisted Shearson Lehman and Prudential Securities to handle its foreign-exchange trades. Remarkably, BNE was successful at reducing its derivative book without suffering losses.

Despite the risks in derivatives and the experience of BNE, foreign banks and broker-dealers are paying top dollar to build trading operations in New York from the ground up. Former Salomon traders recently joined Sanwa Bank and Nomura Securities, Japan's largest securities firm. The list of foreign banks attempting to enter this line of business includes Credit Lyonnais, Barclays Bank, National Westminster Bank, Banque Indosuez, and Union Bank of Switzerland. *Business Week* (June 10, 1991, p. 84) suggests that this trading revolution has freed the securities industry from the boom-and-bust, bull-and-bear market cycles. It is expected that these giant firms can earn huge profits from rising markets and even make money when volume falls off.

CORPORATE RESTRUCTURING WITH
INNOVATIVE FINANCING

In the 1980s, the pace of corporate restructuring quickened. Through mergers, acquisitions, spin-offs, and recapitalization, many U.S. corporations radically changed
their organizational form. Corporate "raiders" such as Carl C. Icahn, Asher B.
Edelman, and T. Boone Pickens played a significant role in this process of industrial
change. A key in this restructuring has been the investment bankers, who advise on
and structure the deals and arrange the financing.

During the 1960s, when a wave of mergers and acquisitions led to the formation
of large conglomerates, such as LTV, Litton, and ITT, investment bankers acted as
the "instruments" of the corporate clients, not the instigators of deals. They were
well-paid advisers to the corporate heads who put together these conglomerates, such
as Jim Ling, Tex Thornton, and Harold Geneen. Then in the 1980s, there was a shift
in power from the corporate chiefs to the corporate raiders and the investment-
banking houses that managed the changes in control. The mergers and acquisitions
specialists of investment-banking firms earned millions of dollars for their firms,
often by instigating the acquisitions and then structuring the deals for the raiders.
The mergers and acquisitions business has been a tight oligopoly dominated by the
large investment bankers, including Morgan Stanley, Goldman Sachs, Merrill Lynch,
and several others.

With more intense competition for securities commissions and underwriting revenues, mergers and acquisitions (M&A) represent a very profitable line of business
for securities firms. Even though the mergers and acquisitions teams are small, they
are generating large revenues for their firms. In 1985, Morgan Stanley's M & A
group included just 120 out of the firm's total employment of 5,000. In that year,
Morgan Stanley's mergers and acquisitions unit produced $300 million of the firm's
total investment-banking revenues of $424 million and one-third of its total operating
revenue (*Business Week,* November 24, 1986, p. 75).

The financing for these deals opened the door to creative new ways to raise capital.
Although corporate raiders were able to borrow from banks to finance these deals,
the rates were relatively high, and each dollar borrowed would likely require a dollar
of collateral behind it. Raiders instead needed unsecured, junior debt in amounts
larger than insurance companies and other traditional suppliers of high-risk capital
would provide. The source of that capital became the junk bond market.

Drexel Burnham Lambert raised billions in high-yield financing to back unfriendly
bids against Gulf, Walt Disney, Union Carbide, Revlon, Owens-Corning, National
Gypsum, and many others. Rival investment bankers, initially reluctant to follow
Drexel into this high-risk market, later followed its lead after seeing the huge profits
it made. The approach of Drexel's rivals was a little different, though. Since they
did not have the lists of investors with experience in this market that Drexel had,
the rival firms started putting their own capital at risk in these deals.

These short-term "bridge" loans are part of these firms' gradual move into "merchant banking." Merchant banks commit capital alongside their clients to make a deal, often taking an equity position. This relatively new activity for broker-dealers started in the late 1980s.

BRIDGE LOANS

Although bridge loans were introduced only in the mid-1980s, by 1989 Wall Street firms had $7 billion worth outstanding in them (*Wall Street Journal,* September 21, 1989, p. C-1). These bridge loans—some as large as $1 billion—are generally made so that a client can complete a major takeover quickly. These loans have been highly profitable. Clients pay interest rates that often are 1 or 2 percentage points above the prime rate and usually several percentage points higher than the broker-dealers' own cost of borrowing. The broker-dealers use bridge loans as a competitive tool to get the deal and then earn a host of takeover-related fees. They can receive tens of millions of dollars in separate fees for arranging the acquisitions, making the bridge loans, and then selling the junk bonds that repay the bridge loans. But of course this is risky business, the main risk being that the junk bond market may experience a slump, making the bonds tougher to sell. In that case, the broker-dealer will end up with what is known as a *hung bridge,* a bridge loan that the borrower cannot refinance.

MERCHANT-BANKING ACTIVITIES

Jensen (1989) argues that the broker-dealers' merchant-banking activities may improve corporate management, and he expects firms such as Morgan Stanley, Lazard Frères, and Merrill Lynch to function as active investors. An active investor holds large equity or debt positions, sits on boards of directors, monitors and sometimes dismisses management, helps with the companies' long-term strategic direction, and sometimes manages them.

Jensen expects these merchant-banking groups to function in the way that leveraged buyout partnerships function and in the way that many Wall Street financial institutions functioned before 1940. For example, partners in the J. P. Morgan and Company bank served on the boards of U.S. Steel, International Harvester, First National Bank of New York; owned a host of railroads; and were powerful management forces in these and other companies. But Jensen also perceives benefits from these merchant-banking activities, as he believes that investment bankers are informed investors who can allocate capital more effectively than a publicly held company's CEO can.

Jensen contends that many large public companies are not effectively managed because of the principal–agent problem. That is, firm managers' and shareholders' interests are not the same. Managers pursue growth in firm size, sometimes at the expense of the shareholders, because executive compensation and prestige are generally related to size. This provides incentives for executives to diversify into unrelated business areas that increase firm size but not firm profitability. This diversification does not benefit shareholders because they can achieve investment diversification more efficiently by adding to their portfolios stock with differing characteristics. Knowledgeable investment bankers functioning as investors will recognize inefficient diversifications into unrelated areas and will either prevent them from happening or sell off previously acquired unrelated businesses.

Merchant banking has given investment bankers effective control over many companies with relatively small equity investments. For example, Morgan Stanley's merchant-banking arm controls directly (or through the leveraged buyout funds that Morgan manages) companies with $21 billion in assets. In each fund, Morgan Stanley is the general partner, and the limited partners include major pension funds like those of General Motors and AT&T. These funds have equity capital exceeding $2.2 billion, 10 percent of which belongs to Morgan. All together, about $250 million in Morgan's equity controls an asset base nearly 100 times as large (*Forbes,* February 19, 1990, p. 94).

THE PRIVATE PLACEMENT MARKET

The Securities and Exchange Commission revised the rules of the game for private placements,[3] and these revisions may dramatically change institutional trading patterns. Rule 144A lifts the minimum two- to three-year period that a primary investor had to wait (under the old rule) before reselling a privately placed security. The new rule allows ''qualified institutional buyers'' (QIBs) to buy private placements and resell them at any time to other QIBs. QIBs are generally institutions such as insurance companies or investment companies that own and invest on a discretionary basis at least $100 million in securities of nonaffiliated entities. Broker-dealers, however, need meet only a $10 million test to qualify as a QIB, and they do not need to meet this test in order to act as a riskless principal or agent in the sale of securities to a QIB. American and foreign banks and savings and loan associations must meet the additional test of having a net worth of $25 million to qualify as a QIB.[4]

One of the SEC's primary reasons for issuing Rule 144A was to attract more foreign issuers to U.S. capital markets. In the past, many foreign firms shunned the U.S. markets because of rigid reporting and registration requirements. By issuing Rule 144A securities, foreigners can easily access a broad market without adapting their own accounting systems to U.S.-style accounting.

The private placement market is an important source of capital for borrowers. In 1989, private placements accounted for more than $170 billion, or about 38 percent of all capital raised in the United States. Many of the important new instruments of the 1980s, including mortgage- and asset-backed securities, found their way to the private placement market.

Banks and insurance companies have played an increasingly important role in the origination of private placements. In the first six months of 1990, commercial banks represented eight of the top twenty managers of private placements. The National Association of Securities Dealers (NASD) developed a screen-based information system for private placements called THE PORTAL^SM MARKET. PORTAL is an acronym for Private Offerings, Resales and Trading Through Automated Linkages.

The computerized system supports negotiated trading, clearance, and settlement of private placements. Subscribers, including investors and investment bankers, are screened to ensure that they meet the definition of QIB under Rule 144A.

CONCLUSION

More than at any other time in the history of the industry, the decade of the 1980s forced securities firms to make difficult decisions about how they should adapt the structure of their firms to the new business opportunities. Our study will show that it was ''natural'' for the firms in the oligopoly group to take over the roles of innovators and the firms that initiated diversification. Based on the economics of the industry and the economics of innovation, oligopoly group firms were in the best position to follow these strategies. It also makes economic sense for medium-size and smaller firms to be willing to let the larger firms act as innovators, and then to wait to see whether the innovations and diversifications are successful before offering a comparable product or service.

NOTES

1. This section is based on Morris (1989b).
2. This section is based on Morris (1989a).
3. Private placements are issues of securities that are sold to sophisticated buyers. These securities do not go through the SEC's registration procedure of public offerings.
4. This section is based on Zysk (1990).

3

An Overview of the Securities Industry

The securities industry is only a small part of the financial sector. Currently, only a small percentage of the almost 5,500 firms in the industry are publicly owned. But through its maintenance of the markets for stocks and bonds, this industry provides one of the most important mechanisms for allocating this nation's capital among competing uses. The efficiency of the industry in performing this allocative function determines in large part the overall growth and efficiency of the economy itself.

The first securities firms in this country were almost exclusively brokers operating out of a single office and dealing in the limited list of bonds and shares then available to the public. Today's firms vary greatly in size and character, ranging in size from giant organizations with elaborate worldwide networks of branch offices to one-person neighborhood offices.

TYPES OF BROKER-DEALERS

In 1990, there were 8,437 broker-dealers who filed regulatory reports with the U.S. Securities and Exchange Commission (SEC) or with self-regulatory organizations. Of these firms, 5,424 dealt directly with the investing public (U.S. Securities and Exchange Commission 1992). Of those firms that dealt directly with the public, 947 operated as clearing or carrying firms. *Carrying or clearing firms* clear securities transactions or maintain possession or control of customers' cash or securities. The remaining broker-dealers operate as *introducing firms,* which means that another firm, or clearing organization, handles the clearing and carrying function for them.[1] Carrying and clearing firms dominate the industry in terms of revenue, pretax income, equity, capital, total assets, and number of employees.

All broker-dealers are members of an exchange or the National Association of Securities Dealers (NASD). Table 3-1 shows the number of firms affiliated with each self-regulatory organization. The New York Stock Exchange (NYSE) had a total of 516 member firms in 1990, of which 327 firms dealt with the public. Of these firms, 183 were carrying firms and 144 were introducing firms. In 1990 the NASD had 6,722 members. (NYSE member firms that deal with the public are also members

Table 3-1. Number of Firms Registered with the SEC, the NYSE, and NASD, 1990

	Number of Firms
Broker-dealers registered with the SEC	8,437
Broker-dealers doing a public business	5,424
Carrying/clearing broker-dealers	947
NYSE member firms	516
Member firms dealing with the public	327
Carrying	183
Introducing	144
NASD member firms	5,827

Sources: U.S. Securities and Exchange Commission (1992), NYSE *Fact Book* (1991), Securities Industry Association, *Securities Industry Yearbook* (1992).

of the NASD.) The NYSE leads the other exchanges and the NASDAQ (over-the-counter exchange) in trading activity, as shown in Table 3-2.

LONG-TERM INDUSTRY TRENDS

The securities industry has switched from relying heavily on the agency business as a source of revenue to relying more on dealers' activities, especially in the debt market. This trend has led to changes in the way that firms structure and finance their inventories of debt securities. Dealing in government securities, which has grown rapidly since the late 1970s, is a highly leveraged business that results in very small margins on enormous transactions. Many developments in investment banking, such as the mergers and acquisitions business and merchant banking, require large asset bases, and the result has been a significant increase in both leverage and the dollar amount of assets needed to generate a given amount of revenue.

Trend 1: Relative Decline in the Importance of the Securities Commission Business

Brokerage commissions, once the mainstay of revenue, have declined in importance, from 53.8 percent of revenues in 1972 to 17.3 percent in 1991 (Figure 3-1).[2] Margin interest, earned on lending related to securities brokerage, also fell, from 8.5 percent in 1972 to 4.3 percent in 1991. These declines were accompanied by changes in the

Table 3-2. Transactions on the NYSE and NASD, 1991

	Number of Shares (Million)	Dollar Volume ($ Million)
New York Stock Exchange	45,266	$1,520,164
National Association of Securities Brokers (NASDAQ)	41,311	693,852
American Stock Exchange	3,367	40,919
Regionals (BSE, CSE, MSE, PSE, and Phlx)	7,107	203,898

Source: National Association of Securities Dealers (1992a).

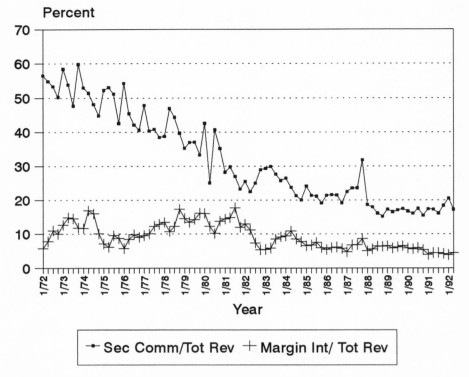

Figure 3-1. Securities commission and margin interest as a percentage of total revenue. (Securities and Exchange Commission data)

composition of the balance sheet. Assets related to the brokerage business, primarily customer receivables (including margin loans), fell from 45.4 percent of assets in 1972 to 6.3 percent in 1991 (Figure 3-2).

On the liabilities side, payables to customers dropped from 16.7 percent of liabilities in 1972 to 9.6 percent in 1991 (Figure 3-2). This account is the source of the free credit balances (excess funds kept by customers in their brokerage accounts) that are the source of funds used for margin loans to customers. Yet securities commissions have increased over the years, from $3.2 billion in 1972 to $10.6 billion in 1991, so it remains a growing source of revenue. But the downward trend in its relative contribution to overall revenues will in all likelihood continue.

Trend 2: Repurchase Agreements Replace Bank Loans as a Source of Funds

A repurchase agreement (repo) is the economic equivalent of a secured loan. The seller (the broker-dealer) provides securities to a counterparty in return for cash and agrees to repurchase those securities. The price at which the securities are exchanged is fixed, and the seller agrees to pay interest for the use of the funds acquired.[3] United

States Treasury and U.S. agency securities are the most common underlying securities in a repo deal. Repos are listed as a liability on the broker-dealer's balance sheet, but a reverse repurchase agreement (or reverse repo) appears as an asset on the broker-dealer's balance sheet. In a reverse repo, the broker-dealer lends cash and receives securities in return for the funds provided to its counterparty.

Repurchase agreements allow securities firms to earn interest on their existing inventory of government bonds, by lending them with an agreement to repurchase them. Reverse repos allow firms to earn interest on excess cash. The SEC estimated that the revenues from repo activity (which is included in other securities-related revenues) accounted for 12.5 percent of total revenues in 1983.

Financing assets with repurchase agreements is less expensive than using bank loans. In addition, repurchase agreements enable broker-dealers to obtain cash equal to nearly 100 percent of the value of securities sold, whereas bank loans enable firms to obtain somewhat less cash relative to the value of collateral. For these reasons, repurchase agreements have replaced bank loans as the primary means of financing dealer inventories.

The growth of broker-dealers' repo activities is due to several factors. First, there

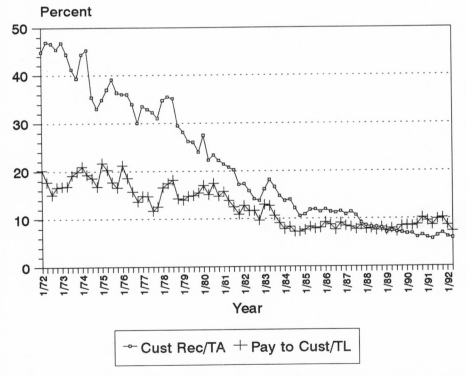

Figure 3-2. Customer receivables as a percentage of total assets and payables to customers as a percentage of total liabilities. (Securities and Exchange Commission data)

has been a substantial increase in the issuance of government securities by the U.S. Treasury. Second, higher interest rates since the 1970s created the need for a less expensive alternative to financing the large inventory positions held by broker-dealers in the form of U.S. government securities and government-related instruments. And third, the development of the secondary mortgage markets expanded the number of instruments available for use in repos and increased the usefulness of repos as a financing tool (U.S. Securities and Exchange Commission 1987, p. 3).

The securities sold under a repo can be obtained from the broker-dealer's own inventory, or they can be obtained under a reverse repo. When a broker-dealer obtains securities under a reverse repo and then sells those securities under a repo, it has a *matched book*. The growth of these ''matched'' transactions represents a large amount of the increase in the industry's financial leverage.

Figure 3-3 shows how repos and reverse repos have come to dominate the industry's balance sheet. On the asset side, securities purchased under reverse repurchase agreements increased from 9.0 percent of assets in 1976 to 36.9 percent in 1991. On the liabilities side, repurchase agreements largely replaced bank loans, which fell from 13.7 percent of liabilities in 1976 to 3.0 percent in 1991, whereas repurchase agreements rose from 26.8 percent of liabilities in 1976 to 52.4 percent in 1991.

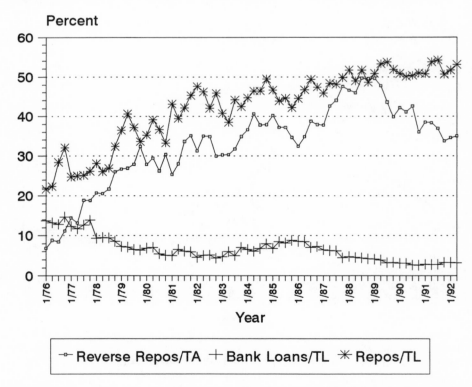

Figure 3-3. Reverse repos as a percentage of total assets, and bank loans and repos as a percentage of total liabilities. (Securities and Exchange Commission data)

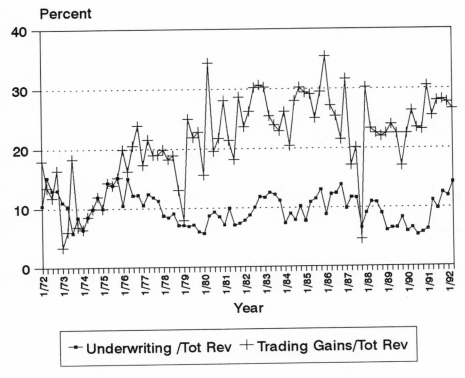

Figure 3-4. Underwriting revenue and trading gains as a percentage of total revenue. (Securities and Exchange Commission data)

Trend 3: Increasing Importance of the Dealer Business

Trading and investment gains increased from 15.2 percent of revenue in 1972 to 28.1 percent in 1991 (Figure 3-4). Throughout the 1980s, more trading gains came from bond market activity than from over-the-counter (OTC) stock market activity. From 1980 through 1988, trading in debt securities contributed 16.2 percent of industry revenues, and market making in OTC securities accounted for 3.4 percent (Security Industry Association, *Yearbook,* various issues). Trading in all other securities accounted for 3.1 percent over this period. Although highly cyclical, the contribution to revenues of underwriting profits does not appear to be moving either upward or downward (Figure 3-4).

Dealer-related assets include long positions in securities and commodities, which increased from 32.2 percent of assets less reverse repos in 1972 to 47.6 percent in 1991, as shown in Figure 3-5. On the liabilities side, short positions became relatively more important as firms used short positions for hedging. Short positions made up 5.5 percent of liabilities exclusive of reverse repos in 1972, but increased to 33.4 percent in 1991.

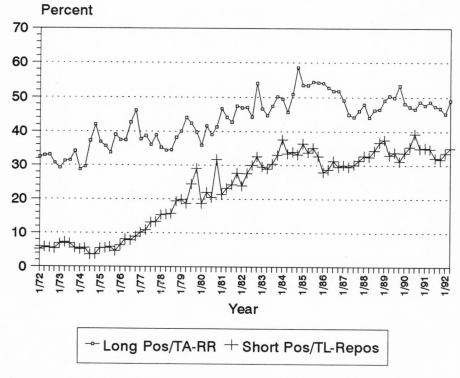

Figure 3-5. Long positions as a percentage of total assets less reverse repos, and short positions as a percentage of total liabilities less repos. (Securities and Exchange Commission data)

Trend 4: Increasing Importance of Mergers and Acquisitions, Merchant Banking, and Other Securities-Related Activities

The category of other securities revenues increased from less than 10 percent of revenues in 1972 to 35.2 percent of revenues in 1991 (Figure 3-6). This category includes revenues from the mergers and acquisitions business, the repo business, and private placement. The mergers and acquisitions and repo businesses barely existed in 1972, but since have become important sources of profit and revenue for securities firms.

Trend 5: Increasing Leverage

The portion of industry assets financed by capital (subordinated liabilities and owners' equity) fell from 12.4 percent in 1976 to 6.3 percent in 1991, even though the industry's capital base grew from $3.9 billion to $39.1 billion during this period (Figure 3-7). The decreasing role of capital in financing assets implies the greater use of financial leverage, and this increased leverage has resulted from the growth of dealer inventories and the financing of those inventories by repurchase agreements. Relatively few firms account for most of this leverage. In 1983, thirteen firms, termed *primary government securities dealers,* accounted for 80 to 90 percent of all U.S. government securities held by carrying and clearing firms or purchased by them under repo agreements. All but one of these firms were either national full-line firms or large investment-banking houses. The financial leverage ratio for these primary government securities dealers substantially exceeded the leverage ratio for all other carrying and clearing firms. In 1983, for the thirteen primary dealers, the ratio of total assets to owners' equity was thirty-five to one, compared with a ratio of eight to one for all other carrying and clearing firms (U.S. Securities and Exchange Commission 1985).

Trend 6: Risk-Based Revenues, a Higher Percentage of Total Revenues

Risk-based revenues now account for almost two-thirds of industry revenues, and that share seems to be growing. These risk-based revenues include underwriting and trading revenues combined with other securities-related revenues. Risk-based revenues are becoming more concentrated among the largest firms because of the heavy capital commitment that most risk businesses require. The trend toward principal

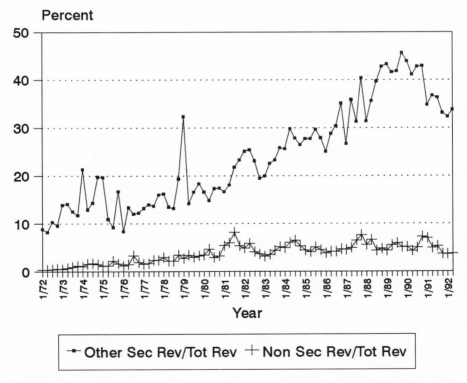

Figure 3-6. Other securities and nonsecurities revenues as a percentage of total revenue. (Securities and Exchange Commission data)

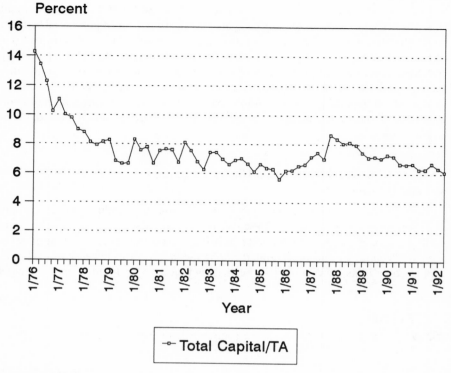

Figure 3-7. Total capital as a percentage of total assets. (Securities and Exchange Commission data)

trading has also changed the way in which business is conducted. For example, in 1988, 82 percent of the value of bond underwritings were completed without underwriting syndicates, compared with under 50 percent from 1984 to 1987 and an even smaller percentage in earlier years. One-third of equity underwritings are now completed without syndicates, although this level has remained more or less constant throughout most of the 1980s (*SIA Trends,* December 29, 1989, pp. 5–8).

Trend 7: The Continuing Cyclicality of Profitability

Figure 3-8 shows pretax profits as a percentage of equity between 1972 and 1991. There is a strong cyclical component in both pretax profits and pretax returns on equity, a cyclicality that reflects the cyclicality in the elements of revenues. The securities industry also is affected by the interrelated cycles that influence our economy. Cycles in personal income, stock prices, bond prices, interest rates, and the like all are exogenous to the industry. Despite the dramatic changes that have taken place since 1974, the industry remains the captive of the macroeconomic cycles of the U.S. economy.

ORGANIZATION AND SERVICES OF SECURITIES FIRMS

Figure 3-9 is a hypothetical organizational chart for a large, fully integrated securities firm. From the core lines of business of securities brokerage, underwriting, and trading and investments, securities firms broadened their scope in the 1980s to include whole departments devoted to arbitrage, junk bonds, mergers and acquisitions, derivatives, merchant banking, and mortgage- and asset-backed securities.

Brokerage Services

Corporate securities: Firms buy and sell equity and debt securities acting as a broker (i.e., agent) for individual and institutional customers by corresponding with other firms through organized securities exchanges, the NASD network, or direct contact. Between 1980 and 1988, brokerage commissions on transactions in listed equity securities averaged 18.5 percent of gross revenues for NYSE firms doing a public business (Securities Industry Association, *Yearbook,* various issues). Commissions on listed options averaged 2.7 percent, and all other commissions averaged 3.6 percent of gross revenues during this period.

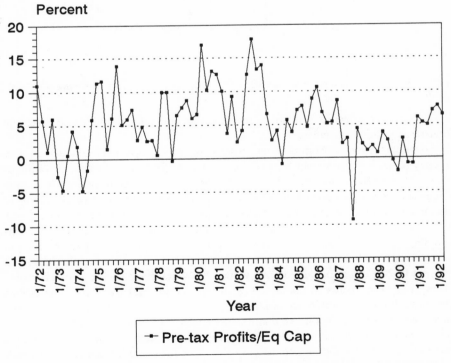

Figure 3-8. Pretax profits as a percentage of equity capital. (Securities and Exchange Commission data)

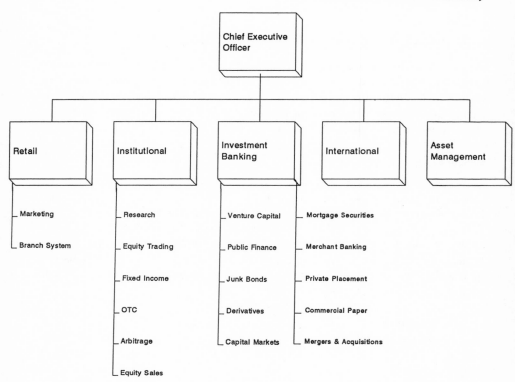

Figure 3-9. A hypothetical broker-dealer. (*Investment Dealers' Digest,* November 30, 1987, p. 46)

Options: Firms act as brokers in the purchase and sale of options contracts on registered options exchanges.

Commodity futures: Commodities business is, for the most part, conducted on an agency basis. It encompasses the purchase and sale of futures contracts of commodities such as coffee, soybeans, wheat, feed grains, livestock and meat, metals, cotton, sugar and cocoa, currencies, and interest rate futures. Brokerage firms belong to major commodities exchanges and compete with specialized commodities brokers who are not involved in a general securities business. Most of the trading in commodities futures contracts is conducted on a margin basis subject to the margin requirements of individual commodities exchanges, ranging from approximately 3 percent to 20 percent of the contract value. Individual traders seek to make profits from price movements in commodities, whereas industrial users of commodities purchase futures contracts in order to protect themselves, or "hedge," against adverse price movements in the commodities needed in their businesses.

Financial futures and options: The relatively new financial futures and options have revolutionized trading and hedging strategies for many large investors as well as broker-dealers. The number of futures contracts on financial instruments traded increased from 0.19 million in 1980 to 1.49 million in 1991 (U.S. Commodity Futures Trading Commission, various issues).

Market-Making Services

In this activity, dealers make markets and trade for their own accounts in government securities and listed and over-the-counter corporate securities. Firms compete with other broker-dealers making markets in the same securities. Interest and dividends on firms' trading are included as trading revenue. An important cause of the revenues' relative increase is the large rise in interest revenues. Also included among dealer services are institutional sales, block positioning, and arbitrage.

Block Positioning and Arbitrage

Block positioning is akin to acting as an "auxiliary specialist," a role necessitated by the inability or unwillingness of exchange specialists to compete in all cases for very large blocks (Welles 1975, pp. 44–46),[4] mainly because the specialist's auction-style order matching does not lend itself to very large orders. Firms that engage in block positioning rely on an aggressive solicitation-and-trade assemblage procedure. Block houses maintain direct communications and close working relationships with all major institutions, from which sufficient buying interest can be determined within minutes. In a typical block transaction, a firm purchases a large block of securities or sells securities short for its own account without full commitments for their resale or repurchase. If buyers cannot be located immediately, the firm will "position" the block. Positioning means that the firm will buy some or all of the block for its own portfolio, with the intent to liquidate the position as soon as possible, since the firm's capital is at risk. Block-positioning firms are usually well capitalized and more willing to take risks than specialists are.

The risk arbitrage business is investing for the broker-dealers' own account in the securities of companies engaged in publicly announced corporate transactions in which the broker-dealer is not acting as an adviser or agent. These transactions include mergers, acquisitions, changes in capital structure, and dividend payments. In the past, risk arbitrage included taking unhedged long or short positions in the securities of companies involved in announced merger transactions. With the new financial instruments, however, firms are better able to hedge their risks. Even so, this business requires the commitment of capital and entails a substantial risk. Returns from this business can be adversely affected if the financial transaction, such as a tender offer, fails.

Margin Lending

Securities transactions are made on a cash or a margin basis. In a margin transaction, the customer pays less than the full cost of the purchase, and the firm lends the balance, subject to various regulatory and internal requirements. Securities in the customer's account provide collateral for the margin loan. The Federal Reserve Board sets the minimum original margin that must be deposited by securities customers; currently the requirement is 50 percent of the value of the equity securities purchased. Exchange regulations also impose minimum margins that customers must maintain. Beyond these requirements, individual firms impose margin maintenance requirements that normally exceed those required by exchange regulations. Firms impose internal limits in order to reduce the risk that a market decline will lower the value of a customer's collateral below the value of the customer's indebtedness before the collateral can be sold. Customers are charged for margin financing at interest rates based on the broker's call rate plus an amount generally ranging from 0.75 percent to 2 percent, depending on their average net debt balance during each interest period. A portion of the funds actually lent to customers is derived from the customers' credit balances, on which interest is paid.

Investment-Banking Activities

Some firms engage in diverse investment-banking activities, including acting as managers, comanagers, or syndicate members in underwriting public offerings of debt and equity securities; assisting in mergers and acquisitions; providing consulting and financial advisory services to corporations; arranging for private placements of securities issued with institutions and other investors; and acting as tender or exchange agents in connection with tender offers.

Profits from underwriting and selling groups contributed around 10 percent of gross revenues between 1980 and 1988, although this figure understates the importance of this line. As Figure 3-1 shows, the important high-profit areas of the 1980s—mergers and acquisitions, junk bonds, and mortgage- and asset-backed securities—are organizationally part of investment banking, but only the revenue from the underwriting part of the deal is reported as underwriting fees. Income from making markets in these areas is reported in trading gains, and other fees associated with these activities are listed with other securities-related revenue.

Asset Management

Broker-dealers provide portfolio management and fiduciary services to taxable and nontaxable institutions, international organizations, and individuals investing in U.S. and international equities and fixed-income securities. Firms also act as fiduciaries for pension funds and trusts, in which capacity firms make asset allocation decisions (determining the choice and timing of different investments) and act as the selector, supervisor, and evaluator of a fund's investment managers. Firms also act as mutual fund managers.

Research

Broker-dealers provide equity and fixed-income research for institutional and individual clients in order to support their sales and trading activities. Research departments produce publications and studies on the economy and financial markets, portfolio strategies, technical market analysis, industry developments, and individual companies. Research activities are oriented to making specific purchase and sale recommendations on individual securities for investment purposes. The broker-dealers own commercial rights to their publications, and some large firms sell "institutional quality" research. In addition to written material, analysts are in direct contact with clients at individual and group meetings sponsored by the broker-dealers.

DISCOUNT BROKERS

Although there was some discounting before commission rates became competitive, the unfixing of rates made it possible for NYSE members to offer discount commissions on transactions regarding NYSE-listed stocks. Discount brokers charge commissions that are up to 70 percent lower than those charged by full-service firms. For the low rates, the customer receives only order execution and confirmation and not any investment advice or "hand holding"—the personal attention available at a full-service firm. The customer places orders with an order clerk rather than a broker; replacing the commission broker with an order clerk saves the 30 to 40 percent of the commission dollar that goes to the broker. According to the Securities Industry Association (*Fact Book* 1992, p. 31), discount brokers increased their share of the retail market to an estimated 9 percent in 1990, up from 4.8 percent in 1983.

Large banks have entered the discount market. It is argued that although many banks do not expect to make money on their discount operations, they feel that it is an essential part of their image as a full-service bank (*Wall Street Journal,* March 6, 1991, p. C-1). However, some large banks have committed capital to build up back-office capabilities and attract clients, with the intention of creating a profit center out of the business.

SECURITIES FIRMS' JOBS

Registered Representatives

Registered representatives are responsible for making sales. They are known as brokers, reps, account executives, or, in earlier days, customers' men. In 1990, there were 82,251 brokers, a 70 percent increase from 1980. The number of brokers per office rose from an average of 10.9 in 1980 to 11.5 in 1990 (NYSE *Fact Book* 1992, p. 94).

Brokers often specialize in one type of security and are therefore known as stockbrokers, bondbrokers, or whatever. They also specialize in retail sales or institutional sales. Retail brokers collect about 35 to 40 percent of the gross fee, with higher percentages or payouts for large producers; institutional brokers collect a lower percentage because they deal with large blocks, but they also usually receive large bonuses (Wright and Dwyer 1990, p. 421).[5] Because pay depends on an individual's production, brokers' income varies considerably, with income ranging from $10,000 to several million dollars a year. Wright (1990) cites industry averages of $50,000 to $60,000 a year for retail brokers and $60,000 to $70,000 for institutional brokers.

Brokers are trained by individual firms and represent a substantial investment for the firms. In 1984 at Prudential-Bache, it cost $34,000 to train a broker (*Institutional Investor,* August 1984, p. 61). Often only one successful salesperson emerges from every three or four trained.

Customers develop personal relationships with their brokers and often move their accounts with the broker if he or she switches firms. Accordingly, a large part of the broker's total production is viewed as transferable. This factor, together with the high cost of training, makes the "pirating" of brokers by rival firms a recurring industry problem (Wright and Dwyer 1990, p. 421).

Traders

Traders specialize in different types of securities: corporate bonds, municipal bonds, OTC stocks, and the like. Traders are highly informed investors who closely follow developments in financial markets that can affect the prices of the securities they trade. Most traders are paid a salary plus a bonus. Bonuses can run from 10 percent to 200 percent or more of a trader's salary (*Wall Street Journal,* January 11, 1991, p. C-1). The average salary for a starting (or assistant) trader is $25,000 to $30,000, and the average salary for a senior trader is $70,000 to $75,000. With bonuses, top traders can earn over $1 million a year. It was reported that the head of Salomon Brothers' oil-trading unit earned $20 million, and a trader in the firm's bond arbitrage group earned $23 million in 1990 (*Wall Street Journal,* March 15, 1991, p. C-1, and January 7, 1991, p. C-1).

Corporate Finance Professionals

Underwriting professionals need a broad understanding of corporate finance, the operations of domestic and international capital markets, and the U.S. business cycle. Therefore, virtually all employees entering the field today have an MBA degree or experience in several phases of the business. Underwriting professionals' high salaries reflect these requirements. This business has a high year-to-year variability in compensation, with bonuses ranging from 25 to 100 percent of salary in good years.

Mergers and acquisitions became one of the highest-paid areas in all of American business in the 1980s. Starting salaries for MBAs from the top business schools were in the $80,000 range. It is not unusual for M & A executives in their mid-thirties to earn up to $200,000, and some M & A specialists earn more than $1 million annually, including bonuses (Wright and Dwyer 1990, p. 424).[6]

Research Analysts

The investment community employs more than 15,000 analysts who collect and analyze data on various companies and the overall economy. Most of their information is considered to be institutional quality and is seen only by portfolio managers and other large customers. Analysts have significant power over a company's stock price, as a pessimistic report by a respected analyst can send down a stock price significantly (*New York Times,* January 31, 1982, sec. 3, p. 1). Former Salomon Brothers' analyst Henry Kaufman was widely respected for his ability to analyze interest rates movements. On April 23, 1980, he predicted that interest rates would be coming down and, therefore, that bond prices would rise. The next day there was a record-breaking rise in the bond market (Wright 1984, p. 555).

Before the unfixing of commission rates, research was provided by securities firms at no cost, as part of the service competition that resulted because firms did not compete on the basis of price. It was argued that the research was offered as part of the tie-in sale by brokerages and was in excess of what would be supplied under competitive rates. Therefore, the output of brokerage research and the number of analysts would decline with competitive rates (West and Tinic 1971, pp. 584–85). From August 1975 to November 1978, the number of analysts employed by securities firms dropped from 2,543 to 2,032, as predicted (*SIA Trends,* December 26, 1978, p. 5).

Following the stock market crash of 1987, the industry experienced another sharp cutback in research capacity. In 1987, Wall Street employed 3,095 senior equity analysts, but by late 1990, the number was down to 2,253, a 27 percent drop (*Institutional Investor,* April 1991, p. 169).

The quality of a firm's staff of analysts is an important competitive tool. Research excellence is touted in television commercials, and *Institutional Investor* annually selects an ''All-American Team'' of analysts by industry covered. Firms use the number of All-Americans on their staff in their advertising materials to signal the quality of the firm.

Although analysts receive their training on the job, an increasing number start with an MBA degree. The industry average salary for analysts reported in 1990 was $100,000. Senior analysts, sometimes called managing directors of research departments, usually earn over $100,000 a year, with the top salary for ''stars'' at $300,000. In addition, analysts may earn bonuses as high as three times their salary (Wright and Dwyer 1990, p. 422).

SECURITIES FIRMS' CAPITAL

The capital employed by broker-dealers consists of the firm's net worth or equity plus various types of subordinated borrowings of cash and securities. Equity in an incorporated brokerage firm normally consists of capital stock, capital surplus, and retained earnings. In addition, the appreciation or depreciation in the market value of exchange memberships represents accretions or diminutions in the enterprise's equity. Equity in the partnership, on the other hand, is reflected in the capital accounts of general and limited partners and the appreciation or depreciation in the market value of exchange membership. Included in the debt capital of broker-dealers are the following loan arrangements: subordinated loans and accounts, secured demand notes, and the accounts of partners subject to equity or subordinated agreements. To the extent that subordinated capital consists of securities, they are subject to the various ''haircut'' requirements in determining their actual value in the regulatory (or ''net'') capital computation.[7]

If the contribution in a subordinated loan arrangement is in the form of securities, the lender can enjoy the benefits of dividends and interest on the securities and also realize any increase in the value of the securities. The lender is also paid interest on the loan. But the agreements subordinate the right of the lenders to receive repayment to the claims of all general creditors of the firm. For the interest paid to lenders on contributed securities or other funds, the loan is used by the broker-dealer as part of the firm's capital and is subject to the risks of the business.

FIRM CLASSIFICATIONS

The Securities Industry Association (SIA) publishes data on securities firms by group. Table 3-3 shows the percentages of industry revenue earned by national full-

Table 3-3. Revenue by Type of Firm, 1988

Type of Firm	Commissions	Trading Profits and Investment Gains	Underwriting	Margin Interest	Mutual Fund Sales	Other Securities Related	Other Unrelated	Fees, Research, and Commodities
National full-line firms	41.0%	41.6%	48.9%	50.2%	76.9%	24.8%	30.0%	48.4%
Large investment banks	13.2	32.8	36.1	16.1	1.3	51.1	36.7	25.3
Regional firms	15.1	7.3	10.5	9.7	18.3	3.7	4.7	5.3
New York City–based firms	12.3	11.1	1.6	5.8	1.9	15.1	9.7	11.5
NYSE discounters	5.5	0.1	—	5.9	0.9	—	—	—

Note: Percentages do not add up to 100 because the SIA does not report breakout of revenues earned by firms that do not fit unto these categories.

Source: SIA Trends, May 30, 1989.

line firms, large investment bankers, regional firms, New York City–based firms, and NYSE discounters.

National full-line firms are general securities firms involved in every aspect of both the agency and the dealer business. They offer all lines of business that are discussed in this chapter. Their customers include individual and institutional investors from small investors to the largest institutions, and they have a nationwide (or multiregional) network of branch offices. In 1988, national full-line firms accounted for 41 percent of securities commissions, 50.2 percent of margin interest, 48.9 percent of all underwriting income, and 41.6 percent of trading profits. They have a large share of margin interest because many of them carry customer accounts for introducing firms and thus generate margin income from the customers of their introducing correspondents. These firms also dominate mutual fund sales, with 76.9 percent of the business with their large base of retail clients.

Large investment-banking houses are known principally as underwriters that organize and manage syndicates of other broker-dealers for the distribution of new securities issues. They service institutions by providing block-trading capabilities primarily intended for the large transactions that accompany institutional business. These houses usually do not seek accounts of small investors but tailor their retail business to the "big ticket" customers. In 1988, large investment bankers earned 32.8 percent of trading profits and 36.1 percent of underwriting revenues. However, the strength of the investment bankers is in revenues earned in the other securities-related area, in which they had 51.1 percent of industry revenues.

The six national full-line firms and the ten investment bankers are identified in Table 3-4. These firms dominate the industry: The national full-line firms had total revenues of $20.2 billion in 1988, and the large investment banks had revenues of

$17 billion. Total domestic broker-dealer revenues were $51.8 billion in 1988; therefore, 71.8 percent of industry revenues went to these firms.

OVERALL INDUSTRY MODEL

The securities industry can be characterized as a loose oligopoly with a multiproduct structure. It has a dominant group of firms, the national full-line firms and the investment-banking firms. We will show in later chapters that these firms' policies set the pace for the industry. They recognize that their price-output decisions and strategic choices are influenced by their interdependence. Thirteen firms of the dominant firm group are among the twenty largest firms in the industry. Firm size gradually tapers down from the largest firms to a competitive fringe.

The industry has multiple lines of business, with different firms holding leadership positions in various lines. For example, Morgan Stanley was the leading managing underwriter in the 1960s and 1970s; Merrill Lynch has maintained the leadership position in securities brokerage for years; Salomon Brothers is known as the leading corporate bond trader; and Goldman Sachs, Kidder Peabody, and First Boston vied for the leadership position in the mergers and acquisitions business. Before its failure, Drexel Burnham Lambert dominated the high-yield (junk) bond market. Identifying the market leader often depends on how the market is specified and what time period is used.

The national full-line firms compete against one another in virtually all securities lines of business. The investment-banking firms do not have much of a retail business, and so they do not compete across a full line of retail services. But the investment bankers do compete with one another and with the national full-line firms for

Table 3-4. National Full-Line Firms and Large Investment-Banking Firms, Based on SEC–SIA Firm Categories

---

National full-line firms
 Dean Witter Reynolds, Inc.
 Donaldson, Lufkin & Jenrette, Inc.
 A. G. Edwards, Inc.
 Merrill Lynch, Pierce, Fenner & Smith, Inc.
 Paine Webber Inc.
 Prudential Securities, Inc.
 Smith Barney Shearson, Inc.

Large investment banks
 Bear Stearns & Co., Inc.
 Dillon, Read & Co., Inc.
 First Boston Corporation
 Goldman Sachs & Co.
 Kidder, Peabody & Co., Inc.
 Lazard Frères & Co.
 Lehman Brothers
 Morgan Stanley & Co., Inc.
 Salomon Brothers, Inc.
 Wertheim Schroder & Co., Inc.

---

all institutional and corporate finance services, as well as competition from firms outside the dominant firm group in various lines of business. Smaller firms tend to compete in fewer lines of business.

The diversity among competitors and the broad range of competitive markets in the industry work against the cohesiveness necessary for an oligopoly to coordinate its policies. In addition, leadership positions can be contested with the ranking of firms in each line of business changing from year to year.

In later chapters we will show that the main axis of competition among the largest national full-line and large investment banks is through innovation and diversification. Innovation and diversification provide a focus for competition because firms do not generally have a cost advantage in the production of securities services. Other competitive strategies, such as advertising, also do not provide the advantages that such strategies offer in other industries.

NOTES

1. The introducing firm retains all sales functions, and the customers of the introducing firm have their accounts administered by the clearing firm, which handles all settlement and credit aspects of transactions.

2. The figures in this section are for NYSE firms doing a public business.

3. Alternatively, no explicit interest may be set; rather, the securities are repurchased at a higher price.

4. Welles (1975, pp. 46–49) also includes a lively account of the action in the trading room during the handling of a block.

5. For retail payout schedules for a sample of the major firms, see *Institutional Investor*, May 1986, pp. 162–68.

6. For a discussion of operations jobs and related salaries in the industry, see Wright and Dwyer (1990), pp. 425–26.

7. *Haircut* is the industry term used to describe the percentage deductions from the market values of proprietary securities operating to reduce net worth in the computation of net capital. This adjustment attempts to take into account market fluctuations.

II

The Legislative and Regulatory Framework

4

The Legislative Framework

Part II looks at those federal securities laws that apply to broker-dealers.[1] Although the U.S. Securities and Exchange Commission (SEC) has direct authority over broker-dealers, much of the day-to-day regulation is carried out by the national exchanges and the National Association of Securities Dealers (NASD). This delegation of regulatory authority to the exchanges and the NASD, referred to as *self-regulation,* takes place with oversight by the SEC.

Securities industry regulation includes the establishment of practices and minimum capital requirements for broker-dealers in order to minimize the risk of insolvency. Another major goal of this regulation is to ensure "fair and orderly markets." The securities laws provide severe punishments for fraudulent and manipulative broker-dealer conduct, and they regulate trading practices at the exchanges and the NASD network and the operation of specialist firms. Issues relating to trading at exchanges, on the NASD network, and by specialists are beyond the scope of this book; rather, we will focus solely on those regulations pertaining to broker-dealers.

THE ORIGINAL LEGISLATION

Federal regulation of the securities markets followed the stock market crash of 1929 (Stoll 1979, pp. 7–11). Congressional investigation of the reports of stock "pools"[2] and other manipulative devices led to passage of the Securities Act of 1933 (1933 act) and the Securities Exchange Act of 1934 (1934 act). With the 1933 act, often called the truth-in-securities law, Congress opted for a disclosure approach to regulating the issuance of securities by corporations. Disclosure of financial data by firms issuing new securities would give investors sufficient information to make informed decisions and would minimize fraud in the sale of securities.

Whereas the 1933 act applied primarily to new issues of securities and required registration by the issuer, underwriter, and "control" persons and provision of a prospectus to all potential purchasers, the 1934 act applied primarily to trading in already issued securities. Major sections of this act are concerned with full disclosure, antifraud, and antimanipulation provisions. The act's periodic reporting requirements necessitated disclosure by publicly held corporations. Provisions against fraud and manipulation are contained in Section 10(b). The 1934 act also required the registration of exchanges and broker-dealers; established standards for transactions among managers of publicly held corporations, board members, and other insiders; and set up proxy and tender offer rules (Phillips and Zecher 1981, pp. 9–10).

The 1933 and 1934 acts attempted to ensure that securities prices did not reflect misinformation, fraud, or manipulation. There was less concern with the efficiency with which brokers and dealers provided their services and the fees charged for these services. To the extent that the business conduct of securities firms was regulated, the emphasis was on preventing manipulative or fraudulent activities, with little attention paid to anticompetitive behavior such as fixed commissions.[3]

The 1934 act regulated the conduct of brokers and dealers that were members of exchanges *only*. It required exchanges to register, file copies of their rules, and enforce the explicit provisions of the 1934 act. Disciplinary power over members was left in the hands of the exchanges. Direct rule-making authority was granted to the SEC in limited areas by the antimanipulative provisions of Section 10 and by Section 14, which gave the SEC authority to make rules with respect to off-floor trading by members and the operations of specialists and odd-lot dealers.

The power to request changes in commission rates, which was based on Section 19 of the 1934 act, was not used until 1968 when the SEC pressured the New York Stock Exchange (NYSE) to adopt volume discounts (before a formal ruling became necessary). Until that time, the SEC had not publicly questioned requests to increase commission rates.

The Maloney Act of 1938—adopted at the urging of the industry—added Section 15A to the 1934 act, which established rules for supervising the over-the-counter (OTC) market, including the registration of any qualified association of broker-dealers. The National Association of Securities Dealers is the only association to have registered under the act. Note that an important difference between the OTC market and the NYSE is that the Maloney Act explicitly prohibits the NASD from imposing minimum rates of commission.

THE GLASS–STEAGALL ACT

Banks Enter and Exit the Securities Business, 1900–1933

Historically, federal banking authorities have viewed commercial and investment banking as incompatible. National banks, therefore, operated for years under a legal regime that restricted their ability to underwrite or make markets in investment securities. Even after the Comptroller of the Currency eased these restrictions at the turn of the century, national banks were prohibited from underwriting, or making markets in corporate stocks.[4]

Federal restriction made it difficult for national banks to compete with private banks and state-chartered banks and trust companies, as these institutions were less constrained. In response, the national banks began to create state-chartered affiliates that could underwrite and deal in corporate securities. Accordingly, the national banks' securities activities began to increase during World War I when they marketed government war bonds.

Although the Comptroller expressed concern over the national banks' securities activities, they continued during the 1920s. Eventually, bank participation in securities underwriting had become a fact of economic life, and any attempt to limit these activities would have caused defections to the state system. The federal government's acceptance of this situation culminated in the passage of the McFadden Act in 1927. The act "reaffirmed" the national banks' authority to underwrite certain investment securities and was designed to prevent any further erosion of the national banking system. Although the Comptroller initially allowed only bond underwriting, this later was extended to underwriting certain equity securities.

Declining Loan Demand Pushes Banks into Securities Underwriting

The banking system experienced a large decline in loan demand during the 1920s, which increased the banks' interest in marketing securities. This reduction in loan demand reflected the bullish securities markets of the 1920s. Corporations reduced their bank loans by selling public securities. In addition, the Federal Reserve pursued an easy money policy until 1928, partly in an effort to help stabilize the value of European currencies. This resulted in a dramatic growth in U.S. bank deposits, which reinforced the banks' tendency to enlarge their securities investment portfolios.

The banks' underwriting activity grew out of their increased purchases of marketable securities for their own accounts. When the banks' bond departments became expert at evaluating various corporate securities, it seemed natural for them to move from recommending securities to underwriting them. By 1929, 459 U.S. banks (out of approximately 27,000) were underwriting securities through their bond departments or some other part of the bank. An additional 132 banks originated securities through a separate firm affiliated with the bank. The affiliate route was necessary because national banks and some state-chartered banks were limited in their ability to underwrite securities within the bank itself.

The banks' underwriting activities differed from traditional investment banking in two ways. First, the banks underwrote almost no equities. Second, the bank affiliates relied heavily on the retail sales of underwritten securities, whereas the private investment banks concentrated on wholesale distributions to sophisticated purchasers. The commercial banks developed a network of branch offices with a large force of securities salesmen, either by merging with local and national brokerage firms or through natural growth. Innovation leadership in investment banking was assumed by the commercial banks. Banks and their affiliates originated 45.5 percent of all new bond issues in their peak year of 1929, up from only 22 percent in 1927 (Flannery 1985, p. 69).

Passage of the Glass–Steagall Act

Before 1933, there had been little public support for separating the banking and securities businesses. But in early 1933, a subcommittee of the Senate Banking Currency Committee held hearings that had a strong effect on public opinion. The hearings documented a number of insider dealings and fraudulent activities. Certain banks had made loans to securities purchasers to help artificially support securities prices, dumped poor-performing securities on correspondents or into trust accounts, used securities affiliates to relieve the bank of their bad loans, and had the affiliates purchase stock in those companies to which banks had lent money (Litan 1987, p. 27).

The hearings did not establish a widespread pattern of abuses by securities affiliates, but they did garner enough support to pass the Glass–Steagall Act, which divorced commercial banking from investment banking, with several significant exceptions. Banks were allowed to underwrite debt instruments of the federal government and general obligation municipal bonds, apparently in the belief that government securities were less risky than corporate securities. It permitted banks to carry out securities brokerage transactions for their customers, and it did not prohibit banks from underwriting securities in foreign markets (Litan 1987, p. 28).

LEGISLATION IN THE 1960s

Following a period of rapid expansion of the securities markets in the late 1950s and early 1960s, Congress authorized a broad study of the rules, practices, and problems of the securities industry. *The Special Study of the Securities Markets* (the *Special Study*) was written in 1963 against a background of concern about "the danger of uninformed public speculation" in the securities markets and "evidences of a substantial amount of manipulations." It was also felt that the tremendous growth in the securities industry since the 1934 act had imposed strains on the regulatory system and revealed structural weaknesses. The Securities Act Amendments of 1964 followed the *Special Study*. The principal provisions of these amendments extended corporate disclosure requirements to OTC stocks, raised requirements for entry into the securities business, and strengthened disciplinary controls of the SEC over brokers and dealers (U.S. Congress, House 1963, pp. 1, iii).

THE SECURITIES INVESTOR PROTECTION ACT OF 1970

Following the turmoil in the industry in the late 1960s, the Securities Investor Protection Act of 1970 was passed as a means of protecting customers beyond reliance on net capital rules. The act also created the Securities Investor Protection Corporation (SIPC), which insures the accounts of customers in the event of a brokerage's failure. The insurance now covers claims up to a maximum of $500,000 for cash and securities (with a cash maximum of $100,000) in the event of a firm's failure. The members of the SIPC are all the broker-dealers registered under the Securities Exchange Act of 1934. All SIPC member firms are assessed $\frac{3}{16}$ of 1 percent per annum of gross revenues from the securities business in order to form a protective fund (Securities Investor Protection Corporation 1992, p. 9).

The SIPC is not an agency or establishment of the United States government; rather, it is a corporation whose members are registered brokers or dealers. The SEC has certain oversight and regulatory functions with respect to the SIPC, and in an emergency, the SIPC may borrow up to $1 billion from the U.S. Treasury through the SEC. The SIPC has no authority to examine or inspect its members; instead, the securities exchanges and the NASD are the "examining authorities" for its members.

THE SECURITIES ACT AMENDMENTS OF 1975

The Securities Acts Amendments of 1975 overhauled the 1934 act. They followed the *Institutional Investor Study of 1971* (U.S. Congress, House 1971), which examined the impact of institutions on the structure of the market, and the *Securities Industry Study* of 1973 (U.S. Congress, Senate 1973), which examined the questions of negotiated commission rates and a centralized market system. The amendments were intended to adjust the regulations to the changing economic environment, which was broadening and making the securities markets more competitive.

The amendments mandated a market system for securities in which competitive forces would play a much larger role, by requiring the SEC to abrogate those rules of exchanges that were anticompetitive and not necessary for a legitimate regulatory objective: "No national securities exchange may impose any schedule as fixed rates of commission, allowances, discounts or other fees to be charged by its members" (Stoll 1979, pp. 9–10). Although competition was emphasized, the amendments also gave the SEC more regulatory authority over exchanges and clarified the jurisdiction of the court and the process for judicial review. The amendments directed the SEC to facilitate the establishment of a "national market system" characterized by the absence of unnecessary regulatory restrictions; fair competition among brokers, dealers, and markets; the availability to all of the information on transaction prices and dealer price quotations; the linking of markets; and the ability to execute orders in the best market. The act permits brokers to charge commissions above those of other brokers in those cases in which research services are provided.

The Municipal Securities Rule-Making Board

The Municipal Securities Rule-making Board (MSRB) was established by the Securities Acts Amendments of 1975, to formulate rules to govern securities firms and banks involved in underwriting, trading, and selling municipal securities, such as tax-exempt bonds and notes. The MSRB was created partly in response to some localized dealer fraud in the industry (*Forbes,* June 17, 1985, p. 202). It consists of fifteen members: five representatives of bank dealers, five representatives of securities firms, and five public members not associated with any bank or securities firm. In the public category, one member must represent issuers and one must represent investors, in order to ensure that all perspectives of the municipal securities market are included.

The MSRB is granted broad rule-making authority over municipal securities dealers' activities, including standards of professional qualifications, rules of fair practice, record keeping, the scope and frequency of compliance examinations, the nature of securities quotations, and the sale of new issue municipal securities. Before the MSRB was created, activity in the municipal securities market was largely unregulated. The current agency is small in size (it had a staff of thirteen in 1985) and relies on the SEC, NASD, Comptroller of the Currency, Federal Reserve System, and Federal Deposit Insurance Corporation for enforcement of its standards, and the MSRB's rule-making authority is subject to oversight by the SEC.

INTEGRATING THE DISCLOSURE REQUIREMENTS OF THE 1933 AND 1934 ACTS

Integrated Disclosure, Rule 415, and Market Efficiency

In March 1982, the SEC adopted a new rule that added flexibility and efficiency to the securities registration process. Rule 415 was the culmination of a series of conceptual changes in the SEC's disclosure scheme. The 1933 act established the disclosure requirements associated with registering and issuing securities by a public company, and the 1934 act established the periodic reporting requirements for securities issuers, including annual, quarterly, and "current" reports on significant issuer events. Although the two acts contain different disclosure concepts, they also have overlapping identical requirements. Whereas the 1933 act was intended to give potential investors the information necessary to make an informal judgment about the quality of the stock being offered, the 1934 act was intended to keep stockholders informed about the management of their investment. Both objectives are accomplished by relying on the same basic information, including audited financial information and management discussion.

Beginning in 1968, the SEC began to integrate the two acts' disclosure requirements, by allowing experienced issuers to incorporate by reference that information already on file in 1934 act reports when they filed a new 1933 act registration statement. However, in order to take advantage of integrated disclosure, an issuer had to be "widely followed" by professional analysts and to have been in the 1934 act's reporting system for three years or more (Auerbach and Hayes 1986, chap. 6).

The SEC's decision was influenced by empirical research that supported various theories about the financial market's efficient valuation of securities. Three forms of market efficiency (the efficient market hypothesis) were distinguished: (1) the weak form, (2) the semistrong form, and (3) the strong form. The weak form asserts that current prices fully reflect the information implied by the historical sequences of prices, meaning that investors cannot enhance their ability to select stocks by knowing the past history of stock prices. The semistrong form states that current prices fully reflect all public information (e.g., annual reports) about the securities, and so efforts to trade on the basis of public information cannot be expected to produce superior investment results. The strong form indicates that not even those with nonpublic inside information can use it to secure superior investment results. Empirical evidence supports the weak and semistrong forms of the hypothesis, but there is no convincing empirical support for the strong form (Lori, Dodd, and Kimpton 1985, chap. 4).[5]

The efficient market hypothesis became both the reason for requiring broadened disclosures under the 1934 act and the justification for considering those disclosures sufficient to meet the requirements of the 1933 act. If 1934 act disclosure was complete and the stock market rapidly incorporated this information into security prices, then new issues of securities could be sold under the 1933 act with confidence that the market price reflected a consensus judgment of the value of those securities of widely followed issues.

Shelf Registration

With Rule 415 in place in 1982, the SEC allowed experienced issuers to register securities for two years, put them ''on the shelf,'' and sell them at a time when the issuer would benefit the most. When Rule 415 was adopted, the SEC argued that these large, experienced firms ''provide a steady stream of high quality information (through 1934 Act disclosure) to the marketplace which is digested and synthesized by financial analysts . . . on a timely basis'' (Securities Act Release 6499, p. 12). The effect of shelf registration on underwriting is discussed in Chapter 13.

ANTITRUST ISSUES

The use of self-regulation in this industry has raised some unique antitrust issues. The SEC oversees the industry's self-regulatory organizations, which have statutorily recognized powers to regulate their members. This statutorily approved, self-regulatory structure has been characterized as ''unique'' and ''curious'' and ''unlike any other system in the world'' (Smythe 1984). Because the rules of the exchanges and the NASD may have been in contravention of antitrust laws, questions arose in the early 1970s as to whether the SEC rulings condoned anticompetitive behavior. If they did, jurisdictional questions related to antitrust issues between the SEC and the Antitrust Division of the Department of Justice would have to be resolved.

Before the 1975 amendments, this issue was important, since ''persons aggrieved by actions of securities exchanges have no avenue of obtaining judicial review of those actions under securities laws, either by the SEC or the courts'' (U.S. Congress, Senate 1973, p. 219). Only those actions taken or explicitly approved by the SEC were subject to judicial review. Individuals were therefore forced to sue the NYSE directly on antitrust grounds (Stoll 1979, pp. 9–10).

The only case prior to the 1975 amendments in which the SEC acted to limit anticompetitive behavior was the *Multiple Trading* case of 1940, in which the SEC abrogated a NYSE rule prohibiting exchange members from acting as odd-lot dealers or specialists in NYSE-listed stocks on other exchanges, on the grounds that the rule was anticompetitive.

The most important case involving the jurisdictional issue was *Silver* v. *NYSE* (373 U.S. 341 [1963]). Silver, not a member of the NYSE, sued the exchange to prevent severing the wire connections between Silver and a member firm. But the U.S. Supreme Court rejected the NYSE's argument that it was immune from antitrust laws, stating that immunity is ''implied only if necessary to make the Securities Exchange Act work, and even then only to the minimum extent necessary.'' The Court noted that it might rule differently in a case in which explicit SEC jurisdiction would be subject to judicial review. In Stoll's view, the ruling applied only to self-regulatory conduct and the SEC's review of such action, not to the SEC's exercise of explicit powers under Section 19(b). The Court later ruled against a plaintiff who argued that fixed commissions violated antitrust laws, on the grounds that the SEC had been granted explicit jurisdiction by Section 19(b)(9) and because to "deny anti-trust immunity . . . would subject the exchanges and their members to conflicting standards" (*Gordon* v. *NYSE* 1975).

Self-regulation was found by Congress to be workable enough to extend it to the commodities business, leading to the establishment of the National Futures Asso-ciation in 1980 as a nonexchange self-regulatory organization patterned after the NASD with oversight by the U.S. Commodities Futures Trading Commission (CFTC).

Antitrust and the Syndicate System

In the early 1950s, the federal government launched an antitrust case against sev-enteen major investment-banking firms, focusing on the syndication system of selling securities. The trial judge, Judge Harold Medina, contended, however, that it was preposterous to assume, as the government prosecutors did, that these firms had first "entered into a combination, conspiracy, and agreement to restrain and monopolize the securities business of the United States" in or about the year 1915. Medina found that neither the shape nor the position of the firms with underwriting syndicates had become frozen. He reasoned that because the flotation of a security issue was so complex, the process was not a standardized arrangement that a few investment bankers could monopolize. Also, because each issue was unique, bankers competed not by offering a commoditylike package of services at the lowest price but, instead, by trying to "establish or continue a relationship with the issuer" based on past performance, current reputation, and faithful adherence to the industry's informed code of conduct. Medina saw the industry as embodying a considerable amount of competitive activity because the "single, entire, unitary transaction" involved in a major underwriting was the sum of many different banking services (Hayes, Spence, and Marks 1983, p. 17).

ECONOMIC ANALYSES OF THE REGULATORY FRAMEWORK OF THE SECURITIES MARKETS

Stigler (1964) was the first economist to question seriously the efficacy of SEC regulation. His examination was directed mainly at the corporate disclosure system and the regulation of trading markets and did not focus on broker-dealer issues.

Schwert (1977) empirically tested the hypothesis that members of the national securities exchanges have received net benefits from the SEC's regulatory activities. The study was a test of the "capture hypothesis," which posits that the *producers* of goods and services receive net benefits from government regulation. The alter-native hypothesis is the "public interest hypothesis," which posits that government regulation benefits the *consumers* of goods and services.

Schwert examined the relationship between stock exchange seat prices and bro-kers' profitability in time periods of major change in the regulation of the securities industry, between 1926 and 1972. A model of the dynamic behavior of seat prices as a function of new information about the future level of stock prices and share-trading volume was estimated and tested for the effects of regulatory actions. As noted in Chapter 6, stock exchange seat prices represent the capitalized value of the expected future flow of profits accruing to stock exchange members. Therefore, changes in seat prices through time reflect changes in the future flow of profits expected by securities brokers.

Schwert believed that if SEC regulation had any significant effect on the long-term profitability of stock exchange membership, changes in regulation would be associated with changes in seat prices. An empirical analysis of the unexpected change in seat prices suggests that the capture hypothesis does not appropriately describe the public regulation of the securities brokerage industry:

There is significant evidence that the expected profitability of NYSE and ASE [American Stock Exchange] membership was permanently reduced by the initiation of SEC activities in 1934. NYSE and ASE seat prices fell by about 50 percent in the month associated with the introduction of the 1934 Securities and Exchange Act to Congress and there is no evidence that seat prices ever recovered from this unexpected fall. There is also evidence that seat prices fell in association with the major changes in the structure of commission rates which have taken place since 1968 at the insistence of the SEC, and there is some indication that seat prices fell in association with increases in SEC activity as measured by budgetary growth during the first ten years of the agency's existence. There is no contradictory evidence that any change in regulatory behavior of the SEC has ever been related to increases in seat prices. (Schwert 1977, p. 147)

He concluded from the analysis that since regulatory change is associated with decreases in NYSE and ASE seat prices, at least some part of the value of the seats prior to the SEC's regulations had to be attributable to monopoly rents of some kind. Whether the current level of seat prices reflects any monopoly rents remains an open question.

Phillips and Zecher (1981) looked at the overall regulatory program at the SEC in the context of the "market failure" and "public choice" theories of regulation. The market failure rationale for regulation identifies regulated industries' failures or deviations from the fully competitive market outcome and sets goals for regulatory processes that would approximate a market solution. Public choice theory utilizes an extended notion of market behavior as expressed in the political system. Groups organize and express their support of or opposition to regulatory programs, depending on the effect that the regulation will have on the wealth of individuals in the group.

The Phillips[6] and Zecher analysis focused on the corporate disclosure system, the effects of the deregulation of rates on competition among exchanges (e.g., the NYSE versus the regional exchanges), and the SEC's efforts to encourage the development of a "national market system." Their evaluation of the SEC's performance is rather negative:

Contrary to the traditional view of the SEC as the New Deal's most successful regulatory agency and protector of investors, the SEC appears to be primarily concerned with maximizing support (net support) for their regulatory programs. This practice results in a net benefit to some groups and a tax on others, but more important it produces regulation insensitive to the costs of programs and to an evaluation of their effectiveness.

Problems with the expansion of the corporate disclosure system, the fixing and the unfixing of commission rates, and many of the actions and inactions in the market structure area are perpetuated rather than repaired. But we have only touched upon a few of the more obvious regulatory failures. (Phillips and Zecher 1981, p. 111)

Phillips and Zecher also identified the interest groups that benefit from SEC regulation:

The public choice theory of regulation has been very useful in explaining the existence and persistence of certain of the SEC's regulatory programs. The SEC has been the most successful in its disclosure regulatory programs, the securities part of the SEC. These programs are characterized by wealth transfers from investors and corporations for whom the cost is not great on a per capita basis to a relatively small group of processors, which includes securities lawyers, accountants, security analysts, and of course the SEC's employees. There is insufficient economic incentive by the members of the taxed groups to organize in opposition to this type of regulation. (Phillips and Zecher 1981, p. 118)

Phillips and Zecher argue that the regulatory programs that the SEC administers should be judged in terms of their costs and benefits and that many of the SEC's regulations are anticompetitive.

Jarrell (1984) examined the causes and effects of the deregulation of commission rates in 1975, describing deregulation as a rational political response to an increasing elasticity of demand of institutions for NYSE brokerage services. He used a political support theory adapted from Stigler (1971) and Peltzman (1976) to identify the forces responsible for deregulation. These were the emergence of the low-cost, off-board alternatives to block trading on the NYSE, and the acceptance by regional exchanges of large financial institutions as members. The dramatic growth of institutional trading between 1965 and 1975 also partly explains the SEC's moves toward discounts on institutional rates and correspondingly higher rates for individuals during those years. Jarrell believes that the growth in institutional trading is not, however, a complete explanation for total deregulation. Competitive brokerage rates become politically optimal because the economic rents to the NYSE cartel had been sufficiently eroded by market forces, including the improved OTC markets and institutions' backward integration into the brokerage business.

NOTES

1. For a current account of the basic securities laws, see Hazen (1990).

2. Stock "pools" ran up the prices of securities on an exchange by means of well-timed transactions, effected solely to "manipulate" upward the market price of a security. Then the pool operators would unload their holdings on the public just before the price dropped.

3. For a discussion of the origins of the concept of self-regulation, see Baruch (1971).

4. This section is based on Kelly (1985).

5. For a discussion of the current state of the evidence supporting the efficient market hypothesis, see Fama (1991).

6. Susan Phillips served as chair of the CFTC from 1983 to 1987.

5

The Safety and Soundness
of Broker-Dealers:
The Net Capital Rule

The U.S. Securities and Exchange Commission's (SEC) primary regulatory tool for ensuring the safety and soundness of securities firms (or broker-dealers) is the net capital rule, intended to protect customers of securities firms who leave large quantities of cash and securities with their brokers. The rule requires that the firms have enough liquid assets to meet their customers' withdrawal demands. It also defines certain securities (e.g., government bonds, stocks) that are owned by securities firms as liquid but automatically reduces (or "haircuts") the value of these securities for the liquidity computation based on the variability of these securities' market prices.

Broker-dealers may choose one of two methods to calculate their required net capital. The traditional *basic capital method* (BCM) defines net capital as a percentage of the firm's aggregate indebtedness. The other, newer method, referred to as the *alternative capital method* (ACM), computes net capital based on customer-related receivables. These rules, coupled with rigorous monitoring of broker-dealers' capital by the self-regulatory organizations, have resulted in relatively few Securities Investor Protection Corporation (SIPC) proceedings among broker-dealers over the past two decades.

THE HISTORY OF THE NET CAPITAL RULE

Since 1934, the Securities Exchange Act has contained net capital provisions,[1] although it was extended to cover all broker-dealers only after the passage of the Securities Investor Protection (SIP) Act in 1970. This act gave the SEC additional authority to adopt rules relating to the acceptance, custody, and use of customers' securities and the carrying and use of customers' deposits and credit balances.

Before 1973, securities firms had almost unrestricted use of customer funds and securities in their businesses. In fact, many brokerage firms ran their businesses on customers' money without using any funds of their own (Mayer 1980). Even though the SEC had no rules before 1973 regarding the segregation of customers' securities, the New York Stock Exchange (NYSE) and the National Association of Securities Dealers (NASD) did have regulations requiring that customers' fully paid and excess margin securities be kept separate from marginable securities and the firm's proprietary securities. The NYSE and NASD did not have rules regarding the use of customers' free credit balances[2] or other balances in the possession of broker-dealers. Firms were able to use customers' free credit balances for any business purpose, such as trading in securities or firm commitment underwriting.

Following the SIP act, the SEC considered a number of alternative approaches to establishing reserves on customers' deposits or credit balances. The economic effects of establishing reserves on broker-dealer financing were analyzed, and it was concluded that establishing reserves as a fixed percentage of customers' deposits or credit balances, similar to that done in the banking industry, would be too restrictive. Instead, the SEC in 1973 adopted a reserve approach with Rule 15c3-3, which permits the use of customers' funds to finance margin loans to other customers and other customer-related brokerage activities. This rule protects customers and also has the beneficial effect of making the broker-dealers' capital structures more responsive to market forces (U.S. Securities and Exchange Commission 1985, p. 6).

THE LOGIC OF THE NET CAPITAL RULE

The underlying logic of the SEC's net capital rule (Rule 15c3-1) is that a broker-dealer should be able to wind down its activities and protect its customers within one month.[3] The SEC evaluates the risk-adjusted liquidity of a firm with a conservative view of those assets that can be sold or collected in order to meet senior obligations in the short run. The rule determines the firm's total capital, applies a series of deductions to derive "net capital," and compares this measure against a required safety margin. Net capital is monitored by the self-regulators and employs several "warning-level" tests. Firms operating with net capital at or below warning levels are subject to special restrictions and close supervisory scrutiny. Broker-dealers with net capital problems must scale down their activities in line with their capital.

The components of total capital reflect the rule's short time frame. Table 5-1 shows the basic net capital calculation. Equity and subordinated debt with more than one year to maturity are the core elements, but other subordinated debt of temporary duration is also allowed as capital. The first set of deductions from total capital

Table 5-1. SEC Net Capital Computation

Total capital	Equity
	Allowable subordinated debt
	Allowable credits
Less deductions	(Illiquid assets)
	(Unsecured receivables)
	(Charges for aged credit exposure)
	(Market risk haircuts)
> Net capital	Compared with
Requirement	6.66 percent aggregate indebtedness or 2 percent aggregate debit items
Excess capital	Net capital less the requirement

Source: Haberman (1987), p. 4.

addresses liquidity and includes intangible, fixed, and other illiquid assets; securities that do not meet a stringent test of marketability; and "dis-allowed" assets such as most unsecured receivables. The deduction of unsecured receivables reflects both liquidity and credit risk concerns. The second set of deductions addresses other forms of credit risk and includes several incentives for efficient market practices. For example, charges against capital are taken for aged credit exposures. Capital adjusted to this point in the calculation can be viewed as "liquid capital."

The third set of deductions, called *haircuts,* gauges potential trading risk—that is, how much securities might decline in value before being sold. Net capital—that is, what remains after all deductions—is compared with a minimum requirement and higher warning levels.

Identifying firms' liquid capital is the heart of the net capital rule. Liquid capital, which differs from total capital, is the excess of marketable and easily liquidated assets over senior liabilities. Unmarketable, unsecured assets are heavily penalized, with a 100 percent capital requirement. The SEC's definition of marketability is quite stringent in most circumstances: The security must be exchange traded, or bid-and-offer quotations must be readily available and the settlement of sales at such prices must be possible within a short time. Marketable assets and liabilities must be valued at current prices, and unrealized gains and losses must be reflected in net worth each day. This is the "mark-to-market" requirement that allows regulations and broker-dealers to know the current value of a firm.

ALTERNATIVE NET CAPITAL RULES

In 1975, the SEC introduced the uniform net capital rule, which provided an alternative to the traditional (BCM) method of calculating regulatory capital. Before the rule was adopted, most of the largest broker-dealers in the industry were exempt from the SEC's capital rules because of the exemption for members of exchanges. But after the 1975 amendment, all broker-dealers were required to meet the SEC's requirements.

Basic Capital Method

A broker-dealer that uses the BCM to compute its net capital must have a net capital equal to at least 6.66 percent of its aggregate indebtedness, or, stated conversely, the aggregate indebtedness may not exceed 1500 percent of the broker-dealer's net capital. The rule defines aggregate indebtedness as the total money liabilities of a broker or dealer arising in connection with any transaction, with certain exceptions. In addition, the broker or dealer must maintain a minimum net capital regardless of its aggregate indebtedness, depending on the nature of its business. Under the BCM, each firm must maintain a minimum net capital of at least $25,000, unless it carries no customer accounts and holds no funds or securities belonging to customers and otherwise limits its businesses as described in particular sections of the rule (U.S. Securities and Exchange Commission 1988, sec. 5).

The rule specifies additional capital requirements for a market maker in securities.

A market maker is required to have and maintain net capital at least equal to $2,500 for each security in which it makes a market if the security has a market value of $5 or more and $500 for each security whose market value is less than $5. The rule provides, however, that a market maker have minimum net capital of at least $25,000, but does not require a market maker to have minimum net capital greater than $100,000 under these additional market-maker capital requirements.

Alternative Capital Method

A broker-dealer that uses the ACM must maintain net capital equal to at least 2 percent of its customer-related receivables, known as aggregate debit items, computed in accordance with the Reserve Formulas. The broker-dealer also must maintain a minimum net capital of at least $100,000. As of December 31, 1982, about 320 broker-dealers, including nearly all of the 25 largest firms, used the ACM. Approximately 3,400 broker-dealers used the BCM, but about 63 percent of these firms did not have enough capital to meet the ACM's minimum dollar requirement ($100,000) (U.S. Securities and Exchange Commission 1985, p. 13).

Early-Warning Levels

In addition to the minimum requirements, the net capital rule and the rules of the various self-regulatory organizations contain early-warning levels below which a firm's net capital cannot fall without adverse consequences. For example, a firm may not withdraw equity capital in any form to pay its shareholders or partners if its net capital is less than 5 percent of aggregate debit items (if it computes net capital according to the alternative method) or if its aggregate indebtedness exceeds 1000 percent of its net capital (if it computes net capital according to the basic method).

Haircuts

The net capital rule uses risk factors, or "haircuts," to adjust a firm's assets for trading risk. The haircuts for investment-grade securities are based on the expected market volatility for various assets. For example, three-month Treasury bills are haircut 0.5 percent and thirty-year bonds are haircut 6 percent of market value. Haircuts are also applied to off-balance-sheet market exposures such as futures, forwards, and options. Many forms of hedging and arbitrage are recognized as having less risk than uncovered positions do. "All other" securities, such as common stock and low-rated bonds, require a 15 percent haircut under the alternative capital rule and a 30 percent haircut under the basic requirement. Table 5-2 summarizes the haircuts.

THE CUSTOMER PROTECTION RULE

The net capital rule's focus on liquidity is designed to work in concert with the SEC's Customer Protection Rule, which is referred to as the reserve/segregation

Table 5-2. Summary of Haircuts Applied to Unhedged Positions

Government and agency securities
  0 to 6 percent in 12 maturity subcategories
  6 percent applies to 25-year bonds

Municipal securities
  0 to 7 percent in 16 maturity categories
  7 percent applies to 20-year bonds

Commercial paper, bankers acceptances, and certificates of deposit
  0 to 0.5 percent in 5 maturity categories
  0.5 percent applies to 9-month paper

Investment-grade corporate debt
  2 to 9 percent in 9 maturity categories
  9 percent applies to 25-year bonds

Preferred stock: 10 percent

Common stock and "all other"
  30 percent under the basic method
  15 percent under the alternative method

Source: Haberman (1987), p. 5.

rule. It compels the broker-dealer (1) to balance its liabilities to customers with receivables due from customers plus its segregated cash reserve and (2) to ensure that the broker-dealer has possession and control of all its customers' securities (Haberman 1987, p. 5). The second requirement ensures that the broker-dealer segregates the firm's proprietary securities from those of its customers and maintains accurate records of customers' securities left with the firm.

The reserve part of the rule provides a "reserve formula" to determine reserves. The rule requires broker-dealers to determine (1) customers' free credit balances, (2) funds realized by a broker-dealer as a result of hypothecation[4] or lending of customers' margin securities, (3) funds derived from failing to receive customers' securities on the settlement date from another broker-dealer, and (4) funds derived from other customer-related sources.

The broker dealer is required to use these data to make a weekly computation to determine how much money it is holding that is either customers' money or money obtained from using customers' securities (i.e., formula credits). If the credits exceed the debits, the broker-dealer must deposit the excess in a special reserve bank account. If the debits exceed the credits, no deposit is necessary. The process is commonly referred to as the Reserve Formula computation.

The 1982 Amendments

Partly in response to the rapid increase in Reserve Formula debits following the introduction of this rule, in 1982 the SEC adopted several amendments to the net capital rule and the reserve/segregation rule. The size of the Reserve Formulas debits and credits had grown rapidly, mainly because of increases in free credit balances and other customer credits. The funds in these accounts grew from $3.1 billion at the end of 1975 to $16.2 billion at the end of 1983. This rapid growth reflects the fact that since the early 1980s, many broker-dealer firms began paying interest on at least some portion of free credit balances and encouraging their customers to retain funds in their accounts. Many of these credits have no offsetting debits, contributing to the tenfold increase in deposits in reserve bank accounts between year-end 1978 and 1981.

The 1982 amendments reduced the amount of regulatory capital that ACM firms were required to maintain relative to their Reserve Formula debits. The amendments also tightened the capital requirements for debt securities. Haircuts on some classes of debt securities were raised to reflect the higher price volatility of these securities. Firms using the ACM experienced a net $610 million reduction in their regulatory capital requirements, and firms using the BCM experienced a $55 million increase in their regulatory capital requirement, owing to the higher capital charges now required on certain debt securities. The net result was a reduction in required regulatory capital held by broker-dealers, of $555 million by year-end 1982 (U.S. Securities and Exchange Commission 1985).

Implications for a Failing Firm

The coupling of the net capital rule requirement for liquidity and the customer protection rule requirement for the coverage of customer payables has important implications for a failing firm. As a broker-dealer weakens toward warning levels of capital, the firm must constrain its business. It cannot engage in larger-scale risky activities with the hope of a big payoff while at the same time relying on Securities Investor Protection Corporation (SIPC) insurance to protect customers. The broker-dealer cannot engage in the "heads I win, tails the insurer loses" strategy that the savings and loans used with Federal Saving and Loan Insurance Corporation (FSLIC) insurance in the early 1980s.

Once a warning level is crossed, the examining authority will seek further constraint, and so a firm's ability to compete when already weak is further undermined at a time when it still has positive liquid capital. In this difficult position, management will try to sell or merge the company before the situation requires a SIPC-managed failure. Haberman (1987, p. 6) argues that approach has been used many times during the past two decades, and when it worked as intended, the SIPC faced little or no loss.

Excess Net Capital as a Market Signal

Wall Street firms place great importance on the amount of their excess net capital because it demonstrates a firm's ability to serve customers and handle large transactions and provides a buffer for firms with volatile assets. The relationship of a firm's total, net, and excess net capital is determined by the composition of its business. Dealing, arbitrage, and underwriting generate high haircuts that reduce net capital but change each day. Haircuts may not be particularly high on those days for which financial statements are prepared. Firms specializing in these activities, for example, the large investment banks, tend to report more than 40 percent of their total capital as "excess," although retail brokerage causes other deductions and the final requirement to be larger. Several of national full-line firms report only 20 percent of their total capital as excess (Haberman 1987, p. 6).

Implications for Holding Companies

If a securities firm is organized as a holding company, the net capital rules will apply to the regulated broker-dealer subsidiary. So as securities firms have broadened their activities to include new products that entail nonmarketable credit exposure, the portion of their business accomplished in the unregulated affiliate has increased. Swaps, whole-mortgage loan trading, and bridge loans are among the innovations handled by affiliates. In response, the SEC has written capital rules to encourage the financial separation of affiliates. Transactions between regulated and unregulated affiliates are treated harshly. For example, unsecured loans require a 100 percent charge and have the effect of transferring liquid capital. This structure does not forbid advances to or investments in affiliates; it merely applies a strict capital evaluation. A firm willing to move capital out of its regulated unit is not constrained by regulation as long as its net capital remains above warning levels. Competitive pressures to report impressive excess net capital figures are a strong incentive to maximize the liquid capital within the broker-dealer subsidiary (Haberman 1987, pp. 6–7).

CAPITAL TRENDS

Figure 5-1 illustrates the rapid growth in the 1980s of both total and equity capital and the industry's response to the slowdown of 1988 to 1990. The security industry

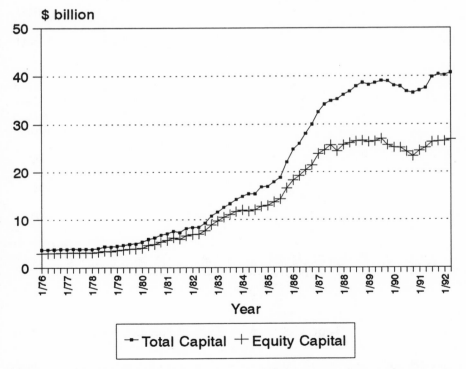

Figure 5-1. Total capital and equity capital. (Securities and Exchange Commission data)

took some time to change direction in response to market factors. Figure 5-2 shows both required net capital and excess net capital. Required net capital had two breaks, one in 1982 in response to revisions of the capital rule by the SEC and the second in response to the stock market crash in October 1987. Excess net capital tracked the total and equity capital series with slightly more volatility after 1987. Finally, Figure 5-3 restates the data from Figure 5-2 as a percentage of total capital, illustrating the significance of its decline in 1982. The ratio format of excess net capital also reveals the cyclical nature of the series that is not evident in the original series.

NET CAPITAL DURING THE 1987 MARKET CRASH

Large Investment Banks and National Full-Time Firms

After the stock market crash in 1987, the SEC examined the financial statements for October 1987 of fifteen of the largest investment bankers and full-line firms (U.S. Securities and Exchange Commission 1988, sec. 5). Between October 14 and October 30, 1987, these firms reported combined losses of approximately $796.5 million in their equity positions. Two of the firms lost over $100 million; one firm did not report its losses resulting from its equity position. The losses of four large invest-

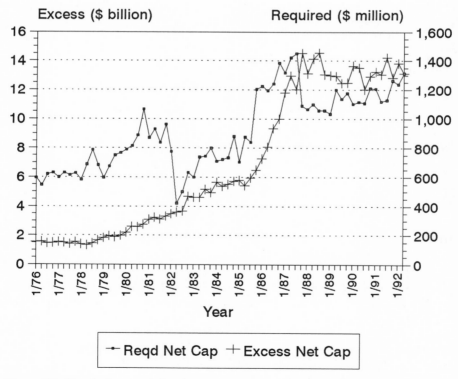

Figure 5-2. Required net capital and excess net capital. (Securities and Exchange Commission data)

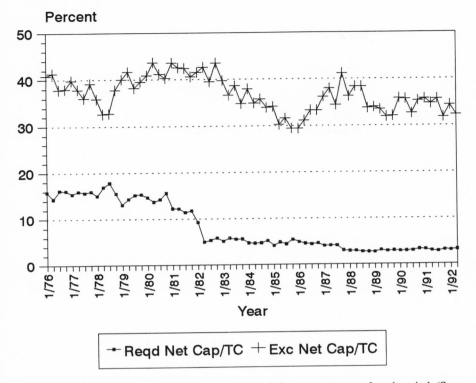

Figure 5-3. Required net capital and excess net capital as a percentage of total capital. (Securities and Exchange Commission data)

ment-banking were exacerbated by contractual commitments that those firms had made in connection with underwriting the common stock of British Petroleum (BP). The break occurred after the syndicate had agreed to buy the securities at a fixed price but before they could be resold to investors. Because the Bank of England ultimately determined that it would offer to repurchase the securities at a price above the postcrash market value, the losses to the four broker-dealers were substantially confined to pretax losses of approximately $325 million. Many of the firms also reported losses from error accounts and bad debts, totaling approximately $235.8 million. Presumably most of these losses arose from losses in cash and margin accounts.

Despite these losses, each of these firms, as well as all other sizable firms, remained above their early-warning levels. At month's end, after the losses, the fifteen firms showed a total ownership equity of approximately $16.9 billion, a total net capital of approximately $9.4 billion, and excess net capital above the required minimum levels of approximately $8.3 billion. In large part, the losses were contained because of the diversity of the firm's assets. The market value of these firms' equity positions at the end of September was only a relatively small fraction of their total assets. The market value of the equity positions in almost every case was less than 20 percent of the total market value of all securities' positions and, in most cases, less than 5 percent of the firm's total assets.[5]

Firms That Ceased Operation

Approximately 6,700 firms that did not transact business solely on the floor of an exchange were registered with the SEC as broker-dealers at the time of the crash. Slightly less than 1 percent of that number (58 firms) had violated the net capital rule for reasons related to the October market crash and so ceased operations at least temporarily. About one-half (30) did not recover from the events of the week of October 19, the great majority falling below the required levels of net capital because of losses in accounts or expected losses in customers' cash or margin accounts (U.S. Securities and Exchange Commission 1988, sec. 5, pp. 7–8).

CUSTOMER PROTECTION PROCEEDINGS: THE EXPERIENCE

Another important measure of the net capital rule's effectiveness is the number and magnitude of broker-dealer failures over time. Table 5-3 shows the number of customer protection proceedings initiated by the SIPC from 1971 to 1991. The 228 proceedings represent less than 1 percent of the approximately 28,800 broker-dealers that were members of the SIPC during these twenty-one years. During this period, cash and securities distributed for customers' accounts aggregated approximately

Table 5-3. Customer Protection Proceedings of SIPC, 1971–1991

Year	Number of Proceedings	Net Distribution from SIPC for Customers Accounts ($ Thousand)
1971	24	401
1972	40	7,343
1973	30	31,706
1974	15	(222)*
1975	8	4,746
1976	4	764
1977	7	254
1978	4	2,518
1979	6	(4,779)*
1980	5	2,848
1981	10	63,238
1982	8	9,359
1983	7	37,138
1984	9	(1,992)*
1985	12	7,674
1986	8	10,472
1987	4	17,828
1988	5	(1,878)*
1989	6	(15,725)*
1990	8	(484)
1991	8	3,625
Total	228	$174,834

*Net recoveries.

Source: Securities Investor Protection Corporation (1992), pp. 6, 17.

$1.8 billion. Of that amount, approximately $1.6 billion came from debtors' estates and $174 million came from the SIPC fund. In 1992 the SIPC had 8,153 members (Securities Investor Protection Corporation 1992, p. 6). From 1980 to 1991, an average of 7.5 proceedings were initiated each year.

The SIPC's statistics on broker-dealer liquidations do not tell the complete story on industry liquidations. Although there were only nine SIPC liquidations in 1987 and 1988, there were eighteen such self-liquidations in which the NASD oversaw the distribution of over $250 million in customers' property involving relatively undercapitalized firms. These cases are examples of potential exposure to the SIPC's fund. In one of the self-liquidations, a firm held $70 million worth of customers' securities, although it had only $61,000 in net capital. In another case, a firm had $8 million worth of customers' securities and only $42,000 in net capital. Since the NASD was aware of these two firms' problems, it was able to have them move the customers' accounts to other clearing firms and thereby avoid SIPC liquidation (SEC Release 27249, September 15, 1989).

BENEFITS OF SELF-REGULATION

In the securities industry, the self-regulatory organizations, including the NASD and the exchanges, monitor firms' net capital positions. Self-regulation enlists the self-interest of members of the securities community to ensure that their industry is not plagued by large numbers of broker-dealer failures. NASD and exchange officials visit those firms having difficulties with net capital—that is, that are frequently at the early warning level. The self-regulators encourage the firms to increase their capital, and if an increase in capital is not sufficient to solve the firm's problems, then the self-regulators arrange for the weak firm to merge with a healthier firm. In this manner, the self-regulators forestall involvement by the SEC.

CONCLUSION

Key elements of the SEC's net capital system include (1) haircuts, which are a risk-adjustment of the broker-dealers' liquid assets; (2) the ability of broker-dealers to readily mark-to-market the value of most of their assets; (3) the ability of regulators to closely monitor the financial position of broker-dealers through net capital reports; and (4) the ability of self-regulators to work with problem broker-dealers to help them solve their problems. This system has worked well in the 1980s in preventing failures and customer losses that would draw down the SIPC insurance fund.

NOTES

1. For a discussion of the development of the net capital rule, see Molinari and Kibler (1983).

2. Free credit balances are customer's funds held by broker-dealers that may be withdrawn by customers on demand. Usually they are generated when (1) a customer gives cash to a broker-dealer with

the advice that instructions for the purchase of securities will follow, (2) a broker-dealer receives interest or dividends on the customer's securities held in "street" name and does not immediately transmit those funds to the customer, or (3) a broker-dealer sells a customer's securities and holds the proceeds pending reinvestment or other instructions from the customer. In December 1983, free credit balances and other credit balances in customers' accounts with NYSE firms exceeded $16 billion (U.S. Securities and Exchange Commission 1985, p. 26).

3. This section is based on Haberman (1987).

4. Hypothecation is the act of borrowing money to finance purchasing or carrying securities using those securities as collateral for the loan.

5. During October 1987, several large firms responded to their equity losses and the volatile market conditions by substantially increasing their net capital, through infusions of equity capital from their parent or affiliated entities or through subordinated borrowings. Even without the infusions, however, all the firms would have remained above the early-warning levels at the end of October.

6

Principal–Agent Problems in the Securities Industry

Multiproduct securities firms face potential principal–agent problems or conflicts of interest in almost all their activities. They may represent both the buyer and the seller in a simple brokerage transaction, or a securities firm's research department may recommend the purchase of a stock in which the firm has a large inventory as a market maker. As an investment banker, a securities firm works with a corporate issuer to set the price of a new offering and then uses its brokerage system to sell the stock to its retail customers.

Conflicts are common because valuable efficiencies result from having one firm perform a variety of functions. Higher transaction costs would clearly result if we eliminated the broker-dealer conflict, by separating various lines of business, but neither Congress nor the U.S. Securities and Exchange Commission (SEC) has found these conflicts to be so severe as to require dismantling multiproduct securities firms. However, legislation does define the fiduciary obligations of the securities firm as broker, dealer, investment banker, investment manager, and so forth. Although the legislation does not guarantee a result, it does reflect the expectation of special conduct by the fiduciary.

With further deregulation in the financial services industry, the potential for conflicts of interest will no doubt expand. This chapter reviews the current conflicts in the securities industry in each line of business and examines the existing economic and regulatory solutions to these conflicts.

FIDUCIARY OBLIGATIONS OF SECURITIES FIRMS

In all business transactions, there exists a conflict of interest between buyer and seller. If a buyer feels mistreated, he or she can shift to another seller, but with professional services, it is more difficult to shop around. Mayer (1980) suggests the following reasons for this difficulty: (1) the need or wish for confidentiality, (2) the importance of the service rendered—the cost of a mistake is too high to justify relying on trial and error—and (3) the inability of the buyer to evaluate not only the value of the service but even what service is required. Even after the transaction is complete, it is difficult to determine whether the service was appropriate and the fee reasonable. In regard to financial services, the government allows the customer to put aside caveat emptor and to trust the seller. In turn, that trust creates a fiduciary obligation for the seller. In transactions between a broker and a customer, the broker is the fiduciary and so has unique responsibilities. The SEC states that those fiduciary duties must be performed with "the same high standard of conduct as the law imposes upon attorneys, administrators, executors, guardians, bankers, public officials, and other persons vested with fiduciary powers" (U.S. Securities and Exchange Commission 1936, p. xiv).

CONFLICTS AS A RESULT
OF GROWTH AND DIVERSIFICATION

Conflicts of interest arise naturally out of many profit-seeking endeavors. As firms attempt to grow, they are attracted to activities that are "closely related" to those in which they are already engaged. These may be either complementary or similar to existing activities, and they often require similar facilities. These additional activities frequently can be undertaken with relatively low marginal costs of production and/or distribution, and they afford not only potential economies of scale and scope but also the greater appeal of a fuller line. For example, a securities firm that buys bonds for its own account can—at no great added expense and with a number of advantages—underwrite and retail bonds, advise on bond purchases, and manage bond portfolios in a fiduciary capacity. But the addition of each of these supplemental activities presents a potential for conflict, for each places the securities firm in a role in which its interests may vary by function and client (Herman 1980, pp. 25–26).

Diversification therefore enlarges the possibilities for conflict of interest. "Related" activities often mean conflict, and the added functions frequently raise the number of choices that an institution must make between its interests and those to whom it has some fiduciary obligation.

CONFLICTS IN THE BROKERAGE BUSINESS

A broker-dealer's ability to use customers' free credit balances as the basis for margin loans leads to conflicts of interest. These balances tend to build up for a number of reasons. When securities are held in "street name," dividend and interest payments to customers are commonly kept in the brokerage house unless a customer gives contrary instructions. There is little pressure to reinvest these sums, which are of little financial significance in the individual account but impressive in the aggregate.

The approach that regulators have selected to minimize this conflict is to allow the firms to pay interest on free credit balances. But because the interest paid is below that charged for funds lent to margin customers, there is an incentive for the broker-dealers to urge their customers to leave funds in these accounts. The SEC and Congress clearly did not intend that cash balances be maintained at broker-dealers in order to earn interest, and the Securities Investor Protection Act of 1970 was not intended to function as deposit insurance.

In 1981, the SEC became concerned that some broker-dealers were implying, in oral communication and in written advertisements, that they paid interest on customers' free credit balances. The payment of interest on these balances normally does not raise regulatory concerns. But when broker-dealers use advertising, promotional, or selling practices to obtain these funds, they may be in violation of the Securities Investor Protection Corporation (SIPC) regulations. The SEC cautioned persons who deposit or leave money with broker-dealers solely for the purpose of earning interest that they would not be entitled to SIPC protection (SEC Release 34-18262, p. 1563-D).

There are, therefore, incentives for firms to encourage customers to leave free credit balances with them. Although firms are restrained from promoting this behavior, they are not restrained from encouraging their customers to engage in margin borrowing. Margin loans, at interest rates significantly lower than those on bank or credit card debt, are promoted as an attractive source of ready cash for brokerages' customers (*New York Times,* November 23, 1986, p. F-13). Brokers typically charge half a percentage point less than banks do for similarly collateralized short-term loans.

Since the SIPC protects these free credit balances, this insurance forms the foundation for margin revenues. In addition, a brokerage firm can pledge a customer's margin securities, which are left with the broker, as collateral to borrow funds (usually from banks or other lenders) in order to make loans to customers. The SIPC insurance gives assurance to customers that the cash left as free credit balances and the margin securities left with brokers will be protected (up to the deposit insurance limits).

Margin interest revenues, which accounted for around 10 percent of the industry's revenues in the 1980s, allow securities firms to expand their business as more revenue is contributed through margin lending. If the extension of their business, made possible by margin revenues, is into more risky endeavors, then the SIPC insurance will be a source of moral hazard, a problem often found in insurance systems.[1] It occurs when insurance creates incentives to take risks against which that insurance provides protection. If the SIPC insurance has encouraged or enabled broker-dealers to pursue riskier strategies and has increased the likelihood of failure or bankruptcy, then it will have created a moral hazard (Fons 1987).

In addition to moral hazard, adverse selection may be a problem, occurring when the insurance protection encourages those most likely to produce the outcome insured against to purchase insurance. Adverse selection would exist if the insurance protection attracted high-risk takers or those willing to engage in fraud.

Table 6-1 offers data on SIPC proceedings initiated between 1975 and 1990. Between the date that the firm registered as a broker-dealer and the date of the initial SIPC filing, the years in business did not change much between the 1970s and the 1980s, suggesting that few newly opened firms were the subject of SIPC proceedings; that is, adverse selection was not apparent in the number of SIPC failures.

Conflicts in the Broker–Client Relationship

A broker provides a wide range of services to clients, foremost among them being the execution of buy and sell orders for stocks and bonds. For this service, the broker

Table 6-1. SIPC Proceedings Initiated and Years in Business of
Liquidated Firms, 1975–1990

	Number of Proceedings Initiated	Average Number of Years Between Registration Date as a Broker-Dealer and Date SIPC Proceedings Initiated
1975	8	6.6
1976	4	4.6
1977	7	7.0
1978	4	1.0
1979	6	2.8
1980	5	6.5
1981	10	12.8
1982	8	5.1
1983	7	10.8
1984	9	9.2
1985	12	5.9
1986	8	6.6
1987	4	11.0
1988	5	10.1
1989	6	4.1
1990	8	11.5

Source: Securities Investor Protection Corporation, *Annual Report,* various issues.

receives a commission based on the value of securities bought or sold. Although some investors base investment decisions on hunches, tips, or personal assessment of securities, the majority rely on broker-dealers for recommendations that will meet their investment objectives, and this suggests an inherent conflict between the interests of the investor and those of the stock broker.[2]

The SEC and the courts have developed three complementary and sometimes overlapping restrictions on this relationship in order to manage these conflicts. These restrictions—the shingle theory, the suitability doctrine, and the antichurning rule—were derived from the express regulatory provisions of the securities acts.

The Shingle Theory
The high standards of conduct required by the securities acts are based on the assumption that investors, particularly unsophisticated investors, are dependent on their brokers' investment advice. Unless the investor has expressed a desire to buy a given security, the investment decision is effectively made by the broker. In hanging out his or her "shingle," the broker implies that he or she will deal fairly with all customers and will have an adequate and reasonable basis for each recommendation. A broker making an investment recommendation also implies that a reasonable investigation has been made and that the recommendation is based on its findings. The broker must disclose the information pertaining to the securities that is known or can be ascertained from public sources. In addition, the broker must disclose whether any information essential to a complete analysis of the security by the broker is lacking.

The Suitability Doctrine

The broker's recommendation must also be suitable for the particular investor. The SEC's "know your customer" rule requires brokers to inquire about each customer's financial status. The intent of these rules is to minimize the possibility of excessively risky recommendations. A suitable recommendation takes into consideration the investor's needs, assets, and objectives. A broker should never recommend an investment whose risk is beyond the client's ability to bear it. The broker is not required to be infallible; rather, suitability is evaluated on the basis of the broker's diligence and prudence in matching the recommendation to the client. Salmanowitz (1977, p. 1086) suggests that suitability is an evolving doctrine, applied on a case-by-case basis and thus incapable of precise definition.

The Antichurning Rule

In contrast with the evolving nature of the suitability requirement, the policy against churning is established in Rule 15cl-7(a). A broker is prohibited from excessive trading for an account in which he or she holds discretionary powers or for an account in which, by virtue of the broker's relationship with the customer, he or she can influence the volume or frequency of transactions. The broker's motivation for churning is to generate high commissions. Churning is often accompanied by unsuitable transactions. The most likely customers to be churned are unsophisticated investors who have come into a large amount of money and who in many cases have given their brokers discretionary control over their accounts.

Brokerage firms have mechanisms in place to detect churning—that is, computer programs that flag excessive trading. Furthermore, compliance departments are in place to investigate possible churning. For some firms, the broker must receive approval from the branch manager before executing trades for discretionary accounts. Despite these safeguards, churning still exists in the securities world. Of 200 pending investigations of abusive trading at the New York Stock Exchange (NYSE) in 1985, 50 involved churning (*Financial World,* September 17, 1985, p. 34). Customers have to clear many hurdles before they can recover full compensation from the brokerage firms, and the brokers have access to an array of legal defenses. Not only are damages are hard to calculate, but churning also is hard to prove, as it is not one trade but a series of trades.

Some brokers have concluded that they face an inherent conflict of interest because they profit from trading commissions whether or not their clients gain. This concern has led some brokers to secure money managers for their clients. The brokers then collect fees only from those trades directed by these investment advisers. These accounts have become big business for broker-dealers as investors have pumped more than $40 billion into these accounts, making them one of the hottest products for individual investors since the mutual fund. They are called "wrap" accounts because the asset-management fees and transaction costs are "wrapped" together into one flat fee based on a percentage of the assets under management. The accounts usually require a minimum investment of $100,000 and an annual fee, which typically amounts to 3 percent of assets under management (*Wall Street Journal,* January 6, 1993, p. C-1).

Broker–Client Contracts

The standard broker–client contract requires that investors' claims be solved through arbitration, not litigation. Some investors have objected to this requirement, however, arguing that arbitration hearings are run for the most part by the self-regulatory groups supported by the securities industry (*New York Times,* March 29, 1987, p. F-1).

The courts have not enforced arbitration clauses in broker–client contracts since the U.S. Supreme Court decided in 1953 that investors have the right to present their claims to judges and juries. In 1987, however, the Supreme Court ruled that clauses in standard customer–broker agreements requiring arbitration of disputes can be enforced. This "victory" for the industry focused attention on arbitration, and soon after, the SEC suggested to the industry that it make a number of reforms in the arbitration system, and the industry complied (Clareman 1991, pp. 207–208). As a result of these reforms, most of the investors' disadvantages in arbitration have been swept away. Although one of the arbitrators on a panel may continue to be from the securities industry, the public members must be what their names imply; anyone with a meaningful tie to the industry is disqualified or must be counted as the industry arbitrator. In practice, arbitrators are often business people, lawyers, university business professors, and retirees from these professions.

Clareman reports that arbitration panels have an inherent tendency to reach a compromise that gives something to the investor. Statistics from the *Securities Arbitration Commentator* show that between May 1989 and January 1990, investors won 532 (or 55 percent) of the 964 cases brought to arbitration. Of the $63.8 million claimed as compensatory damages by the winners of these cases, the aggrieved investors won $27.7 million (or 43 percent) of what they asked for.

CONFLICTS IN THE DEALER BUSINESS

Conflicts arise whenever a dealer maintains an inventory in a security that the firm's sales force is recommending to its clients. The customers, of course, assume that their broker is acting as their agent. But a favorable research report works as a very effective selling tool, for even if the research is accurate and the stock is a good buy, the increased demand for the security will increase the value of the broker-dealer's inventory. Another aspect of this conflict is that the broker usually receives a higher commission payment from the firm when a customer purchases an over-the-counter security in which the firm makes a market (Mayer 1980).

The most troublesome dealer conflict arises when the stock price is falling. If the customer has a position in the stock and the firm has a trading inventory, what type of advice should the broker give to the customer?

Block Trading

Many of the largest securities firms provide block-trading, investment-banking, and investment management services for their clients, but these three activities within the same firm present a potential for multiple conflicts. If a firm is both a block trader and an investment manager, a conflict can arise when the block positioner places its discretionary accounts on the passive side of a trade. This allows the positioner to avoid a very risky activity but still permits the firm to collect the commission for the deal (Mayer 1980).

Another kind of conflict may be created if a positioner makes a bid for the firm's own account that is rejected by the seller. Then the firm may buy the securities for the discretionary account at a slightly higher price and pocket the brokerage commission. Buying securities from a managed account for the broker-dealer's account at a price below a previous sale also suggests a possibility of conflict. If a block positioner purchases a large block, breaks it up, and sells it to its retail customers, it can create a conflict. It may be argued that the retail clients are getting a good deal if they do not have to pay commissions and benefit from the positioner's wholesale purchase price. On the other hand, a large block is usually distributed to retail customers when wholesale customers (generally institutions) do not want to participate, perhaps because of superior information.

CONFLICTS WITH INSTITUTIONAL CUSTOMERS
Money Management

When an institutional customer, such as a mutual fund, is affiliated with a brokerage house, possible conflicts abound. Here a committee of ''disinterested directors'' of the fund meets monthly and reviews all business relations between the fund and the brokerage house. As a dealer, a firm cannot sell to its own fund without prior SEC approval. But this approval is generally not sought because it would take a month and yield unfavorable publicity. Under the terms of the Investment Company Act of 1940, the fund also is barred from taking any action in connection with blocks that the firm positions or any underwritings in which the firm participates. And under the 1975 amendments to the Exchange Act, brokers managing mutual funds are compelled to trade their funds through other brokers.

The rules are not quite as strict when the money that a broker-dealer manages comes from a pension fund or a source other than a publicly offered mutual fund. To avoid the types of conflicts that arise between money management and brokerage, some broker-dealers avoid money management altogether (Mayer 1980).

Front Running

Complaints that some securities firms profit by ''front running''—trading in advance of customers' orders—were noted by the SEC following the October 1987 market crash. In several instances, firms traded in futures ahead of their customers' futures and stock programs. Large institutions' customers also raise questions of fairness regarding this practice.

In its report on the 1987 crash, the SEC tried to determine whether securities firms that provided portfolio insurance traded ahead of customers' orders on October 16, 19, and 20, but it found that the practice was not general or widespread (*Wall Street*

Journal, February 3, 1988, p. 6). Nevertheless, the NYSE tightened its rules on how brokers could trade for their own accounts. It has been argued that the SEC should improve its monitoring capabilities so as to be able to detect front running directly (*Business Week,* May 16, 1988, p. 38).

CONFLICTS IN INVESTMENT BANKING

Due Diligence

Before underwriting a securities offering, securities laws require investment bankers to investigate the financial and operational details of a company and to identify its weaknesses—that is, to use "due diligence" to protect and inform potential investors. Investment bankers are exposed to civil liabilities for misstatements in a prospectus unless they had, "after reasonable investigation, reasonable grounds to believe and did believe" that the material in the prospectus was true (Auerbach and Hayes 1986). This is the SEC's main method of protecting the public from misrepresentation of a corporation's financial and business status.

Conflicts arise because the investment banker as an underwriter has several strong economic incentives to sell an issue to anyone who can be convinced to buy it. In a *firm commitment* underwriting, investment bankers incur a significant risk by purchasing the stock or bond from the issuer. They must then sell it quickly, for if the stock or bond price were to drop, the underwriter would suffer a severe financial setback.

Merchant Banking

Large Wall Street firms are providing more of their own capital to make deals work; that is, they are taking an equity position in some deals, as London's merchant bankers have been doing for centuries. The conflict centers on how investment bankers will be influenced by the money they invest in such deals. The customers of investment bankers assume that the bankers will put their customers' interests first, but in the new environment there is evidence that new conflicts have been created: To the extent that the investment bankers have become a potential buyer of a company, they are competing with their own clients in the market for corporate control, which may make some companies less likely to trust their investment bankers.

Inside Information and the Chinese Wall

Multiproduct firms that have investment banking as one line of business constantly gain access to inside information while working with an issuer. Often this inside information, if known by the public, can significantly affect the price of the issuer's stock. To protect themselves from liability to those investors who do not have access to the same information, multiproduct firms have attempted to isolate their investment-banking departments from their trading departments, by erecting a "Chinese wall." This "don't-tell-your-partner" technique is offered as a practical solution to the conflict problem of (1) the duty of confidentiality to the investment-banking client, (2) the duty to deal fairly with the firm's brokerage and market-making customers and the obligation of the securities firm to know the merchandise,[3] and (3) the obligation of the securities firm possessing the inside information either to disclose it or to refrain from using it.

Some firms have "reinforced" the Chinese wall by additional policies, including a "no recommendation" policy and a "restricted list" procedure. These policies are intended to solve problems that arise when the firm's investment bankers acquire inside information about a client (1) while the firm's brokers or investment advisers are making recommendations with respect to that company's securities, (2) when the firm's investment management department is purchasing or selling the company securities for accounts managed by the firm, or (3) when the firm's trading department is purchasing or selling such securities for accounts managed by the firm (Lipton and Mazur 1975, p. 465).

The "no recommendation" approach is a policy of not making any recommendations with respect to securities about which a firm is likely to obtain inside information through investment-banking, directorial, or other relationships. This policy avoids situations in which a firm's brokers recommend the purchase or sale of a security to customers on the basis of public information, even though the investment bankers in the same firm know that this public information is incomplete, misleading, or false.

A further step is the restricted list: If a firm places a security on its restricted list, the firm is precluded from investing in the securities for its own account. A rigorous form of the restricted list prohibits firms from investing in the securities of an investment-banking client.

Although all securities firms construct a Chinese wall within their firms, not all add the additional reinforcement steps of the no recommendation and the restricted list. They cite difficulties with the restricted list; for example, adding a security to or deleting it from the restricted list would send a signal that some significant inside information exists about the investment-banking client. For this reason, some firms prohibit their salespersons from recommending for purchase the securities of its investment-banking clients.

The SEC's position is close to the more cautious Brothers' position. That is, the SEC endorses the Chinese wall technique of isolating inside information from traders and brokers, but it also suggests that to eliminate the signaling of a problem, the securities firm should restrict the security of a client at the same time it enters into an investment-banking relationship with a client.

THE GENERAL ECONOMIC VIEW OF AGENCY PROBLEMS

Economists have used price theory to examine the ways that firms and individuals have structured their relationships to resolve or at least manage conflicts. With frictionless markets (e.g., Coase 1960), incentive conflicts are assumed to be costlessly controlled. That is, it is assumed that contracts can be costlessly negotiated, administered, and enforced in order to control the conflict by restricting individuals' and firms' behavior. It is also assumed that in this scenario there are zero transaction costs (Mayers and Smith 1981, p. 408).

In the real world, the costs of writing and enforcing contracts to manage these conflicts or agency problems are substantial. Therefore, incentives exist to structure relationships and institutions to reduce these costs. The current institutional arrangements in the industry represent contractual solutions to these conflicts that are efficient from the standpoint of all contracting parties.[4] And as Alchian stated, "Whenever successful enterprises are observed, the elements common to those observed successes will be associated with success and copied by others in pursuit of profits or success" (1950, p. 218). So as this industry grows and changes, the new conflicts that emerge will be managed through negotiation among the interested parties. Some of these problems can be resolved by market forces, some by government, and some by a combination of both.

OVERALL CONFLICT CONTROL

Three kinds of institutional arrangements and controls (economic, regulatory, and legal) exist in the securities business to limit the exploitation of potential conflicts (Saunders 1985).

Economic Controls

Most conflicts involve a probable trade-off between short-term and long-term profits for a firm. When there are no internal controls limiting managers' incentives to exploit such conflicts, or if those controls are weak, there are at least three external "market controls" preventing managers from exploiting conflicts for short-term gains: the market for corporate control, the monitoring role provided by various third parties, and the value of reputation for long-term profit maximization.

The Market for Corporate Control
If managers pursue short-term profits by exploiting conflicts, thereby adversely affecting or damaging the enterprise's long-term value, shareholders will have an incentive to replace them with managers whose objectives are more closely aligned with their own long-term objectives. However, shareholders often have difficulty replacing existing management. When managers are not maximizing the shareholders' wealth and the stockholders are unable to replace them, the firm will become a target for a takeover. This financial discipline, enforced through the stock market, is one of the most important elements in the market for corporate control.

Performance Monitoring by Third Parties
Various securities-rating agencies, such as Moody's and Standard & Poor's, monitor externally and independently the financial performance of securities firms that issue securities. Securities analysts closely follow the public securities companies; the financial press and trade publications are constantly searching for important stories about the conduct and behavior of financial firms; and there is substantial movement of employees at all job levels in securities firms. All these factors work against a firm's successfully exploiting a conflict. Although exploitation may be possible for a time, it is not likely to continue indefinitely.

Numerous sources of information publish comparisons of firms' performance in the management of funds (e.g., *Forbes Annual Mutual Fund Survey*) and in the performance of stock recommendations by brokers. Pension fund performance is also evaluated and compared. This monitoring makes it difficult for firms to exploit their customers.

The Value of Reputation and Long-Term Profit Maximization

Because stockholders, through boards of directors, want to maximize long-term profits, they naturally will be concerned with building and maintaining a good long-term reputation with their customers. This reputation, or a stock of ''goodwill,'' can be viewed as an asset of a firm that has real value to existing shareholders and is reflected in binding commitments or implicit contracts with its customers.[5] For example, securities-underwriting activities undertaken by a firm with its customers are similar to economic games taking place in a repeated, or dynamic, market setting. Although the securities firm may earn a net profit in the short term from exploiting a conflict with a given customer—such as promoting the sale of tainted securities— in the long term the exploitation of conflicts, or the breach of the implicit contract, may damage the reputation of the securities firm and its various affiliates, as well as its future growth and profit prospects. Specifically, customers who feel they have been exploited will move their business to another firm, and adverse publicity will deter new customers from forming permanent relationships with an exploitative securities firm. In particular, the greater the flow of information among customers, the higher will be the cost to the firm for exploiting conflict.

Institutions are sophisticated purchasers of securities services and so are less likely to be exploited. Individuals, however, probably have to rely on the protection of the self-regulatory organizations and the SEC, and there still are a few securities firms that use ''boiler rooms'' and various other scams to exploit poorly informed individual investors.

Regulatory Controls

In addition to economic disincentives, regulatory controls restrain the exploitation of conflicts. Margin requirements and collateral requirements, combined with direct monitoring and examination by regulatory authorities, impose regulatory nonmarket constraints on conflict exploitation. Margin requirements substantially limit the amount of credit that investors can use to purchase securities. Therefore, high margin requirements limit securities firms' ability to support the price of securities underwritten by their affiliates with loans to individual investors. Violations of these restrictions can lead to costly penalties' being imposed on managers and shareholders if discovered by the SEC. Regulatory examination and surveillance thus provide an additional disincentive to exploit conflicts. The more efficient the examiners are, the higher the expected cost of exploiting a potential conflict will be, with potential costs or penalties ranging from fines to criminal prosecution.

Rules of Fair Practice

The National Association of Securities Dealers (NASD) adopted the Rules of Fair Practice to form a code of ethics by which its member firms are obligated to conduct their business. The rules spell out fair treatment of customers as well as behavior toward customers in regard to influencing their investment decisions. The rules also define a registered representative's permissible actions in regard to discretionary accounts and customers' securities or monies and spell out the disciplinary procedures for rule violations (National Association of Securities Dealers 1985).

Legal Recourse

Customers also have the option of turning to the courts in the event of conflict exploitation, although the costs of legal action may often be prohibitive for the small investor. Such recourse has often been taken with respect to the investment management activities of securities firms, when a customer felt that a securities firm had violated its fiduciary responsibilities (Schotland 1980). Class action suits in the courts also are becoming more common in cases in which investors feel that their underwriters failed to exercise due diligence, such as in fully disclosing information prior to a new issue. The bad publicity surrounding such court cases acts as clear disincentive for securities firms to exploit conflicts, apart from the legal costs of defending such cases. An example of a class action suit is the one in 1982 and 1983 against several investment firms alleging failure to show due diligence in regard to Washington Public Power Supply System bonds.

ECONOMIC MODELS OF SPECIFIC AGENCY PROBLEMS IN THE SECURITIES INDUSTRY

The path-breaking work of Ross (1973) and Holmstrom (1979) provided a framework for analyzing the relationship in which a principal hires an agent to supply an input that affects the distribution of an outcome of interest to the principal. The input is costly to the agent and is assumed to be impossible or prohibitively costly for the principal to monitor, either directly or indirectly; thus the agent has an incentive to supply less input or effort than the principal demands. To avoid a breakdown in exchange, an optimal incentive contract is devised that aligns the preferences of the principal and the agent (Golec 1990, pp. 1–5).

Issuer–Investment Banker Contracts

Baron (1982) developed a theory of the demand for investment-banking advice and distribution services for the case in which the investment banker is better informed about the capital market than is the issuer and the issuer cannot observe the distribution effort expended by the banker.[6] Baron describes the optimal contract under which the better-informed investment banker makes offer price decision. The contract is structured to deal with the adverse selection and moral hazard problems resulting from the informational asymmetry between the issuer and banker and the issuer's limited ability to observe the banker's effort.

Under the optimal contract, the offer price decision is delegated to the banker who sets the offer price based on his or her superior information about the capital market. The issuer must compensate the banker for use of this information, and so the banker shares in the gains from this superior information. Distribution by the banker may also have value to the issuer: An investment banker may be able to facilitate distribution because of his or her ability to "certify" the issue to the market by putting his or her reputation behind it.

Investment Company–Investment Adviser Contracts

Starks (1987) analyzed the agency problems between investment company owners and their agents, the financial management advisers. Two types of performance fee contracts have been used most often in this relationship: *symmetric* performance incentive fees and *bonus* performance incentive fees. Under the symmetric fee approach, the manager receives a percentage of the market value of the asset, plus a bonus or penalty, depending on whether the portfolio return was higher or lower than the return on a particular market index, usually the Dow-Jones Industrial Average or Standard & Poor's 500 index. Under the bonus incentive fee, the manager receives a percentage of the market value of the assets plus a bonus if the managed portfolio's return exceeds the index return. Under this approach, no penalties are assessed if the return is lower than the benchmark return. Thus the bonus performance fee schedule is an asymmetric form of the symmetric performance fee schedule.

Starks found that when the performance standard was a market index, symmetric fee schedules eliminated one of the potential agency problems, but not another problem. When the manager's only decision was to select the portfolio's risk level, the symmetric performance contract provided the appropriate incentives for selecting the investor's desired risk level. On the other hand, if the manager's decisions included the amount of resources to expend on managing the portfolio, the agency problem was not be resolved by the symmetric fee schedule. The portfolio manager always chose less effort or resources to manage the portfolio than the investor (here, the investment company) wanted.

Starks concluded that the symmetric approach motivates the portfolio managers to choose the optimal risk level but a lower-than-optimal resource level. But, if given the bonus performance contract, portfolio managers will choose an even lower level of resource expenditures and a higher-than-optimal risk level. Starks argues that therefore the SEC's decision in 1971 to abolish the bonus performance fee contract is consistent with the results of her model.

CONCLUSION

Conflicts expand with diversification, but they can be managed through industry and regulatory mechanisms. One benefit of diversification is that it allows firms to lessen the impact on the soundness of the overall firm of risk that originates in one line of business. On the other hand, the organizational steps that a firm must take to control conflicts, including the erection of Chinese walls, tends to limit the firm's ability to take advantage of potential economies of scope across lines of business.

More research is needed to identify the agency and transaction cost issues that underlie the existing relationships in the industry. This additional work will provide a more complete framework for policymakers, who will then be better able to judge whether a market solution is adequate to manage a conflict problem or if regulation is necessary.

The recent breakdown in conflict control on a large scale with the insider trading of the 1980s and the government bond–trading scandal of 1991 show that there are many opportunities to take advantage of the conflicts inherent in this business. However, these violations were also discovered and punished.

NOTES

1. For a discussion of the problem of moral hazard in the savings and loan industry, see White (1991).

2. This section is based on Salmanowitz (1977).

3. The obligation to deal fairly with customers rests on the "shingle" theory. The broker-dealer must reveal to the customer any information about a security that might reasonably be expected to affect a trading decision (Lipton and Mazur 1975, p. 474).

4. For a discussion of the survivorship principle, see Alchian (1950) and Stigler (1958).

5. Bull (1983, p. 659) argues that concern by the firm for its brand name or reputation may lead the principal to fulfill his or her contract.

6. In earlier, related models, Mandelker and Raviv (1977), Baron (1979), and Baron and Holmstrom (1980) characterized the optimal contract between an issuer and an investment banker in the context of a negotiated sale.

III

Elements of Securities Industry Structure

7

Characteristics of Demand

Institutional investors increasingly dominate U.S. securities markets in terms of volume of trading. These huge institutions trade large blocks of securities and allocate or hedge their portfolios in ways that can move markets, especially when they act in unison. Their needs therefore strongly influence the types of products offered by broker-dealers and exchanges. Although individual investors are increasing their participation in the securities markets, their participation is increasingly through mutual fund ownership rather than direct stock ownership.

INDIVIDUALS

Individual investors now own just over 50 percent of U.S. equity and account for less than one-fifth of all trading. Over half the population owns some type of equity investment, although most of it is through participation in institutional investments, such as mutual, pension, and insurance funds. Direct stock ownership is concentrated among a relatively small proportion of investors. The United States nevertheless, has the highest level of individual participation in the securities markets of any country in the world. For instance, less than 25 percent of British citizens hold stock investments (U.S. Office of Technology Assessment 1990, pp. 6, 7, 33).

The New York Stock Exchange (NYSE) occasionally conducts surveys of share ownership among individual customers in the United States, and the results are presented in Table 7-1. By 1970, 30.9 million individuals owned stock in a publicly traded company or in a stock mutual fund, more than doubling the number of shareholders in 1959. The increased ownership was, in part, a response to the bull market in the 1960s. The NYSE composite index, which was at 30.94 at year-end 1960 reached a record high of 61.27 in late November 1968, an increase of almost 100 percent. The market fell in 1969 and 1970, reaching a low of 37.69 in May 1970.

Individual investors left the stock market in the 1970s as inflation reduced the returns from holding stocks, and accordingly, individual ownership dropped from 30.8 million in 1970 to 25.3 million in 1975. Ibbotson and Sinquefield (1982, p. 19) examined the impact of the relatively flat stock market of the 1970s and inflation on returns to stockholders and constructed long-term cumulative wealth indexes for

Table 7-1. NYSE Share Ownership Survey, Selected Years Between 1959 and 1990

	1959	1962	1965	1970	1975	1980	1981	1983	1985	1990*
Number of individual share owners (thousands)	12,490	17,010	20,120	30,850	25,270	30,200	32,260	42,360	47,040	51,440
Number owning shares listed on NYSE (thousands)	8,510	11,020	12,430	18,290	17,950	23,804	24,504	26,029	25,263	29,580
Share owners as percentage of population	7.1%	9.2%	10.4%	15.1%	11.9%	13.5%	14.4%	18.5%	20.1%	21.1%
Median household income (unadjusted; prior year)	$7,000	$8,000	$9,000	$13,000	$19,000	$27,000	$29,200	$33,200	$36,800	$43,800
Median age	49	48	49	48	53	46	46	45	44	43
Portfolio										
Under $10,000	N/A	N/A	N/A	8,810	11,647	17,912	17,038	22,187	24,292	20,910
$10,000–$14,999	N/A	N/A	N/A	9,001	3,072	2,290	1,945	2,783	2,674 ⎤	9,240 ⎤ 20.9
$15,000–24,999	N/A	N/A	N/A	8,272	2,760	1,847	2,115	2,068	3,214 ⎦	⎦
$25,000 and over	N/A	N/A	N/A	4,437	5,909	4,489	5,871	8,187	8,019	14,080

*1990 results are not strictly comparable with previous studies because of differences in methodologies.

Source: NYSE *Fact Book*, various issues.

various securities. These indexes measure the year-end value of investments made between 1925 and 1981; for example, one dollar invested at the end of 1925 grew in the Standard & Poor (S&P) composite index to a nominal value of $65.64 by 1968 and to $133.62 by 1981. But when adjusting the index for inflation, that same original investment grew to only $32.95 by 1968 and actually declined to $25.13 by 1981. Clearly, stock market investments were wealth-losing for investors in the 1970s.

Individuals were drawn back to the stock market in the late 1970s and were almost back to 1970 levels by 1980, with 30.2 million shareholders. The bull market that started in 1982 increased share ownership to 47 million by 1985 and 51.4 million in 1990. Perhaps because of the perceived increased volatility of the 1980s, individual investors moved to stock ownership through mutual fund ownership. Table 7-2 shows that the percentage of share owners that owned stock mutual funds increased from 23.9 percent in 1983 to 59.8 percent in 1990. Thus instead of ''leaving the market,'' as is often reported, the number of Americans owning stock actually rose in the 1980s, although most of the increase was in ownership of mutual fund shares. Table 7-2 also shows a tiering of equity ownership, with 47.3 percent of all investor portfolios holding less than $10,000 in 1990, another 20.9 percent with between $10,000 and $24,999, and a further 31.8 percent with over $25,000 invested. In 1985, 21 percent of individual investors held portfolios with over $25,000 invested. The median family income of investors was the highest ever at $43,800, with the median age of forty-three the lowest over the history of the survey. The 30 million small investors with portfolios of less than $24,999, although better off than the ''average American,'' clearly did not depend on securities market profits for the bulk of their household income and probably did little trading. Those 14 million investors with portfolios of $25,000 and above were wealthier Americans who might trade more frequently. These are the customers that many broker-dealers prize. In terms of ownership or volume of trading, however, institutions are more important than individuals on the NYSE and particularly in the larger issues. Individuals continue to be important on the American Stock Exchange (ASE), on regional exchanges, and on the over-the-counter markets. Institutions historically have been more risk averse than individuals and therefore are less likely to buy not only the smaller and less liquid seasoned equity issues but also the unseasoned new issues. In recent years, however, institutions have been increasing their holdings of non-NYSE equities.

INSTITUTIONS

Table 7-3 shows the increasing pool of institutional assets owned by type of financial institution between 1950 and 1989. Total assets grew from $107 billion in 1950 to $5,733.4 billion in 1989. The relative growth of private and state and local pension funds substantially exceeded the growth of other institutions: Private and state and local pension funds made up 11.2 percent of total institutional assets in 1950 and 33 percent in 1989. Average annual growth rates for private pension funds were 14.7 percent and 13.8 percent for state and local pensions for this period.

The 500 largest corporate pension plans together had over $640.2 billion invested in securities in 1988. The four largest—General Motors, AT&T, General Electric,

Table 7-2. Total Number of Share Owners of Public Corporations, by Type of Security (Multi-Market Basis)

Type of Security	1990		1985		1983	
	Number of Share Owners	Percentage of Total*	Number of Share Owners	Percentage of Total	Number of Share Owners	Percentage of Total
New York Stock Exchange (listed)	29,580,000	70.0	25,263,000	69.7	26,029,000	75.5
Other stock exchange (listed)	6,670,000	15.8	3,224,000	8.9	1,928,000	5.6
Over-the-counter	11,050,000	26.2	8,344,000	23.0	10,221,000	29.6
Stock mutual funds	25,260,000	59.8	10,994,000	30.3	8,257,000	23.9

*Percentages reported exceed 100 percent because investors own different types of securities.

Sources: New York Stock Exchange (1986), p. 4; New York Stock Exchange (1991), p. 11.

Table 7-3. The Increasing Pool of Total Institutional Assets, 1950–1989 ($ Billion)

	1950	1960	1970	1980	1989	Average Annual Growth Rates 1950–1989
Private pension funds	$ 7.1	$ 38.1	$112.0	$469.6	$1,163.5	14.74%
State and local pension funds	4.9	19.7	60.3	198.1	727.4	13.81
Life insurance companies	62.6	115.8	200.9	464.2	1,268.0	8.03
Other insurance companies	11.7	26.2	49.9	174.3	491.3	10.23
Open-end investment companies	3.3	17.0	46.8	61.8	555.1	15.63
Foreign sector	17.4	38.9	99.0	401.0	1,528.1	12.58
Total	$107.0	$255.7	$568.9	$1,769.0	$5,733.4	

Source: New York Stock Exchange (1991), p. 3.

and IBM—each had assets of more than $26 billion, among the public pension funds, the New York City Employees Retirement Fund had over $30 billion, and California's employment fund had over $50 billion invested in 1988 (U.S. Office of Technology Assessment 1990, pp. 32–33). Life and other insurance companies managed $1.76 trillion in securities investments in 1989. Historically, stocks were only a small part of the insurance companies' assets, for reasons related to both the industry's investment philosophy and the laws regulating the industry. State laws now, however, commonly allow more investment in stocks, although often require them to be maintained in a separate account.

Institutional ownership of NYSE listed stocks has risen from 13 percent in 1949 to nearly 50 percent. Institutions did 54.6 percent of the trading on the NYSE in 1988, up from 42.4 percent in 1969, as shown in Table 7-4. Individuals, or retail customers, did only 18.2 percent of NYSE trading in 1988, down from 33.4 percent in 1969. Institutions own about 39 percent of the stocks listed on the NASDAQ (over-the-counter market) and dominate the market for privately placed corporate securities.

Schwartz and Whitcomb (1988, p. 8) looked at this institutional activity in another way. If institutional trading is measured by the (very arbitrary) definition of block volume (trades of over 10,000 shares), the share of institutional trading on the NYSE

Table 7-4. Volume of Stock Trading on the NYSE

Year	Institutional	Retail	Member Firms
1969	42.4%	33.4%	24.2%
1980	47.4	25.7	26.9
1988	54.6	18.2	26.2

Source: U.S. Office of Technology Assessment (1990), p. 33.

rose from 3.1 percent in 1965 to 49.9 percent in 1986, and the daily average number of block trades grew at more than a 23 percent compound annual rate. The relative constancy of the size of large-block trades may be due to a tendency of institutional traders to trade very large blocks off the exchange and to break up very large orders in order to minimize the impact on the market.

Berkowitz and Logue (1987) examined the reasons that the amount of stock-trading activity by large institutional investors has risen so dramatically since the early 1960s. A substantial portion of this activity is due to the growth of institutional portfolios. For example, if a pension plan sponsor makes a large cash infusion, the pension fund manager must invest it. Some trading, therefore, is motivated by the growth or contraction of a portfolio and is not really discretionary; rather, contractual relations and obligations dictate much of the fund's activities.

There still remains an increase in discretionary trading by pension managers beyond that related to the inflow and outflow of funds. Berkowitz and Logue argue that there are two possible reasons for the greater turnover. First is the increase in attractive investment opportunities, and second is the decrease in the cost of exploiting opportunities that are not otherwise better than they had been but have become less costly to exploit. They also considered a number of new opportunities for investment: more publicly traded companies, the use of options as hedging tools, and more market-timing opportunities. But they found that even with these changes, there does not seem to be a greater potential for profitable stock trading; they believe that this is not the primary cause of the higher turnover.

There is evidence, though, that trading costs have fallen. Roll (1984) found that NYSE specialists' bid–ask spreads have generally declined. To the extent that these costs have dropped, it should lead to more trading generally and higher turnover as well. Brokerage costs also fell after the introduction of competitive commissions. Piecing together the fragmentary evidence, Berkowitz and Logue decided that the increase in wholly discretionary trading (turnover) seemed to be closely related to the declining trend in trading costs. Lower trading costs allow for more frequent portfolio revision, even when potential gains from trading are no greater than they ever have been.

Impact of the Market's Institutionalization

Shiller (1991) contents that there are two possible results of the institutionalization of the stock market. One is that with the higher percentage of financial assets held by institutional investors, financial markets should have become more efficient, and prices should now better reflect true investment value than before. Professional investors should be able to do a better job of managing financial assets than amateurs could, and by buying and selling in competition with one another to take advantage of price discrepancies, they should push prices closer to the true values of assets. Financial options, futures, swaps, and other derivative assets are used heavily by institutional investors, which is a trend that would also seem to imply that the original financial markets should become more efficient. Derivative securities have lowered the cost of trading, which has allowed investors who have certain information to form better-hedged portfolios to take advantage of this information, thereby causing it to be reflected in prices.

Some observers point to another possibility, arguing that institutional investors are contributing to volatility in financial markets that is unwarranted by information about fundamentals. Institutional investors are blamed for the stock market crash of 1987 and other recent large movements in the market, and for forcing corporate managers to emphasize maximizing short-term profits over the long-term consequences of their actions.

After reviewing the evidence, Shiller concluded that we cannot say with any assurance from theoretical considerations whether institutionalization has helped or hurt market efficiency and what the effect of institutionalization will be in the future. He believes that some recent examples suggest that the development of new theories or trading strategies by institutional investors might destabilize the market. On the other hand, Shiller argues, if there were a tendency toward greater swings away from efficient prices, there would tend to be more profit opportunities, although perhaps not short-term profit opportunities and not riskless profit opportunities, but nonetheless opportunities that institutional investors should be able to understand and exploit.

DEMAND CHARACTERISTICS

For the securities firms, the increased investing by institutions and individuals has meant a greater demand for brokerage, trading, and underwriting services throughout the 1980s. Another characteristic of the demand for securities firms' services is that it is cyclical in nature, subject to the "bull-or-bear" pattern in the securities markets. Figure 7-1 illustrates this cyclicality, showing NYSE volume and the NYSE composite index from 1972 to 1991. Trading volume rose sharply as the NYSE composite index increases and dropped off sharply as the index fell, resulting in a "boom-or-bust" revenue pattern for securities firms as revenues from securities brokerage, margin lending, and trading activity felt the direct impact of this cycle. The demand for securities firms' services is influenced by factors that are exogenous to the industry, such as changes in interest rates, exchange rates, and tax laws; investment, consumer, and government spending; and oil price shocks. These changes or shocks force investors to realign their portfolios. Because these economic changes and shocks are often unpredictable, the duration and magnitude of any cycle are uncertain, and so this demand for services is both cyclical and uncertain.[1]

DEMAND IN THE CORE LINES OF BUSINESS

Table 7-5 shows the increase in trading on the NYSE. The average monthly trading activity, a measure of securities brokerage, rose dramatically from 1975 to 1991 on the basis of both number of shares sold and dollar value, with the average monthly number of shares traded climbing by almost 800 percent and the average monthly value traded increasing by over 1000 percent during this period. The table also shows the standard deviation of monthly shares sold from each year's average. There was a substantial increase in the *absolute* value of the month-to-month variation in the value and volume of shares traded. The coefficient of variation is used to determine

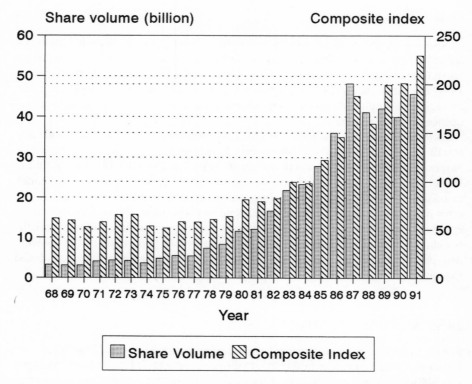

Figure 7-1. New York Stock Exchange composite index (high) and reported share volume.

Table 7-5. Average Monthly Number of Shares and Value Traded on the NYSE, 1975–1991 (Round Lots)

	Shares Traded (Millions)			Value Traded ($ Million)		
	Mean	Standard Deviation	Coefficient of Variation	Mean	Standard Deviation	Coefficient of Variation
1975	420	75	0.18	11,152	1,908	0.17
1976	471	98	0.21	13,712	2,330	0.17
1977	468	36	0.08	13,104	905	0.07
1978	635	159	0.25	17,536	4,874	0.28
1979	723	121	0.17	20,925	3,716	0.19
1980	1,032	157	0.15	33,139	6,458	0.19
1981	1,070	119	0.11	34,659	4,603	0.13
1982	1,518	428	0.28	42,855	13,800	0.32
1983	2,021	165	0.08	67,926	6,233	0.09
1984	1,922	250	0.13	63,727	9.672	0.15
1985	2,292	302	0.13	80,872	11,282	0.14
1986	2,973	221	0.07	114,528	8,867	0.08
1987	3,983	701	0.18	156,132	28,631	0.18
1988	3,404	443	0.13	113,004	15,286	0.14
1989	3,475	365	0.11	128,570	18,190	0.14
1990	3,305	403	0.12	110,280	17,237	0.16
1991	3,772	344	0.09	126,680	10,494	0.08

Source: NYSE *Fact Book,* various issues.

whether there has been an increase in the *relative* value of variation.[2] The coefficient remained relatively stable over this period, which suggests that although the monthly variability of exchange trading increased in an *absolute* sense, it did not increase in a *relative* sense.

Trading on NASDAQ is a measure of market-making activities. In this market, securities firms act as dealers and trade securities from their own accounts. Table 7-6 lists the average monthly number of shares traded on NASDAQ by volume from 1975 to 1991 and by value from 1978 to 1991. Share volume increased by over 2800 percent, and share value rose by over 1800 percent over the periods shown. Here also, the standard deviation of month trading increased, but the coefficient of variance remained relatively stable.

Table 7-7 shows average monthly new issues of corporate stocks and bonds from 1975 to 1991 as a measure of underwriting activity. Over this period, the average monthly dollar value of new stock and bond offerings rose; average monthly stock offerings increased by 518 percent; and bond offerings climbed by 636 percent. The coefficient of variation for this measure of underwriting activity also did not increase.

The Demand for Securities Brokerage

The demand for securities brokerage services is derived from the demand for securities. It is difficult to estimate the demand for securities, and also the demand for securities brokerage services, because securities are traded on speculative markets, for which the usual concepts of supply and demand do not hold (Godfrey, Granger,

Table 7-6. Average Monthly Number of Shares by Volume and Value Traded on NASDAQ, 1975–1991

	Shares Traded (Millions)			Value Traded ($ Million)		
	Mean	Standard Deviation	Coefficient of Variation	Mean	Standard Deviation	Coefficient of Variation
1975	116	13	0.12	N/A	N/A	N/A
1976	140	21	0.15	N/A	N/A	N/A
1977	160	16	0.10	N/A	N/A	N/A
1978	230	54	0.24	$ 3,012	$ 902	0.22
1979	304	51	0.17	3,692	803	0.30
1980	558	117	0.31	5,722	1,529	0.28
1981	652	63	0.10	5,921	1,067	0.18
1982	701	208	0.29	7,015	3,228	0.46
1983	1,325	151	0.11	15,690	2,096	0.13
1984	1,263	122	0.10	11,958	3,922	0.33
1985	1,725	205	0.12	19,456	2,457	0.13
1986	2,395	228	0.10	31,518	3,644	0.12
1987	3,158	358	0.11	41,654	7,948	0.19
1988	2,589	271	0.10	28,923	4,005	0.14
1989	2,794	236	0.08	35,948	4,613	0.13
1990	2,781	398	0.14	37,702	7,605	0.20
1991	3,442	404	0.12	57,820	8,159	0.14

Source: NASD, *NASDAQ Securities Fact Book,* various issues.

Table 7-7. Average Monthly New Securities Issued by U.S. Corporations, 1975–1991

	Stock ($ Million)			Bonds (% Million)		
	Mean	Standard Deviation	Coefficient of Variation	Mean	Standard Deviation	Coefficient of Variation
1975	880	349	0.40	3,563	947	0.27
1976	925	445	0.48	3,521	1,064	0.30
1977	972	395	0.41	3,407	914	0.27
1978	846	296	0.35	2,970	565	0.19
1979	949	276	0.29	3,339	837	0.25
1980	1,705	564	0.33	4,416	1,987	0.45
1981	2,049	681	0.33	3,646	1,446	0.40
1982	2,507	751	0.30	4,366	1,850	0.42
1983	4,298	983	0.23	3,939	1,519	0.39
1984	1,886	418	0.22	6,103	2,436	0.40
1985	2,960	860	0.29	9,959	3,242	0.33
1986	5,153	1,115	0.22	19,772	5,016	0.25
1987	4,446	2,547	0.57	19,463	4,972	0.25
1988	3,538	973	0.28	18,602	3,982	0.21
1989	2,606	1,385	0.53	16,681	4,407	0.26
1990	1,953	987	0.51	17,623	4,873	0.28
1991	5,439	2,670	0.49	26,235	4,289	0.16

Source: Federal Reserve Bulletin, various issues.

and Morgenstern 1964). Epps (1976) overcame these difficulties in estimating the elasticity of demand for brokerage services by developing a probability model with links to portfolio theory. His model implies, for any security, (1) that the expected number of transactions per unit time is a decreasing linear function of the ratio (r) of transaction costs to the security's price per share and (2) that both the expected number of shares exchanged on any single transaction and the expected trading volume over any fixed time interval are decreasing—but more complicated functions of r. Epps also estimated a demand function for each of twenty stocks and found that volume was measurably responsive to changes in transaction costs: The overall estimate of the elasticity of demand was -0.26.

The Elasticity of Demand by Market Segments

Individuals and institutions represent two distinct markets for securities brokerage services and so are easily segmented. Institutional purchasers make transactions in the name of their institutions, and individuals make transactions in their own names. Registered representatives are usually in either institutional sales or retail (individual investor) sales.

Many individuals maintain their accounts with one "full-service" broker and execute their transactions through that broker. But instead of full-service brokerage, which includes execution and additional services (e.g., research), individuals may substitute the services of a discount broker, or they may use a discounter in conjunction with a full-service firm. In addition, individuals may also substitute mutual fund ownership for direct securities ownership,[3] alternatives that provide elasticity in the short-term demand for brokerage services.

Institutional purchasers, on the other hand, normally have accounts with and transact through a number of different brokers. They trade at ''wholesale'' prices that are substantially less than those that individuals pay. Institutions sometimes use discount brokers.

The most important difference between institutions and individuals as purchasers of brokerage services is switching costs, the one-time cost of switching brokers. Switching costs are high for individuals, since they include such things as transferring securities held in the name of the broker and breaking a satisfactory relationship with a registered representative. For an institution, switching costs are much lower because institutions transact through a number of different brokers, and so switching from one broker to another for a transaction is almost costless. Low switching costs result in a high cross-elasticity of demand among different suppliers of institutional brokerage services. Therefore, although the Epps estimate of price elasticity of brokerage services of −0.26 is suitable for individuals, a more appropriate elasticity concept for institutions is the cross-elasticity of demand. This analysis suggests that there would be a relatively inelastic response by individuals to a small increase in prices by a securities firm. But for institutions, the response would be different. An institution would be more likely to switch to another broker in response to a firm-specific increase in commission fees.

CONCLUSION

The demand for securities firms' services in the core lines of business has grown dramatically over the last twenty years, and there does not appear to be anything on the horizon to slow that growth. In fact, with investment opportunities in Eastern Europe expanding, this rate of growth may accelerate.

Individuals have not been driven from securities markets by institutions. Rather, individuals continue to increase their participation in the securities markets but appear to have switched to mutual funds as a primary means of owning securities. The reasons for this change are not well defined, although several may be hypothesized: concerns about the perceived greater volatility of the markets and concerns that changes in the equity markets—particularly the use of certain new trading strategies—have somehow tilted the U.S. equities markets unfairly against the individual investor (New York Stock Exchange 1990a, p. 1). A more likely economic rationale is that investors realize that they can obtain a more diversified portfolio at a lower cost by purchasing mutual funds rather than directly buying corporate shares.

Volatility is a complicated issue for broker-dealers. From a business perspective, the month-to-month *relative* volatility of their business is not substantially different from that of the 1970s, although the *absolute* volatility of business and specific asset markets' volatility have increased,[4] and the days of large price changes have generated particular concerns among firms with large trading inventories.[5] Given (1) the concern about volatility, (2) the increased understanding of the importance of portfolio diversification, (3) the rising role of institutions in equity markets, and (4) the technological and communication advancements that have lowered the costs of financial innovation, it is expected that the industry will develop new products and investment strategies to respond to these stimuli (Furbush 1990, p. 1).

The fact that more small investors are choosing to own stock through mutual funds has regulatory implications, as this trend has broadened the base of participation and given more Americans a stake in the liquidity, efficiency, and fairness of securities markets. Traditional public policies or U.S. Securities and Exchange Commission procedures and regulations, framed around the objective of protecting the ''small investor,'' may not recognize the implications of these changing patterns of market participation. Although it is important to ensure investment opportunities and fair treatment for small investors, even more Americans may be adversely affected if the needs of institutional investors are not also met (U.S. Office of Technology Assessment 1990, p. 7).

NOTES

1. For a discussion of stock market cycles, see Cohen, Zinbarg, and Zeikel (1987).

2. The coefficient of variation measures the relative dispersion of a distribution. It is calculated by dividing the standard deviation by the mean (Chiswick and Chiswick 1975, p. 19).

3. Schreiner and Smith (1980) show that for investors who want a diversified portfolio of sixteen or more equity securities, the purchase of a mutual fund will result in lower brokerage costs than a direct purchase will.

4. A New York Stock Exchange panel reported that by most common measures, the U.S. equity markets have experienced high volatility in recent years (New York Stock Exchange 1990a, p. 1).

5. This point was made by Robert Greenberg, assistant director of research, NYSE, in an interview with me.

8

Costs and Entry Barriers
in the Securities Industry

Costs and entry barriers are the next elements of structure that we will examine. In this chapter, we will begin to see how various firms' strategies help determine the structure of the securities industry. Consistent with the contestable markets analysis, we will use Baumol, Panzar, and Willig's approach to analyzing costs and entry barriers.

FIXED COSTS, SUNK COSTS, AND ENTRY BARRIERS

Baumol, Panzar, and Willig (1982, pp. 280–83) distinguish among fixed costs, sunk costs, and entry barriers:

1. Long-run fixed costs: those costs that are not reduced, even in the long run, by decreases in output so long as production is not discontinued altogether. But they can be eliminated in the long run by total cessation of production.
2. Sunk costs: costs that (in the short or intermediate run) cannot be eliminated, even by total cessation of production. Once committed, sunk costs are no longer a portion of the opportunity cost of production.
3. Entry barriers: an entry barrier is anything that requires an expenditure by a new entrant into an industry, but imposes no equivalent cost upon an incumbent. More generally, an entry barrier is any advantage over an entrant that an incumbent firm enjoys if that advantage produces a welfare loss. An advantage is a barrier if its consequences are undesirable, and it is not an entry barrier otherwise. The magnitude of entry costs can be affected by deliberate acts of incumbent firms such as legal countermoves, capacity expansion or advertising.

Sunk costs need not be fixed, and fixed costs need not be sunk. Examples of sunk costs for a securities firm are expenses for advertising and promotion, costs of training registered representatives, costs of research and development required to produce a new product, and costs of regulatory approvals to enter a line of business. The cost that bears a resemblance to fixed costs is occupancy and equipment expenses. Examples of entry barriers for the securities industry include required net capital, exchange memberships and broker-dealer registration fees, and associated legal costs, as well as the delays to obtain the regulatory agency's permission to enter.

Fixed Costs Versus Sunk Costs as Entry Barriers

Fixed costs are not, and do not raise, entry barriers. They offer an advantage to incumbents only to the extent that if their output is greater, they can spread their costs more thinly than entrants can. Sunk costs share to some degree with entry barriers an ability to impede the establishment of new firms. The need to sink money into a new enterprise—whether into physical capital, advertising, or legal expenses—imposes a difference between the incremental cost and the incremental risk that are faced by incumbents and entrants. Sunk costs, unlike fixed costs, can constitute barriers to entry.

In the securities industry, sunk costs are generally not important as a barrier to small-scale entry, as there is no large investment necessary in plant and specialized equipment. Rather, small, newly formed brokers generally lease office space and can lease or buy any computer and office equipment necessary. An individual firm may invest in advertising or promotion and in training registered representatives and other employees, but often new firms are started by experienced securities professionals with established clients. A firm usually invests in training and advertising, sunk costs in the securities industry, after its initial entry.

Large-scale entry is attempted only through the acquisition of an existing securities firm. Examples are Sears Roebuck's purchase of Dean Witter Reynolds and American Express's purchase of Shearson Hayden Stone. The costs of these acquisitions are not sunk costs, since these brokerage subsidiaries can be later spun off or sold (possibly at a profit). The initial purchase does, however, represent a considerable barrier to entry into the national full-line business or the large-scale investment-banking business. When a securities firm enters a new line of business that requires some regulatory approvals, sunk costs may be very high and result in entry barriers.

Sunk Costs for New Product Development

Sunk costs associated with development of new products can be substantial and can form a barrier to small firms trying to enter. Tufano (1989) reports that investment bankers estimate that developing a new financial product requires an investment of $50,000 to $5 million per product. This investment includes (1) payment for legal, accounting, regulatory, and tax advice; (2) time spent educating issuers, investors, and traders; (3) investment in computer systems for pricing and trading; and (4) capital and personnel commitments to support market making. All but the last item are sunk costs. In addition, investment banks that are innovators typically pay $1 million annually to staff product development groups with two to six bankers. The stakes are high, in that individual investment bankers stake their reputations and careers on the success or failure of new products. This investment is undertaken even though the new securities they create generally have not been patented; indeed, the U.S. Securities and Exchange Commission (SEC) requires innovators to reveal information on product design, and so rivals can ride free on innovators' investments in educating regulators, issuers, and investors. Tufano also reports that imitators invest up to 50 percent to 75 percent less than innovators do to create "knock-off" products.

One result of the high sunk costs associated with new products is that it is difficult for smaller firms to compete effectively with the large investment bankers and full-line firms in this area. Although mid- and small-size firms do eventually introduce some of these products, there tends to be a lag between the introduction by the innovators and quick imitators (or fast seconds) and the remaining firms in the industry. Firms that are fast seconds rapidly imitate a new product with a similar product of their own. In Chapter 11, this lag is shown to be able to increase concentration in the industry.

BARRIERS TO ENTRY INTO THE SECURITIES INDUSTRY

Regulatory Barriers to Entry

In order to enter the securities business as a broker or dealer, an individual must apply for registration with the SEC as a broker-dealer.[1] This application must be accompanied by a statement of financial condition, including financial data and a computation of the applicant's net capital. In addition, a registered broker-dealer must join the National Association of Securities Dealers (NASD) or an exchange. Every registered broker-dealer must also become a member of the Securities Investor Protection Corporation (SIPC) unless the principal business is conducted outside the United States or is the sale or distribution of investment company shares.

The net capital requirement is the primary financial entry barrier to the broker-dealer business, with a basic minimum requirement of $25,000. Certain broker-dealers who do not carry customer accounts must maintain a minimum net capital of either $5,000 or $2,500, depending on circumstances described by SEC rules.

NASD Requirements

The basic membership fee for the NASD is $500, as part of the annual assessment. In addition, a member must pay an amount equal to the greater of $350 or the total of (1) 0.21 percent of annual gross income from state and municipal securities transactions, (2) 0.25 percent of annual gross income from other over-the-counter securities transactions, and (3) 0.25 percent of annual gross income from U.S. government securities transactions. In addition, there are small annual fees for each registered representative and each branch office. The NASD also charges for corporate financing, $500 plus 0.01 percent of the gross dollar amount of the offering, up to the maximum gross dollar amount of $300 million.

Entry into the New York Stock Exchange

Until 1979, to become a member of the New York Stock Exchange (NYSE), a broker-dealer had to purchase a seat from an existing member, but then "physical access memberships" were introduced. Through this method, a broker-dealer can lease seat privileges on an annual basis. As of December 31, 1987, there were 583 seats leased by members, and in 1990, lease prices ranged from a high of $85,200 to a low of $48,000 (NYSE *Fact Book* 1991 p. 67).

The number of seats on the NYSE is fixed at 1,366, with some of them held by commission brokers who execute orders for large firms. To handle their greater volume, large broker-dealers control more than one seat. The price of a seat is related to earnings in the industry. Any company that contemplates buying a seat would clearly pay no more than the expected return from participating in NYSE brokerage, nor would a brokerage house owning a seat be induced to sell it for less. Doede (1967) demonstrated that the value of NYSE seats capitalizes the expected profit of the NYSE brokerage business, by developing a complex expectations model under the assumption that industry profit is a constant proportion of exchange volume. His empirical tests confirm the hypothesis that seat prices are determined by capitalizing the expected value of the economic profit accruing to NYSE firms from the brokerage business.

Table 8-1 shows member (seat) prices since 1955. Seat prices before competitive rates were introduced in 1975 included a capitalized value of the cartel's monopoly

Table 8-1. NYSE Yearly High and Low Seat Prices, 1955–1991

Year	High	Low
1955	$ 90,000	$ 80,000
1965	250,000	190,000
1966	270,000	197,000
1967	450,000	220,000
1968	515,000	385,000
1969	515,000	260,000
1970	320,000	130,000
1971	300,000	145,000
1972	250,000	150,000
1973	190,000	72,000
1974	105,000	65,000
1975	138,000	55,000
1976	104,000	40,000
1977	95,000	35,000
1978	105,000	46,000
1979	210,000	82,000
1980	275,000	175,000
1981	285,000	220,000
1982	340,000	190,000
1983	425,000	310,000
1984	400,000	290,000
1985	480,000	310,000
1986	600,000	455,000
1987	1,150,000	605,000
1988	820,000	580,000
1989	675,000	420,000
1990	430,000	250,000
1991	440,000	345,000

Source: NYSE *Fact Book* (1992), p. 94.

profits. The elimination of fixed rates imposed a windfall capital loss on seatholders that was reflected in the decline of seat prices in the period surrounding deregulation. In the 1980s, with the upswing in NYSE volume, seat prices climbed to record levels in nominal dollars, but in inflation-adjusted dollars, they peaked in 1987 at a level below the highest value in 1968.

Entry into the Discount Brokerage Business

The SEC monitored the entry of firms into the discount brokerage business following the introduction of competitive rates, and this record gives some indication of the relative ease (or difficulty) of entering into a business that is primarily securities brokerage. By the end of 1980, there were approximately 125 discount brokers with an estimated 6 percent of all retail commissions (U.S. Securities and Exchange Commission 1981b, pp. 85–87). These figures represent an increase from 90 discounters with 3.5 percent of the market in 1977. Whereas the firms that entered the business in 1977 started with an average of $37,000 in total capital, the firms that started their businesses in 1978 had substantially more capital, an average of $130,000. This suggests that although firms can start their businesses with capital close to the SEC minimum ($25,000), many firms establish their business with a comfortable cushion. The main component of cost that is lowered when dealing with a discount broker is the registered representatives' compensation. Orders are taken and processed by clerks, which indicates that discount brokers' charges may be a good measure of the costs associated with straight brokerage transactions.

STRATEGICALLY CREATED BARRIERS TO ENTRY

In the industrial organization literature, there has been a recurring debate about the forces responsible for the economic structures of the industries we observe. One group takes the view that the economic structures are the natural adoption of an industry to environmental conditions. Another group believes that structure is related to strategic decisions and manipulation of the environment by firms in the industry.[2] The first view suggests that the natural selection that results from the competitive forces within an industry probably will ensure the emergence of optimal market structures. Baumol expressed this viewpoint in presenting the theory of "contestable markets": He said that although the industry structures that emerge in reality are not always those that minimize costs, they constitute reasonable approximations to the efficient structure (1982, p. 8). According to this view, the selection criteria that determine whether an industry is to be constituted as a natural monopoly, a duopoly, or an oligopoly are based on the relation between the firm's cost function and the given output vector.

The other view suggests that the characteristics of the industry and the strategic behavior of economic agents lead to industrial configurations that can be explained not by considerations of technical efficiency but by the pursuit of advantages linked to market power. In the strategic models used to analyze this behavior, firms take positions financially and psychologically so as to discourage and to constrain the actions and reactions of actual and potential rivals. That is, firms try to shape the environment by altering the institutions and rules of the game relevant to an industry.

Strategic choices made by broker-dealers help explain the structures of the industry and the form of competition among broker-dealers. Those strategic choices that relate to barriers to entry include (1) the choice of innovation and fast-second strategies by larger firms in the industry, (2) potential increases in net capital requirements proposed by the SEC and endorsed by the larger firms in the industry, and (3) the use of investment-banking reputation as a barrier to entry into the managing underwritten business.

Innovation and Fast-Second Strategies

Innovation and fast-second strategies, pursued by the largest firms in the industry, create two types of barriers for small and mid-size firms. Since the large firms act as fast seconds to any important innovation in the industry, small and mid-size firms are discouraged from innovating because they know that large firms will be fast seconds to any innovation they may initiate, because without patent protection, the large firms will be able to duplicate rather quickly the characteristics of any new product in the industry.

A barrier to small and mid-size firms' imitating an innovation by the larger firms is the strategy of an innovator underpricing its services (perhaps following a limit pricing strategy) (Tufano 1990). The innovator facing the prospect of the competitive fringe of smaller firms entering will keep the price of the new product low enough to signal the smaller firms that they will not profit from imitating this new product.

Raising Net Capital Levels

The SEC proposed raising required net capital in 1989 (Securities Exchange Act Release 27249, September 15, 1989). Under the proposed changes, broker-dealers that hold customer funds or securities would have to maintain at least $250,000 in net capital, and firms that clear customers' transactions, but do not hold customers' funds or securities, would need to maintain at least $100,000. Firms that introduce customers' accounts would be required to maintain $50,000 or $100,000, depending on whether they occasionally or routinely receive customers' funds and securities.

The SEC noted that it was mindful of the arguments that increased minimum capital requirements would restrict free entry to the broker-dealer business. Nevertheless, it was proposing an increase for several reasons. First, it was concerned that undercapitalized new entrants to the business would harm customers and could be a financial drain on the SIPC's insurance fund. Second, the SEC argued that the $25,000 net capital minimum requirement for broker-dealers was adapted in 1976 but that now the dollar was worth less than 50 percent of its 1976 value, making the minimum requirements less than half of what they were in absolute terms. Third, the SEC contended that with the greater volume and volatility of transactions involving more complex products, and the substantially larger positions of customers' and proprietary funds that the broker-dealers were holding, the possibility that an individual firm's failure might trigger substantial exposure to other broker-dealers had increased.

This proposal by the SEC was supported by the larger firms in the industry, as it would raise entry barriers for new entrants, while the larger firms would have no trouble meeting the more stringent requirements. The opposition of the smaller broker-dealers was so strong, however, that the SEC planned to repropose a capital increase that would probably not raise capital requirements as much as the original proposal did.[3]

Investment-Banking Reputation

Investment bankers use their reputations as an entry barrier to prevent competitors from gaining the much soughtafter positions as managing underwriters for the nation's leading corporations. Firms at the top of the investment-banking rankings follow strategic approaches to maintain the perception that they are "prestige" underwriters. Until the early 1980s, Morgan Stanley maintained the position that the firm would not share the managing underwriter position on any offering with another firm, in order to keep its position as the industry's "premier" underwriter.

MEASURES OF FIXED COSTS

Research on Fixed Costs Prior to Competitive Rates

In 1968, the NYSE argued that the practice of fixed commission rates should be continued, taking the position that the industry was characterized by high fixed costs and increasing economies of scale. These structural characteristics would result in destructive competition among the many firms in the industry if rates were determined through competition. The NYSE also presented data to support the high fixed cost position (New York Stock Exchange 1968, p. 64). The NYSE contended that it was reasonable to consider as fixed clerical and administrative salaries, communications costs, occupancy and equipment costs, and other expenses, including promotion, licenses, dues, and assessments. Commissions paid to others, floor brokerage paid to others, clearing charges, commission fees, registered representatives' compensation and employee bonuses, and profit-sharing plans were named as variable costs. Based on this allocation, variable costs were 49 percent of expenses and fixed costs were 51 percent.

The NYSE also estimated fixed costs with a regression that related the dependent variable, total expenses, to the following independent variables: (1) the number of transactions that were handled by each firm and (2) a series of six dummy variables that accounted for the firm's size. The fixed costs for the firms in each group were determined by adding the coefficient of the appropriate dummy variable to the intercept term. The NYSE concluded from these data that nearly 90 percent of the firms in the sample had a cost structure in which fixed costs constituted about 50 percent of total costs.[4]

An analysis by Mann (1975), prepared for the Department of Justice, took issue with the NYSE study. He rejected the assumption implicit in the NYSE model that the variable costs of providing brokerage services are the same for all firms. He thereupon added a variable to the regression that allowed for differences in variable costs for firms of different sizes: the number of transactions squared. Mann's model showed that fixed costs were substantially less that variable costs for each firm group.

Friend and Blume (1973) also investigated costs in the industry, examining year-to-year changes in expenses for NYSE firms from 1961 to 1970. Their analysis showed that only occupancy and equipment expenses did not drop when revenue fell off from 1968 through 1970, the only significant decline in the period. They concluded that only occupancy and equipment expenses behaved over this period as fixed costs would be expected to behave.

COST ESTIMATES USING BROKERAGE COMMISSION DATA

A number of studies have examined commission costs since 1975, based on costs charged to customers for brokerage services rather than actual broker-dealer internal cost data. Assuming that commission charges are representative of broker-dealer costs in a competitive environment, these studies indicate the relevant costs of providing institutional and individual brokerage.

Commission Costs for Individuals

Blum and Lewellen (1983) and Blum, Kracaw, and Lewellen (1986) investigated commission costs for individuals using a large data base of agency transactions for a large, full-service broker. The 1983 study found that discounts from posted rates following the deregulation of rates in 1975 did become fairly common, that they increased in size over time, and that they were related to certain distinctive characteristics of both the investors and the securities transactions. The discounts were not sufficient, however, to offset fully the appearance of a general trend since 1975 for small investors' commission costs to rise, at least at full-service brokers.

Although discounts were provided on only 16 percent of small (under $2,000) orders, they were offered in 86 percent of orders of more than $50,000, and the majority of the large trade discounts were more than 30 percent off the scheduled rates. Individuals whose annual trading volume was less than $25,000 realized discounts on approximately one-seventh of their trades, and these were generally only small reductions.

Customers who traded more than $250,000 worth of common stock annually, however, paid below-schedule commission rates on nearly three of every four transactions, and less than half the scheduled rate about one time in six.

The investigators also found, contrary to expectations, that cash-account customers seemed to have done better at obtaining discounts than had individuals with margin accounts. In a multivariate analysis of variables that influenced the discount, the customers' past year's trading volume explained 60 percent of the variance. Transaction size was also an important explanatory variable, but other characteristics of the order—purchase versus sale, solicited, or round lot—did not contribute substantially to the analysis's explanatory power.

The 1986 article used an expanded version of the sample used in the 1983 article. Those variables used to explain transaction-execution costs include (1) the size of the trade, (2) the exchange on which it took place, (3) the year in which it occurred, (4) whether the trade was an odd lot or a round lot, (5) the price of the security, (6) the volatility in that price, (7) the trading volume in the security on the day of the trade, and (8) whether the trade was "with" or "against" the price movement in the security on the trading day. The execution costs calculated were found to be positive and statistically significant for all categories of trades and generally smaller than the commission charges for the same trades. Blum, Kracaw, and Lewellen found that the exchange where the security was traded, whether it was bought (sold) in a rising (falling) market, and the round- or odd-lot status of the trade had detectable influences on costs. But they discovered no systematic effect on execution costs based on the absolute or relative size of the trade or the price volatility of the security. They also uncovered no evidence of a reduction in execution costs for individual investors following the deregulation of rates in 1975.

Commission Costs for Institutions

Offer and Melnick (1978), Tinic and West (1980), Condon (1981), Loeb (1983), Berkowitz and Logue (1987), and Berkowitz, Logue, and Noser (1988) all examined institutional brokerage orders, and they all used large samples of actual transactions by institutions such as pension funds or banks.

Offer and Melnick used the following factors to explain brokerage commission rates: the size of the transaction, the brokers' total assets, a measure of the brokers' execution quality, average trading in the stock, the price of the stock, and a trend variable. They estimated the regression model for each of ten banks' trust departments between May 1, 1975, and May 1, 1976, and found that the price of the stock was positive and highly statistically significant, indicating that it was an important determinant of the commission charged. The number of shares traded was negative and statistically significant for all ten banks, indicating that volume discounts were in effect during this period. This finding points to economies of scale by transaction size. The coefficients for the brokers' asset size were positive but significant for only five of the ten banks. The coefficients for the average monthly number of shares traded were mixed between positive and negative coefficients and significant and insignificant results. The trend variable was negative for all banks and statistically significant for eight of the ten banks, indicating that commissions were reduced over this period. Offer and Melnick suggested that the reason that the coefficient for price per share was positive and highly significant for all banks was that the price variable reflected the broker's risk exposure, which commands a premium.

Tinic and West (1980) examined the expected relationship between brokerage commissions and the marginal cost of providing brokerage services. In a competitive market, a profit-maximizing firm would equate the commission charged on these various orders with the marginal cost of servicing them. Tinic and West used the securities firms' cost data from the *Institutional Investor Study* (U.S. Securities and

Exchange Commission 1971) and estimated a regression between the average brokerage cost per share and the order size. They concluded that their finding of an elasticity of average cost per share to order size of −0.1448 was consistent with the finding by Offer and Melnik of an elasticity of brokerage commission per share to order size of around −0.1342. Comparing these findings, Tinic and West found it remarkable that there was nearly perfect correspondence between commission rates and the cost of servicing different size orders, after only a year of price competition. They thus decided that competition forced brokerage firms to reflect the economies in the rates charged when executing larger orders.

Condon's (1981) analysis was motivated by an interest in determining whether market inventory funds incurred lower transaction costs than did actively managed portfolios. Transaction costs are defined as the sum of (1) commissions, (2) taxes and SEC fees on sales, and (3) market-impact costs. The important findings of Condon's study are that the dollar-weighted transaction cost of purchases significantly exceeded the cost of sales, even though taxes were paid on sales but not purchases. The reason was the market-impact cost, which reached 0.92 percent for purchases versus 0.18 percent for sales, thereby overwhelming the tax differential. Although transaction costs of broker-initiated and bank-initiated sales were not significantly different, broker-initiated purchases cost significantly less than did bank-initiated purchases.

Loeb (1983) focused on the increase in total trading costs that resulted when trading stocks of smaller companies. He discovered that the round-trip trading costs (including the spread plus price concessions and brokerage commissions) on a $5,000 block of small capitalization issues (under $10 million) consumed 17.3 percent of the price; the total cost for an equivalent block of large capitalization issues (over $1.5 billion) will be 1.1 percent. He concluded that it would be unreasonable to expect small-stock strategies to perform positively after being adjusted for risk and transaction costs.

CONCLUSION

Entry into the basic brokerage business is relatively easy. Neither sunk costs nor regulatory barriers are particularly high. However, high research and development costs may prevent many smaller firms from entering the innovation game; this important aspect of competition is generally left to the large investment banks and national full-line firms.

Low fixed costs in the industry imply that the industry can be expanded rather quickly as demand increases because the industry does not require increments of physical capital that require long lead times. This ability to rapidly expand the size of the industry has resulted in a pattern of overhiring during bull markets.

Research on commission costs consistently showed that the costs associated with increasing order size were declining. That is, there were economies of scale by transaction size. But risk also plays a role in brokerage charges. The high-priced transactions are riskier for brokers to handle, and so they require an extra risk premium as compensation.

In this industry, fixed costs, sunk costs, and entry barriers all are low, suggesting that the industry is contestable and that the Baumol, Panzar, and Willig approach is useful for analyzing it.

NOTES

1. Information on registration is contained in the *Broker-Dealer Registration Package* (U.S. Securities and Exchange Commission 1990).

2. For a discussion of these views, see Jacquemin (1987), chap. 1.

3. The SEC did revise the capital rules to gradually increase minimum capital requirements (SEC Release 34-32737, August 18, 1993).

4. West and Tinic (1972) provide an accessible source for the NYSE's equations.

9

Mergers, Concentration, and Multiproduct Economies of Scale and Scope

One has only to look at the names of today's securities firms to understand the importance of mergers in the industry (e.g., Merrill Lynch, Pierce, Fenner & Smith, Inc.); indeed, most large firms have undergone significant mergers. Until the early 1980s, mergers played a major role in increasing concentration in the industry, whereas in the mid-1980s, this concentration was more closely related to firm innovations and diversifications. Mergers have progressed from horizontal to vertical to conglomerate. Those mergers that were intended to develop a complete financial service company, or a financial "supermarket" (e.g., American Express and Shearson, Prudential and Bache), have not worked out as well as expected. In Chapter 14, I will argue that this is due to the lack of any real economies of scope or shared know-how among these entities. I also will examine multiproduct economies based on two studies, which show the somewhat surprising result that there is little in the way of economies of scale or scope among the core lines of business in this industry.

MERGER HISTORY

The weight of transaction processing during the high-volume periods in the late 1960s adversely affected a number of large broker-dealers. During that time, 57 firms, including several large firms, left the New York Stock Exchange (NYSE) through either dissolution or merger.[1] During the economic recession of 1973 to 1975, 60 more firms left the NYSE (between the first quarter of 1973 and the first quarter of 1975) as the industry sustained estimated (after tax) losses of $25 million (Schneider 1981, p. 68). This period was characterized by horizontal mergers among investment bankers in response to the variability of the new issues business (Schaefer and Warner 1977, p. 31). A drop in registered offerings in 1973 and 1974 resulted in a decline in the number of firms managing any corporate issues, from a peak of 504 in 1972 to 128 in 1974 (Schneider 1981, p. 69).

Between 1972 and 1974, a number of vertical mergers took place in which several major brokers and investment banking houses began to integrate new issue management with distribution. Schneider (1981) cites the following as examples of mergers of investment bankers and retail brokers: W. E. Hutton & Co. merged into broker Thomson & McKinnon Auchincloss Kohlmeyer, Inc.; broker Clark Dodge & Co. merged into Kidder Peabody, Inc.; CBWL-Hayden Stone, Inc., merged into Shearson, Hamill & Co., Inc.; and investment banker White Weld & Co., Inc., acquired broker G. H. Walker Laird, Inc.

Competitive rates also increased firms' desire to internalize their complementary functions and diversify their securities business (Schneider 1981, app. E). In 1976 and 1977, for example, firms with a primarily retail business acquired firms with an institutional business (e.g., Drexel Burnham Lambert, Inc., acquired institutional broker William D. Witter, Inc.; institutional broker Shields Model Roland, Inc., merged into Bache Halsey Stuart, Inc.; and Shearson, Hayden Stone, Inc., acquired institutional broker Faulkner, Dawkins and Sullivan). Firms with well-known research capabilities also were acquired by larger, full-line firms (e.g., Reynolds Securities acquired research house Baker Weeks & Co.; and Paine Webber, Inc., bought research house Mitchell Hutchins Inc.). In addition, a large investment banker bought a retail brokerage with a ''big ticket'' retail clientele (Morgan Stanley purchased Shuman Agnew). The period from late 1977 through 1978 was marked by mergers among seven of the ten largest firms in the industry, including the merger of Merrill Lynch & Co. with White, Weld & Co.; Loeb, Rhoades & Co. with Shearson Hayden Stone; Dean Witter & Co. and Reynolds Securities, Inc.; and Lehman Brothers, Inc., and Kuhn Loeb & Co.

One view of these mergers is that they reflected the conviction among Wall Street executives that the successful securities firm of the future had to be better capitalized than they were in the past and had to have a much larger sales force. This was believed important because the securities market of the future was expected to be dealer oriented and so a large order flow would be needed in order to compete (*The Economist,* February 10, 1978, p. 16).

In another analysis, Schneider suggested that these consolidations were intended to achieve two basic objectives. One set of mergers was primarily horizontal combinations that were expected to improve the firms' opportunities and performance in their current lines of securities business, building on the combined firms' strengths. The mergers of Reynolds Securities with Dean Witter, Kuhn Loeb with Lehman Brothers, and Loeb Rhoads with Hornblower seemed to fit this pattern. These mergers were expected to achieve greater economies by trimming or building aspects of the operation common to both firms.

Another set of mergers was thought by Schneider to facilitate the expansion of business activities into new products or customer markets. These mergers were mainly vertical or conglomerate and were carried out to allow both firms to diversify into new lines of business or to take advantage of complementary service capabilities. The mergers of Paine Webber with Mitchell Hutchins, Morgan Stanley with Shuman Agnew, and Merrill Lynch with White Weld fit this pattern.

In 1981 and 1982, a number of conglomerate mergers took place between securities firms and large financial institutions and nonbrokerage retail firms. Some of the largest securities brokerage firms were acquired in this period, including Shearson Hayden Stone by American Express; Bache by Prudential Life Insurance Co.;

Dean Witter Reynolds by Sears Roebuck; and Salomon Brothers by Philbro Corporation.

The general motive offered for these acquisitions was that the traditional businesses of banks, insurance companies, retailers, stock brokers, and consumer lenders were breaking down and thus would lead to widely diversified providers of a full range of financial services (*New York Times*, March 7, 1982, sec. 3, p. 1). That is, the relevant market for financial services was expanding, and so these firms were preparing for future changes. In some cases, synergy was offered as a motive for the acquisition, although some acquirers argued that even if the expected synergy did not result, the acquisition was important to introduce the acquirer into the market for securities-related services. Expected economies of scale in operation did not appear to be a motive in any of the acquisitions, since the securities firms operated autonomously. However, the acquisitions by the larger firms were intended to allow the securities firms to broaden their capital base and become more aggressive in their trading and underwriting activities. Some of these mergers have not been successful. Chapter 14 examines these diversifications and suggests that these combinations may not have achieved their anticipated success because they did not have the kind of know-how that could be transferred across financial lines of business. It is the ability to transfer know-how that enables diversification to succeed.

CONCENTRATION IN THE SECURITIES INDUSTRY

Concentration ratios have long been used by industrial organization analysts as an indicator of the market power of firms in an industry, with high concentration levels generally associated with the presence of the large firms' market power.

Concentration in total capital among the 100 largest firms from 1968 to 1991 is shown in Table 9-1.[2] Total capital is used to calculate concentration ratios because it is the only measure of individual firm size that is publicly available for all NYSE member firms doing a public business over a long time. Since many of the firms still remain partnerships or private corporations, individual firm data on total revenue or other measures of concentration are not available. Total capital has the additional complication that in the 1980s several of the largest firms acquired capital from parent corporations (e.g., Salomon Brothers, Shearson/Hutton), and some acquired capital by going public. Nonetheless, total capital does give some indication of trends in firm growth.

Concentration increased between 1968 and 1991 for each group of firms shown and increased more rapidly between 1968 and 1974 under the fixed-rate regime than after it, as shown in Table 9-2. Immediately after May 1975, from 1975 to 1981, this increase slowed for all groups except the top eight. By 1982, the effects of deregulating commission rates had diminished, although firms were now competing through the introduction of new products and through diversification into new lines of business. From 1982 to 1991, concentration increased for all groups of firms, with the share of the eight largest firms increasing more than that of any other group. This group of firms was doing better in the new lines of business in the 1980s than was any other group of firms, as shown in Chapter 14. The Herfindahl index, an

Table 9-1. Concentration Ratios and Herfindahl Index of the 100 Largest Securities Firms by Total Capital, Selected Years Between 1968 and 1991

Number of Firms	1968	1970	1972	1974	1976	1978	1980	1982	1984	1986	1988	1990	1991
Top 1	9.6	12.3	13.7	18.0	17.2	18.0	16.4	15.0	12.6	10.8	17.3	19.8	17.5
Top 4	19.5	23.0	23.8	29.4	29.2	33.4	35.6	37.7	40.3	37.4	40.3	49.8	55.6
Top 8	29.1	32.3	33.8	40.1	39.9	47.4	49.6	51.8	58.3	56.6	57.3	66.0	72.3
Top 10	33.2	36.1	38.3	44.4	44.4	52.6	54.5	56.9	64.7	63.5	64.3	71.4	76.6
Top 20	49.7	52.3	55.2	62.9	63.2	70.2	72.5	74.9	80.3	80.4	80.0	82.9	86.1
Top 50	77.6	78.9	81.4	85.3	86.5	85.5	90.5	91.2	92.4	93.0	93.0	93.9	95.3
Herfindahl index	.022	.028	.032	.046	.045	.052	.052	.052	.056	.052	.059	.079	.083

Source: 1968 to 1976: *Finance Magazine*, various issues; 1978 to 1991: *Institutional Investor*, various issues.

Table 9-2. Concentration Ratio Change* and Herfindahl
Index Growth, 1968–1991

	1968–1974	1975–1981	1982–1991
Top 1	8.4%	−2.8%	2.5%
Top 4	9.9	7.1	17.9
Top 8	11.0	11.3	20.5
Top 10	11.2	11.7	19.7
Top 20	13.2	10.8	11.2
Top 50	7.7	5.2	4.1
Herfindahl index	0.024	0.004	0.011

*The change in concentration was calculated by subtracting the initial year's
concentration from the final year's concentration.

overall measure of concentration for this 100-firm group, increased by 0.024 from
1968 to 1981, by 0.004 from 1975 to 1981, and by 0.011 from 1982 to 1991.[3]

Table 9-3 shows securities industry concentration changes in the 1980s, based on
Securities Industry Association (SIA) data. Of all NYSE member firms doing a
public business, the share of industry revenue for the top ten firms rose from 52.9
percent in 1980 to 56.2 percent in 1991; the shares of the top eleven to twenty-five
increased from 20.1 percent to 21.0, and the rest of the industry declined from 27.0
percent to 22.8 percent. Total capital concentration also grew for the top ten as their
share of *total industry capital* climbed from 50.7 percent to 62.1 percent; the share
held by the top eleven to twenty-five declined from 18.8 percent to 17.4; and the
rest of the industry fell from 30.5 percent to 20.5 percent. The SIA figures show
further support for the finding that in the 1980s the largest ten firms in the oligopoly
group increased their size relative to that of their competitors.

Table 9-3. Concentration in Total Revenues and Total Capital in All NYSE Firms Dealing
with Public, 1980–1991 (In Percent)

	1980	1981	1982	1983	1984	1985	1986	1987	1988	1989	1990	1991
Total revenues												
Top 10	52.9	55.5	57.4	54.3	58.8	57.5	57.3	54.5	54.0	58.5	56.9	56.2
Top 11–25	20.1	19.5	18.7	19.6	17.1	19.7	19.8	20.9	20.8	19.3	21.1	21.0
Rest of industry	27.0	25.0	23.9	26.1	24.1	22.8	22.9	24.6	25.2	22.2	22.0	22.8
Revenues (% billion)	16.0	19.8	23.2	29.6	31.2	38.6	50.1	50.8	51.8	59.5	54.0	60.7
Total Capital												
Top 10	50.7	52.6	54.8	52.9	57.3	63.2	61.9	58.3	57.5	61.8	63.6	62.1
Top 11–25	18.8	19.6	19.0	18.8	15.7	14.8	16.0	18.5	17.8	16.4	15.9	17.4
Rest of industry	30.5	27.8	26.2	28.3	27.0	22.0	22.1	23.2	24.7	21.8	20.5	20.5
Capital ($ billion)	6.7	8.1	10.7	14.2	16.7	21.9	29.8	35.8	39.1	39.3	35.8	39.1

Source: Securities Industry Association, *Fact Book,* various issues.

Effect of Mergers on Concentration

Table 9-4 examines the impact on concentration of the large mergers of the late 1970s. The table shows the 20 largest firms at the end of 1979 on the basis of total capital and also the firms among the largest 100 that were combined between 1975 and 1979 to form the 1979 entity. The component firms are listed along with the amount of total capital that each firm held and the capital ranking of each firm at the end of 1974. The 20 largest firms in 1979 represented a combination of 33 of the largest 100 firms in 1974. In 1979, the 20 largest firms held 70 percent of the total capital of the largest 100 firms, and in 1974, the component firms held 69.9 percent of the total capital of the 100 largest firms.[4] Thus most of the increase in concentration between 1975 and 1979 can be explained by mergers and acquisitions. Internal growth did not play a major role in the increased concentration of the 20 largest firms, and so mergers are therefore important to determining the structure of the securities industry.

The smaller share of the largest firms and the failure of the largest to increase substantially their share of the total capitalization from 1975 to 1979, despite the mergers among the largest firms, suggest that the industry is not characterized by great economies of scale. Competitive rates also have not given large firms an opportunity to engage in "destructive competition." Rather, the slowdown in the rate of increase in concentration indicates that the mergers that took place from 1975 to 1979 resulted in more optimally sized firms than had existed before the introduction of competitive rates.

Concentration continued to increase in the 1980s despite less merger activity among the top eight and top twenty firms. Part of this greater capital came from injections of capital by parent firms. Also, a number of private firms (e.g., Morgan Stanley, Bear Stearns) went public in order to raise capital to compete in the important new areas of junk bonds, mortgage- and asset-backed securities, and mergers and acquisitions. The increased concentration is thus at least partially driven by the firm's need for capital in order to compete in these new and expanding areas. (Chapter 13 shows why most of this new product development comes from the oligopoly group and why this pattern also increases industry concentration.)

ECONOMIES OF SCALE AND SCOPE IN THE SECURITIES INDUSTRY

In our analysis of economies of scale in the securities industry, we will use three approaches. The first examines minimum efficient scale in the industry; the second is based on the "survivor test" developed by Stigler (1958); and the third uses the multiproduct economies of scale and scope approach developed by Baumol, Panzar, and Willig (1982).

Minimum Efficient Scale

An important concept in examining economics of scale is that of minimum efficient scale (MES), the minimum size at which costs become constant. Alternatively, MES

Table 9-4. Largest Twenty Firms in 1979 by Total Capital and Component Firms in 1974

Rank by Total Capital in 1974	1979 Firm and 1974 Component Firms	Total Capital 1974 ($ Thousand)	Total Capital 1979 ($ Thousand)
	Merrill Lynch (1)		$784,245
1	Merrill Lynch, Pierce, Fenner & Smith, Inc.	$546,002	
17	White, Weld & Co.	50,745	
	Shearson, Loeb, Rhoades (2)		246,255
7	Loeb, Rhoades & Co.	78,320	
10	Shearson Hayden Stone, Inc.	65,733	
29	Hornblower & Weeks–Hemphill, Noyes	26,529	
45	Spencer Trask & Co., Inc.	14,969	
69	Faulkner, Dawkins & Sullivan, Inc.	9,207	
	The E. F. Hutton Group (3)		237,954
4	E. F. Hutton Group Inc.	99,895	
	Paine Webber (4)		236,000
6	Paine Webber, Jackson & Curtis, Inc.	84,384	
57	Mitchell, Hutchins, Inc.	11,015	
	Salomon Brothers (5)		228,700
2	Salomon Brothers	123,700	
	Dean Witter Reynolds (6)		193,727
5	Dean Witter & Co., Inc.	85,519	
16	Reynolds Securities, Inc.	55,051	
52	Baker, Weeks & Co., Inc.	13,182	
	Goldman Sachs & Co. (7)		181,000
8	Goldman Sachs & Co.	76,000	
	Bache Halsey Stuart Shields (8)		162,549
3	Bache & Co., Inc.	120,431	
30	Shields Model Roland, Inc.	24,310	
46	Halsey, Stuart & Co., Inc.	14,734	
	Stephens, Inc. (9)		145,098
15	Stephens, Inc.	56,139	
	First Boston Corporation (10)		127,200
13	First Boston Corporation	61,655	
	Morgan Stanley & Co. (11)		107,542
32	Morgan Stanley & Co., Inc.	22,522	
	Drexel Burnham Lambert (12)		107,250
19	Drexel Burnham & Co., Inc.	49,059	
60	William D. Witter, Inc.	10,498	
	Allen & Company (13)		104,700
9	Allen & Company	70,302	
	Lehman Brothers, Kuhn, Loeb (14)		103,784
18	Lehman Brothers, Inc.	49,998	
40	Kuhn, Loeb & Co.	17,762	
	Kidder, Peabody (15)		92,389
20	Kidder, Peabody & Co., Inc.	48,486	
	Donaldson, Lufkin & Jenrette (16)		81,000
12	Donaldson, Lufkin & Jenrette, Inc.	63,122	
43	Pershing & Co., Inc.	15,625	

Rank by Total Capital in 1974	1979 Firm and 1974 Component Firms	Total Capital 1974 ($ Thousand)	Total Capital 1979 ($ Thousand)
	A. G. Becker/Warburg Paribus Becker (17)		80,747
14	The Becker and Warburg–Paribus Group Inc.	56,580	
	Shelby Cullon Davis & Co. (18)		79,959
36	Shelby Cullon Davis & Co.	20,084	
	Bear, Stearns & Co. (19)		73,675
27	Bean, Stearns & Co.	30,000	
	Smith Barney, Harris Upham & Co. (20)		69,099
22	Smith Barney & Co., Inc.	39,829	
35	Harris, Upham & Co., Inc.	21,035	

can be thought of as the size at which a firm becomes a viable economic entity. MES is often expressed as a percentage of the total relevant market. More than 6,000 broker-dealers deal with the public; some firms are only small proprietorships and operate out of just one office. Many of these small firms specialize in only one line of business (e.g., discount brokerage, over-the-counter (OTC) securities dealership) and are profitable with less than a 0.1 percent share of the market. A minimum efficient scale with one line of business is therefore very small. But for firms that provide a full range of services, the MES is large. According to 1979 data from the U.S. Securities and Exchange Commission (SEC), seventy firms reported activity in all the three core lines of securities brokerage, underwriting, and market making, although the smallest of the firms providing all three services represented less than 1 percent of total industry assets. The MES for a full-service firm thus remains rather small, indicating that firms can be viable at nearly any size and that economies of scale do not constitute an entry barrier. The diversity of firm sizes also is consistent with Baumol, Panzar, and Willig's analysis. One of the reasons for their research was to develop more conceptual tools to explain such diversity.

Survivor Test

The survivor test is based on the following notion: Firms that survive and contribute increasing proportions of an industry's output are assumed to be optimal, whereas those that supply a declining share are thought to be either too large or too small. Table 9-5 shows that firms in the first group (1–10) increased their share of total capital over the entire period, from 1968 to 1991. Those firms in the second group (11–20) increased their capital between 1968 to 1977, but their share then declined from its 1977 peak.

All other groups of firms lost their share of capital between 1968 and 1991. Table 9-4 shows that much of the growth among firms 1 through 10 occurred between 1975 and 1979 and was due primarily to mergers, suggesting that the strategy pursued by most firms to increase their share of industry output was through mergers. That is, firms did not rely on "natural" economies of scale to improve their relative position in the industry following the introduction of competitive rates.

Table 9-5. Survivor Test Growth Ratios, Selected Years Between 1968 and 1991

Firm Rank	1968	1970	1972	1974	1976	1977	1978	1980	1982	1984	1986	1988	1990	1991
1–10	33.2	36.1	38.3	44.4	44.4	47.7	52.6	54.5	56.9	64.7	63.5	64.3	71.4	76.6
11–20	16.5	16.2	17.0	18.7	18.7	19.3	17.6	17.9	18.0	15.6	16.9	15.6	11.5	9.5
21–30	11.9	11.4	11.6	10.7	11.4	11.0	8.7	9.3	8.4	5.8	6.3	6.1	5.0	4.2
31–40	9.0	8.4	8.4	6.8	7.0	6.1	5.6	5.2	4.6	3.6	3.7	4.1	3.5	3.0
41–50	7.1	6.8	6.2	4.9	4.9	4.3	4.0	3.6	3.3	2.6	2.7	2.9	2.5	2.0
51–60	5.9	5.5	5.0	3.9	3.8	3.3	3.1	2.7	2.7	2.2	2.1	2.0	1.9	1.5
61–70	4.9	4.7	4.4	3.3	3.1	3.1	2.7	2.2	2.2	1.8	1.7	1.7	1.5	1.2
71–80	4.2	4.1	3.5	2.8	2.4	2.1	2.2	1.8	1.3	1.5	1.3	1.3	1.0	0.9
81–90	3.8	3.7	3.0	2.4	2.2	2.0	1.9	1.6	1.3	1.2	1.0	1.1	0.8	0.7
91–100	3.5	3.2	2.7	2.2	2.0	1.7	1.6	1.2	1.1	0.9	0.8	0.9	0.7	0.5
Total capital ($ million)	2,653	2,485	3,398	3,028	3,667	3,928	3,917	6,502	11,200	17,562	29,813	38,098	48,350	67,161

Based on the survivor analysis, the ten largest firms in the sample had more rapid growth in capital than did any other group. Therefore, the survivorship analysis demonstrates that they are closer to optimal size than are the smaller firms.

Movement Among the Top Ten Firms

Tinic and West (1980) examined the SEC data to determine whether the elimination of fixed commission rates enhanced the ability of larger securities firms to maintain or enhance their positions in the industry. They found that the transition relative frequencies of ranking based on commission income, gross revenues, and equity capital from 1975 to 1978 were virtually identical with those between 1972 and 1975. They concluded that the end of fixed commission rates had no significant impact on the degree of fluidity in the securities industry (Tinic and West 1980, p. 34).

Total capital rankings continued to exhibit fluidity, as shown in Table 9-6. Merrill Lynch, the leader in capital since the 1940s, was displaced by both Salomon Brothers

Table 9-6. Total Capital of the Ten Largest Securities Firms, Selected Years Between 1960 and 1991 ($ Thousand)

1960		1965	
Merrill Lynch, Pierce, Fenner & Smith, Inc.	$ 71,240	Merrill Lynch, Pierce, Fenner & Smith, Inc.	$133,389
Equitable Securities Corp.	36,710	Equitable Securities Corp.	55,888
Lehman Brothers	35,211	Allen & Company	50,000
Allen & Company	32,756	Francis I. du Pont & Co.	46,315
Blyth & Co.,	29,108	Bache & Co.	46,251
Francis I. du Pont & Co.	26,121	Dean Witter & Company	35,938
Bache & Co.	26,054	Eastman, Dillon, Union Securities Co.	32,032
First Boston Corporation	22,737		
Halsey, Stuart & Co., Inc.	22,480	Blyth & Co., Inc.	30,506
White, Weld & Company	21,640	Lehman Brothers	29,540
		Walston & Co., Inc.	27,986

1970		1975	
Merrill Lynch, Pierce Fenner & Smith, Inc.	$304,549	Merrill Lynch & Co., Inc.	$567,417
		Salomon Brothers	142,700
Bache & Co., Inc.	99,059	Bache Halsey Stuart, Inc.	124,257
Salomon Brothers	92,700	E. F. Hutton Group, Inc.	114,883
Allen & Company	75,000	Loeb, Rhoades & Co.	92,349
Loeb, Rhoades & Co.	67,346	Paine, Webber Incorporated	91,053
Hornblower & Weeks– Hemphill, Noyes	57,169	Goldman Sachs & Co.	90,000
Walston & Co., Inc.	56,980	Dean Witter & Co. Incorporated	88,229
F. I. du Pont, Glore Forgan & Co.	50,500	Blyth Eastman Dillon & Co. Incorporated	77,708
Goldman Sachs & Co.	49,000	First Boston Corporation	72,319
Eastman Dillon, Union Securities & Co.	45,700		

(continued)

Table 9-6. Total Capital of the Ten Largest Securities Firms, Selected Years Between 1960 and 1991 ($ Thousand) (continued)

1980		1985	
Merrill Lynch & Co.	$1,065,000	Salomon Brothers	$2,315,287,716
Shearson Loeb Rhoades	469,883	Shearson Lehman Brothers	2,251,000,000
E. F. Hutton Group	448,037	Merrill Lynch, Pierce,	2,169,521,000
Salomon Brothers	330,700	Fenner & Smith	
Paine Webber	243,000	Prudential-Bache	1,259,260,000
Bache Halsey Stuart	233,788	Securities	
Shields		Goldman Sachs & Co.	1,201,000,000
Goldman Sachs & Co.	219,000	First Boston Corp.	1,042,200,000
Dean Witter Reynolds	216,338	Drexel Burnham Lambert	958,250,000
Stephens	167,250	Dean Witter Reynolds	884,030,000
First Boston Corp.	153,000	Bear, Stearns & Co.	800,000,000
		E. F. Hutton & Co.	755,998,000

1988		1990	
Merrill Lynch & Co.	$ 9,767,500	Merrill Lynch & Co.	$ 9,567,000
Shearson Lehman Hutton	8,157,000	Shearson Lehman Brothers	7,499,000
Salomon Brothers	4,440,000	Salomon Brothers	7,162,000
Holding Co.		Holding Co.	
Goldman, Sachs & Co.	2,771,000	Goldman Sachs & Co.	4,700,000
Morgan Stanley & Co.	2,413,900	Morgan Stanley Group	3,380,400
Drexel Burnham Lambert	2,143,000	CS First Boston	1,612,000
First Boston Corp.	1,864,000	Prudential Securities	1,585,000
Prudential-Bache	1,497,800	PaineWebber Group	1,552,900
Securities		Dean Witter Reynolds	1,405,000
PaineWebber Group	1,464,000	Bear, Stearns & Co.	1,387,700
Integrated Resources	1,435,500		

1991	
Merrill Lynch & Co., Inc.	$11,782,500
Salomon, Inc.	11,097,000
Shearson Lehman Brothers	8,079,000
Goldman Sachs & Co.	6,390,000
Morgan Stanley & Co.	5,820,000
Paine Webber	1,866,000
Bear, Stearns & Co.	1,835,800
C. S. First Boston	1,700,000
Dean Witter Reynolds	1,424,000
Prudential Securities	1,420,000

Source: Finance Magazine and Institutional Investor, various issues.

and Shearson Lehman in 1985. E. F. Hutton, tenth largest in 1986, was acquired by Shearson Lehman and no longer exists as a separate firm. Drexel Burnham Lambert advanced in the rankings through its strong hold on the high-yield bond market to capture the sixth position at the end of 1988, only to file for bankruptcy in 1990. Also note that in the short three years from 1988 to 1990, all firms changed rank at least once.

In sum, the MES analysis suggests an industry in which firms may be economically viable at a relatively small size. The survivor analysis shows that the largest ten firms grew at the expense of the smaller firms, but the turnover analysis suggests that position in the oligopoly group is not stable but changes from year to year. Firms compete with one another and contest the relative positions within the industry. Firms such as Drexel Burnham Lambert, Morgan Stanley, and Bear Stearns entered the top ten group of firms in the 1980s, indicating that the largest firms did not affect some type of oligopoly coordination that would have allowed the position of the leading firms to remain stable (Shepherd 1979, p. 207).

Estimates of Economies of Scale and Scope in the Securities Industry

Background

At hearings held by the SEC in 1968 on commission rates and other topics, the NYSE was formally required to justify its practice of fixing commission rates. The NYSE argued at the hearings that the securities industry was characterized by declining average costs (or economies of scale) and high fixed costs, and so the abolition of fixed rates would result in "destructive" competition.[5] If there are unrealized economies of scale over the whole range of output for the securities industry, in the absence of collusion, competitive pressures will ultimately result in an industry of only one firm. That is, the industry would be a natural monopoly.

The hearings prompted a number of studies that tested for the existence of economies of scale in the securities industry. Studies by the NYSE and the Antitrust Division of the Department of Justice (Mann 1975), in addition to examining fixed costs, also estimated economies of scale. The cost function used in both of these studies estimated economies of scale with a function that assumed securities brokerage as the only output for securities firms. Friend and Blume (1973) estimated economies of scale with a profit function that included a dummy variable to distinguish between firms that provided underwriting services and those that did not. Mann (1975) concluded from a review of those studies that economies of scale seemed to be present but disappeared at a level that permitted a large number of efficient-size firms.

Since these studies did not explicitly account for the multiproduct character of this industry, they may have been inadequate to make judgments about the existence of such economies. Baumol and Braunstein (1977) note that the usual scale economy concepts do not apply to the multiproduct case without considerable amendment. The next section analyzes the multiproduct character of the securities industry using a multiproduct cost function developed by Baumol, Panzar, and Willig (1982, pp. 453–57). This cost function, which relates costs to outputs, is useful for studying the securities industry because the industry is characterized by joint costs, which makes traditional cost analysis difficult.

Economies of Scope

In addition to the economies derived from the size or scale of a firm's operation, cost savings may result from jointly producing several different outputs in a single enterprise. That is, economies of scope will occur if it costs less to produce two products together than to produce the two products separately. With economies of scope among different lines of business, specialty firms would be unstable, and it would be profitable for them to merge with firms in other lines.

Economies of scope describe the basic phenomena that distinguish the multiproduct firm from the single-product firm. In an industry that enjoys no economies of scope, an improvement in efficiency could result if a multiproduct firm were broken up into several specialized firms.

Multiproduct Tests Using a Quadratic Cost Function

In an earlier study, I (Matthews 1984) used 1979 data from FOCUS Reports to estimate scale and scope economics.[6] The firms I included in my sample reported activity in the three core lines of (1) customer brokerage transactions, (2) market-making activity, and (3) underwriting activity on Schedule I of the FOCUS Reports. There were seventy firms in this sample, and all were among the largest 2 percent of broker-dealers. The variables used in this analysis include the following:

Total brokerage transactions (TRANS) are the sum of securities transactions carried out on a national securities exchange; equity securities transactions carried out on other than a national securities exchange; and commodity, bond, option, and other transactions carried out on or off a national securities exchange.

Underwriting output (UNDDOL) is the aggregate cost to the public of securities sold by respondents, which is the sum of total corporate securities and total government securities.

Market-making output (POS) includes securities and commodities positions in trading accounts and is the sum of total trading accounts including both long positions and short positions.

Total cost (TEXP) for each broker-dealer is equal to total expenses.

Only those firms that reported $100 million or more in securities business revenue were required to report dollar values for underwriting or positions in trading accounts. These were the industry's largest firms.

The functional form used for the analysis is the quadratic cost function introduced by Baumol, Panzar, and Willig (1982, pp. 449–50):

$$C(Y) = F + \sum_i a_i Y_i + 1/2 \sum_{ij} a_{ij} Y_i Y_j \tag{9-1}$$

Where $F < O$; $a_{ij} = a_{ji}$; C is a cost measure; and Y_i and Y_j are output measures.

Results

The results for the regression are

$TEMP = 315.229 \quad + 0.8205\ TRANS \ + 0.4844\ UNDDOL\ + 0.9954\ POS$
$\quad\quad\quad (0.55) \quad\quad (5.44) \quad\quad\quad\quad (3.49) \quad\quad\quad\quad (2.26)$
$+ 0.0106\ (TRANS \times UNDDOL) - 0.003\ (TRANS \times POS)$
$\quad\quad (1.36) \quad\quad\quad\quad\quad\quad\quad\quad (-0.00)$
$+ 0.0008\ (POS \times UNDDOL) - 0.0064\ TRANS^2$
$\quad\quad (0.04) \quad\quad\quad\quad\quad\quad (-0.92)$
$- 0.0091\ POS^2 - 0.0042\ UNDDOL^2$
$\quad (-0.70) \quad\quad\quad (-1.07)$

$\tag{9.2}$

$$F = 213.84$$
$$R^2 = 0.96$$

(*t* statistics in parentheses)

Size-related economies were analyzed for three types of firms in the sample: the "typical" firm, which represents the sample mean; "large" firms, which are all those with over $100 million in total assets; and "small" firms, which are those with under $100 million in total assets. The sample was divided about evenly between large and small firms.

Within the content of the cost function used in this analysis, overall economies of scale, S_N, are measured by

$$S_N = \left[F + \sum_i a_i Y_i + 1/2 \sum_i \sum_j a_{ij} Y_i Y_j \right] \bigg/ \left[\sum_i a_i Y_i + \sum_i \sum_j a_{ij} Y_i Y_j \right] \quad (9\text{-}3)$$

and the degree of product specific return to scale is given by

$$S_i = \left[a_i Y_i + 1/2 + \sum_{i=j} a_{ij} Y_i Y_j \right] \bigg/ \left[a_i Y_i + a_{ii} Y_i^2 + \sum_{i=j} a_{ij} Y_i Y_j \right] \quad (9\text{-}4)$$

Overall economies of scope, S_c, are measured by

$$S_c = [C(Y_1, 0,0) + C(0, Y_2,0) + C(0,0,Y_3) - C(Y_1,Y_2,Y_3)] \bigg/ C(Y_1,Y_2,Y_3) \quad (9\text{-}5)$$

and product specific economies of scope are measured by

$$SC_i = [C(Y_i) + (Y_{N-i}) - C(Y_1,Y_2,Y_3)] \bigg/ C(Y_1,Y_2,Y_3) \quad (9\text{-}6)$$

where for S_N and $S_i > 1$ indicates economies of scale and < 1 indicates diseconomies of scale, and for S_c and $SC_i > 1$ indicates economies of scope and < 1 indicates diseconomies of scope.

At the grand sample means and at the sample mean of the large and small firms, the multiproduct scale and scope economies are given in Table 9-7. The measure of overall economies of scale for the typical firm is 1.124; for the large firm it is 1.119, and for the small firm it is 1.172. This evidence suggests that all groups of firms enjoy moderate economies of scale, although economies of scale appear to decline slightly as the firm size increases. Economies of scope will be greater than zero if joint production is more efficient than nonjoint production. Of the three groups, only the small firms indicate any economies of scope, and the typical and large firm groups exhibit minor diseconomies of scope.

According to Table 9-8, product-specific economies of scale and scope increase for brokerage, underwriting, and market making as firm size increases. Small firms enjoy product-specific economies of scope, however, and the typical and large groups of firms in some cases show diseconomies of scope in each product line.

These findings may explain why overall economies of scale appear to decline

Table 9-7. Overall Economies of Scale and Scope at
Sample Means

	Economies of Scale	Economies of Scope
Large B/D	1.119	−0.0809
Typical B/D	1.124	−0.0480
Small B/D	1.172	0.2785

somewhat as firm size grows. The slight diseconomies of scope found in the large
and typical firm groups reduce the advantage that large firms have in regard to
product-specific economies of scale. The implication of this finding is that for the
largest of the large firms (above $100 million in assets), the separation of various
lines of business into autonomous units would be more efficient from an organizational perspective. These results generally agree with the conclusion of Mann (1975)
and Friend and Blume (1973) that economies exist but are not very strong.

Multiproduct Test Using a Translog Cost Function
Goldberg, Hanweck, Keenan, and Young (1991) also examined economies of scale
and scope in the securities industry, using a multiproduct translog cost function that
included the following variables:

C = total expenses

Q_1 = revenue from brokerage operations (commissions, margin interest, and fees
from mutual fund trading)

Q_2 = revenue from underwriting operations and capital-positioning operations
(underwriting fees and gains in trading and investments for firms' own
accounts)

Q_3 = revenues from account supervision, account management fees, research services, merger and acquisitions, and other revenues

B = number of offices

P_1 = labor costs (annual salary)

P_2 = cost of rental space per square foot

The data used for the estimation were obtained from a survey of New York securities firms conducted in 1984. The survey was sent to 202 firms, and 74 responded.

Table 9-8. Product Specific Economies of Scale and Scope at Sample Means

	Brokerage		Underwriting		Market Making	
	Scale	Scope	Scale	Scope	Scale	Scope
Large B/D	1.213	−0.093	1.203	0.0003	1.093	0.0185
Typical B/D	1.194	−0.073	1.131	0.077	1.092	0.0248
Small B/D	1.007	0.138	1.019	0.131	1.001	0.405

This sample of 74 firms was then divided into four groups with the following characteristics:

Group 1   National in scope
         national full-line firms (9)
         large investment banks (6)
Group 2   Regional multiproduct firms
         smaller New York–based (7)
         larger New York–based (9)
         large regional (4)
         medium regional (1)
Group 3   Specialized brokerage
         commission brokerage (9)
         other specialized (9)
         discounter (1)
         clearing (1)
Group 4   Other specialized
         not elsewhere classified (18)

Ray scale economies (RSCE) are defined as the proportional effect on cost of a scale expansion along a ray in multiproduct cost space, holding constant the proportion of each of the outputs to the others. RSCE values > 1.0 show scale diseconomies; RSCE values $= 1.0$ show constant returns to scale; and RSCE values < 1.0 show scale economies.

Table 9-9 shows the ray scale economies from their multiproduct cost function. The RSCE estimates are provided for each securities firm classification and the overall sample mean. Group 1 firms exhibit statistically significant scale diseconomies, but at the other extreme, the smaller, more specialized firms (Group 4) show statistically significant economies of scale. The general conclusion of Goldberg and his colleagues with regard to the presence of scale economies is that securities firms experience economies of scale at smaller sizes but that these economies are exhausted when the firm reaches between $14 million and $36 million in total revenue. By contrast, many of the larger and more diversified firms show scale diseconomies.

The results in Table 9-10 show that Group 1 securities firms have diseconomies

Table 9-9. Estimates of Ray Scale and Scope Economies

	Total Q ($ Millions)	Number of Observations	RSCF	Scope
Group 1	825.69	14	2.08*	0.83
Group 2	66.42	20	1.39*	0.15
Group 3	35.70	20	1.16*	0.04
Group 4	13.70	14	0.82*	−1.42
Sample mean	186.51	68	1.82*	0.44

*Statistically different from 1.0 at the 5 percent level of significance on a two-tailed test.
Source: Goldberg et al. (1991), p. 99.

Table 9-10. Interproduct Cost Complementaries by Group and at the Mean of the Sample (Q_iQ_j Interaction Coefficient in Parentheses)

Output Combination	Group 1	Group 2	Group 3	Group 4	Sample Mean
Q_1Q_2	0.006	0.017	0.033	0.021	0.002
	(0.139)*	(0.139)*	(0.139)*	(0.139)*	(0.139)*
Q_1Q_2	0.0003	0.003	0.004	−0.166	0.0002
	(0.019)	(0.019)	(0.019)	(0.019)	(0.019)
Q_2Q_3	−0.0004	−0.002	−0.001	−0.055	−0.0001
	(−0.038)	(−0.038)	(−0.038)	(−0.038)	(−0.038)

*Statistically significant at the 1 percent level of significance for a two-tailed test. No other coefficients are significant.
Source: Goldberg et al. (1991), p. 104.

of scope, but that the smaller, specialty firms in Group 4 show economies of scope. Goldberg and his colleagues did not run statistical tests for scope economies (because they are nonlinear and complex), but the results are consistent with those for scale economies. Specifically, the smaller, specialty firms exhibit economies of both scale and scope. Therefore, expansion by these firms toward Group 2 firm sizes in terms of total production and changes in product mix suggests that marginal costs can be reduced in the provision of all products. The opposite is the case for the larger, multiproduct firms, which suffer from diseconomies of scale and scope. They could lower their marginal costs by reducing their size and moving toward a product mix similar to that of Group 2.

Table 9-10 also shows the results of tests for interproduct cost complementarities, which measure the change in the marginal cost of one product as a result of a change in another, jointly produced product. Although the sign of the product pairs Q_2 (underwriting) and Q_3 (account supervision) are negative, indicating cost complementarities, the interactive terms are not statistically significant. Since the coefficient is not statistically significant, it is not likely that there are significant economies of scope between Q_2 and Q_3. However, the product pair Q_1 (brokerage) and Q_2 has a coefficient that is positive and statistically significant, indicating that there are interproduct cost noncomplementarities and supporting the case for diseconomies of scope between underwriting and brokerage. This also suggests that there are cost advantages to producing these two lines of business separately rather than jointly under certain output mixes and at large scale.

The results of Matthews (1984) and Goldberg, Keenan, Schrier, and Young (1989) taken together illustrate that larger firms have exhausted economies of scale and that their organizational forms do not provide economies of scope. Yet these firms have continued to grow and prosper in terms of total assets, revenues, and profits. Since economies of scale and/or scope in the core lines do not explain this result, we must look elsewhere. Chapters 14 and 15 suggest that the combination of product innovation and firm diversification, driven by many economic forces, has enabled securities firms to continue to gain advantage from increased size.[7]

CONCLUSION

Because economies of scale are not large in any of the core lines of business, securities firms must rely heavily on mergers for growth. However, mergers in this industry are a risky way to grow, because when a firm is acquired as part of a merger, its most talented people often became the objects of recruitment efforts by other firms.[8] Since the securities industry is a ''people'' business, sometimes the acquiring firm does not get the acquired firm's best ''assets,'' and therefore other strategies, especially innovation and diversification, are pursued by securities firms in order to continue their growth.

Concentration has been increasing in the industry over the last twenty years. Part of this increase can be explained by mergers, but no substantial economies of scale in the industry can explain the continuing increase in concentration. Instead, we must look to innovation and diversification by firm.

NOTES

1. The collapse of these firms is examined in detail by Welles (1975). Scherer and Ross (1990, p.159) observe that mergers occur for many reasons and that in any given case, several different motives may simultaneously influence the merging parties' behavior.

2. The largest 100 firms are used because this is the only group for which data are available between 1968 and 1991.

3. For a discussion of the Herfindahl index, see Hay and Morris (1979).

4. If these firms had been combined in 1974, there would have been 13 more firms included in the 100 firms for 1974. But since capital figures for firms smaller than the 100 largest are not available for several years in the study, no attempt was made to adjust for the additional 13 firms.

5. For a discussion of the evidence used to support this argument, see New York Stock Exchange (1968).

6. FOCUS Reports are reports on financial condition filed by broker-dealers with their regulatory organizations.

7. Economies of scale and scope are one type of measure of industry and firm efficiency. There are, however, other approaches to examining efficiency. For example, how effectively do the producers of securities services combine their productive inputs? One approach based on the work of Färe, Grosskopf, and Lovell (1985) uses a nonparametric, linear-programming approach to calculate a set of efficiency measures. With these measures, firms in a data set can be ranked by productive efficiency, and sources of inefficiency can be isolated. Inefficiency can then be attributed to operating at an incorrect scale of operation and/or inefficient technical choices made by management. In Grosskopf and Matthews (1985), this approach was used to evaluate the productive efficiency of publicly held broker-dealers between 1971 and 1980.

8. Merrill Lynch's acquisition of White Weld was troubled by this problem (*Fortune*, October 23, 1978, pp. 78–90).

IV
Conduct

10

Securities Brokerage Pricing

As predicted by West and Tinic (1971) and Friend and Blume (1973), commission rates declined for institutions and individuals following the introduction of negotiated commissions. Figures 10-1 and 10-2 show commission rate trends monitored by the U.S. Securities and Exchange Commission (SEC) for institutions and individuals from April 1975 (the last month under the New York Stock Exchange [NYSE] schedule) to the end of 1981 when the survey was discontinued. These figures show that commissions fell for institutions and individuals both on a cents per share basis and as a percentage of principle value for each share group.

This chapter argues that the pricing system that emerged with competitive rates for individuals closely resembles barometric pricing, whereas between 1978 and 1984 institutional pricing was characterized by stability or kink in the demand curve. The kink in the demand curve for institutions is related to a regulatory approved practice known as *soft dollars*, which allows broker-dealers to bundle research and other services along with the execution of transactions for the commission dollar. In the late 1980s, institutional pricing was characterized by more price flexibility. This chapter also offers an economic rationale for the industry's preference for bundling securities services rather than individually pricing research, execution, and other services.

PRICING FOR INDIVIDUALS

The individual (or retail) side of the business is characterized by low barriers to entry, thousands of competitors, slight economies of scale, and low fixed costs. Pricing for individual brokerage services, therefore, should be relatively competitive, although industry concentration is at loose oligopoly levels. Competitors should therefore be aware of competitors' pricing initiatives. Elasticity of demand on the retail side is relatively inelastic, and so firms should not be reluctant to raise prices to reflect increasing costs.

Under these structural conditions, "barometric" price leadership often emerges. This is a type of noncollusive price leadership in which the price leader sets prices approximating those that would emerge under competitive conditions (Stigler 1947).

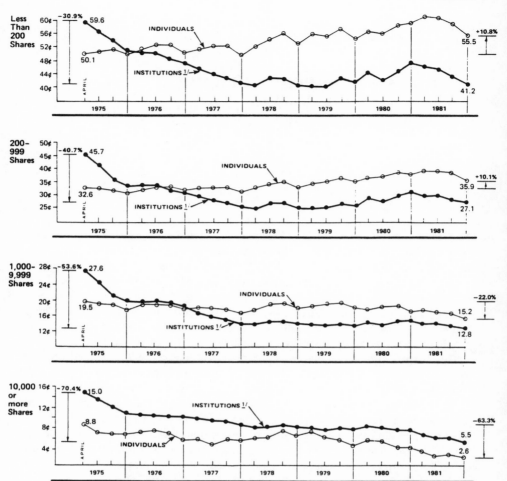

Figure 10-1. Effective commission rates, New York Stock Exchange firms, April 1975 through fourth quarter 1981: commission cents per share. (Securities and Exchange Commission, Survey of Commission Charges on Brokerage Transactions)

The distinguishing characteristics of this type of price leadership include occasional changes in the identity of the price leader, the absence of leader power to coerce others into accepting its price, upward leadership only when rising costs or demand warrants price hikes, and occasional lags in following or outright rejecting the leaders' initiatives (Scherer 1980, pp. 176–77). These characteristics appear to describe the pattern of price changes found in the industry.

Merrill Lynch attempted to assume the role of dominant price leader in the early years of competitive pricing, and just before the introduction of competitive rates, it announced that it would raise brokerage fees an average of 3 percent from the NYSE schedule on most standard transactions under $5,000 (*Wall Street Journal,*

April 30, 1975, p. 5). A second round of price increases for individual investors also appeared to have been led by Merrill Lynch in early 1978 (*New York Times,* December 30, 1978, p. D-2). The firm increased its commission rates to retail customers by an average of 7 percent and also instituted custodial charges for inactive cash accounts holding securities. A third round of price increases on the retail side was instituted by Smith Barney in early February 1979 and was quickly followed by Bache (*New York Times,* March 31, 1979, p. 27). Merrill Lynch joined the price increases in late March 1979 with an average increase of 4.25 percent. Once Merrill Lynch joined in the price increases, the remaining firms that had not raised their commissions joined in, thereby suggesting that Merrill Lynch remained the dominant

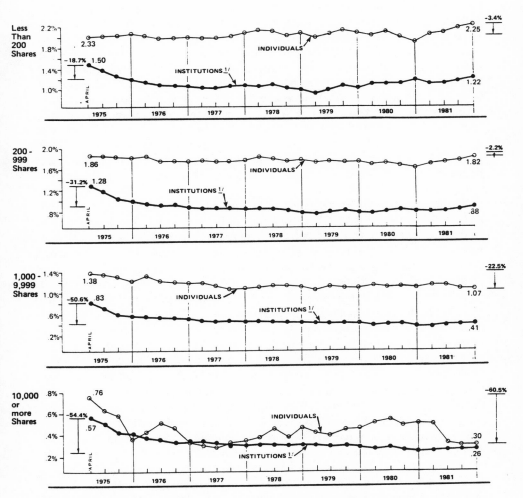

Figure 10-2. Effective commission rates, New York Stock Exchange firms, April 1975 through fourth quarter 1981: commissions as a percentage of principal. (Securities and Exchange Commission, Survey of Commission Charges on Brokerage Transactions)

firm up to this point (*Wall Street Letter,* April 2, 1979). Another round of price increases took place in the spring of 1980, led by Donaldson Lufkin, Bache, and Lehman Brothers. Merrill Lynch did not raise its rates until November 1980, with an increase of 5 percent (*Wall Street Letter,* November 10, 1980, p. 2). Smith Barney implemented a small increase in rates in June 1982 that did not appear to have been followed (*Securities Week,* June 10, 1982, p. 1). Dean Witter Reynolds initiated a rate increase in June 1984 that was immediately followed by E. F. Hutton, Paine Webber, and Merrill Lynch (*Securities Week,* June 25, 1984, p. 1). The increase was the first by Merrill Lynch since 1980.

The evidence suggests that Merrill Lynch was a strong price leader immediately following deregulation but gradually surrendered that role to a number of other firms. Price increases now appear to occur on a firm-by-firm basis, but commission fees still appear to cluster around those of Merrill Lynch. The loss of securities commission revenues by Merrill Lynch may have caused the firm to give up the role of price leader. From 1975 to 1977, Merrill's share of industry securities commissions declined from 12.4 percent to 11.2 percent, while the share of other national full-line firms increased. Shearson's share increased from 2.5 percent to 2.7 percent; Dean Witter's share, from 3.4 percent to 3.7 percent; Paine Webber's share, from 3.2 percent to 3.6 percent; and E. F. Hutton's share, from 4.2 percent to 4.8 percent (*Wall Street Letter,* May 18, 1981, p. 2). By early 1979, Merrill Lynch appeared to have abandoned its role as price leader, thereby allowing a number of other "barometric" firms to take the lead. With Merrill Lynch following the lead of other barometric firms, its share of commissions rose in 1979 and 1980, although the firm's share declined slightly in 1981.

Barometric price leadership is generally viewed as consistent with competition and its results (Shepherd 1979, p. 287). According to Stigler, the barometric firm commands adherence of rivals to its price only because, and to the extent that, its price reflects market conditions with tolerable promptness (1947, p. 445). Barometric price leadership also suggests that pricing in the retail brokerage business is competitive, although securities firms have not made their pricing schedules readily available to individual investors (*New York Times,* June 4, 1980, p. D-8). This may represent the firms' attempt to develop market power. Research in information theory indicates that in a market with imperfect information, each firm obtains market power in the short run and often in the long run as well (Salop 1976), but there does not appear to be any evidence that the firms have been successful in obtaining market power based on this strategy. Discount brokers regularly place advertisements in financial publications comparing their rates for various types of transactions with those of national and regional full-line firms. A quick glance at these comparisons can give the individual investor a rough idea of the rates charged by various firms.

There have been no reported rounds of price cutting on the retail side, despite the cyclical nature of the business. Since the industry has low fixed costs, firms are not inclined to cut prices in the event of a downturn in order to generate revenue to cover high overhead costs. Another important factor that would minimize price cutting is the interactive nature of the securities business. On many transactions a firm deals with its competitor, and the interrelated nature of this business offers many opportunities to punish a price cutter. For example, since most major retail firms take part in other firms' underwriting syndicates to distribute new securities offerings, a price cutter could be invited to participate in fewer syndicates.

PRICING FOR INSTITUTIONS

Like the individual side of the market, the institutional side has low fixed costs, a cyclical demand, and a large number of purchasers and sellers. Concentration among institutional sellers is probably higher than that among retail sellers,[1] and it may be substantially higher. For example, Goldman Sachs reported that it made 17.8 percent of its institutional trades of 20,000 or more shares between December 1984 and November 1985 (*The Economist,* December 1985). These structural conditions, together with the industry practice of providing research and other services along with execution services for the commission dollar, lead to a pricing structure that tended to be more rigid than that of the individual side from the late 1970s into the early 1980s.

The SEC survey showed that commissions on large blocks (10,000 or more shares) remained stable from early 1978 to late 1981, at around eight cents a share (Figure 10-3). Press reports also imply that eight cents a share represented a stable price for institutions and that it remained the large block price until 1984. In 1984, press

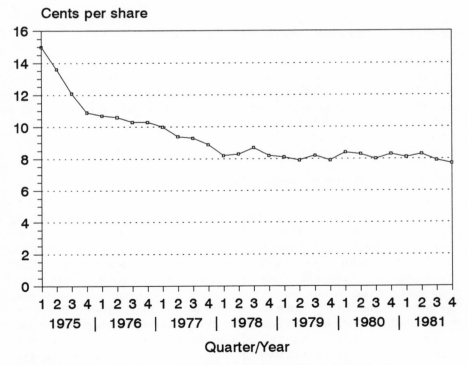

Figure 10-3. Commission rates. (Securities and Exchange Commission data)

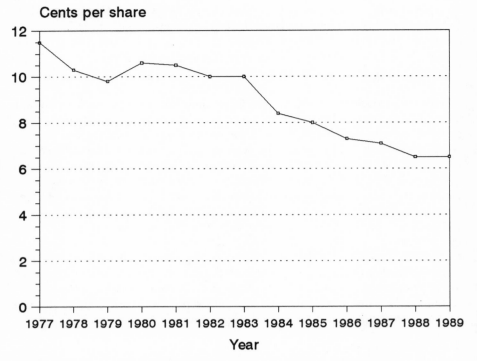

Figure 10-4. Average commissions per share. (Greenwich Associates data)

reports stated that a new price had been established at five cents a share.[2] Survey data from Greenwich Associates also reveal stability in institutional pricing (Figure 10-4). The average commissions charged on all transactions for institutions that did in excess of $5 million in commission business a year remained around ten cents a share from 1978 through 1983. In 1984, average rates were adjusted downward to around eight cents a share.

Current Perspective on Institutional Rates

Based on extensive interviews, Greenwich Associates (1990) reports that broker-dealers are now more determined to manage their institutional business on the basis of each client's contribution to profitability rather than on total revenue. Firms are tiering their accounts—that is, looking closely at those with low profit potential and reducing or eliminating service to those that offer no real prospect of an adequate return. Greenwich argues that for some years the institutional business has not been profitable for broker-dealers. One of the reasons is the declining commission rates, as shown in Figure 10-4. Another reason is the use of soft dollars—especially significant in the relationship between broker-dealers and medium-size and smaller institutions. A third reason is the use of index funds, especially by pension funds. Greenwich's research shows that the proportion of funds investing in passive domestic equities is greater than in any other investment category, and the commissions on index funds tend to be very small. Although some large broker-dealers attempted to enlarge their share of the institutional business in the early 1980s, that no longer appears to be the case. Market shares have stabilized. Greenwich also reports that in the future institutional brokers will be unbundling more of the research and other services from execution. Part of the problem with what is perceived to be low profitability results from the continued lack of cost-accounting systems that can precisely allocate institutional brokerage costs.[3]

Based on its survey data (Figure 10-4), Greenwich contends that institutional commissions may rise from the low of 6.5 cents a share reported in 1988 and 1989. Although this rise is only to 6.6 cents, the fact that the decline is stopping could be very important. Based on its consulting and research, Greenwich (1990, p. iv) stated that very large, savvy institutions are willing to pay an extra cent or half cent a share if that will get the best market.

Institutional Commissions and Soft Dollars

The stability of institutional rates from 1978 to 1984 was accompanied by an increase in "soft dollar" payments in the securities industry. Soft dollars represent credits accumulated by an investment manager when he or she directs transactions through a broker that charges more than the lowest possible price for securities transactions. Investment managers are typically hired by corporations, unions, and state and local governments to manage and invest their pension fund monies. When these outside portfolio managers accumulate enough soft dollar credits with the institutional brokerage firms to which they direct transactions, the managers are entitled to obtain services such as specialized investment research, computer software, or research seminars. This "paying up" or paying more than the lowest rate for commissions is approved by the SEC as long as the soft dollar services are among those that it specifically allows.

Soft dollars are a significant portion of equities commissions. In 1989, for institutions that generated over $5 million in equity commissions, soft dollar allocations typically represented 10 to 20 percent of commissions. For smaller, more research-oriented institutions, the portion of soft dollar allocations was 30 to 50 percent (Greenwich Associates 1990, p. 4). The soft dollars of the 1980s were preceded in the 1960s by the customer-directed "give-ups" or sub-rosa commission rebates that resulted from the fixed-commission rate system. Even though the give-ups led to abuses that were so flagrant that the practice was finally restricted by the SEC in December 1968, this practice never completely left the industry. As late as 1975, institutions could use these "soft dollars" to buy such items as newspaper subscriptions and office furniture.

Regulatory View of Soft Dollar Systems

Congress and the SEC have been sensitive to investment managers' need for access to the investment and other research generated by brokers. Historically, brokerage firms have provided research in addition to execution services in exchange for brokerage commissions. But investment managers have always been charged with a fiduciary duty to pay the lowest costs for commission services. They were therefore reluctant in 1975 to pay a higher commission rate that would include payment for research in the new negotiated rate environment.

In response to these concerns, Congress added Section 28(e) to the Securities Exchange Act of 1934, which provided a "safe harbor" for investment managers paying up for research.[4] In 1976, the SEC issued an interpretative release that addressed two outstanding questions about payment for research. First, the release spelled out a policy that any product or service that was customarily available and offered to the general public on a commercial basis was not within the safe harbor of Section 28(e) (3). The release outlawed certain services and products that had been exchanged for soft dollars before 1975 (e.g., subscriptions to periodicals, airline tickets, office furniture, and quotation equipment).

The second item related to third-party research. The SEC took the position that Section 28(e) "might, under appropriate circumstances, be applicable to situations where a broker provides an investment manager with research by a third party" (Freedman 1982, p. 218). Provision of third-party research was permitted because research might not be produced by the broker "in house" and so the broker might, under appropriate circumstances, contract with a third party to provide research services to investment managers.

The SEC revised its soft dollar guidelines after its 1976 release. In a 1986 release, the SEC recommended liberalizing the regulations to broaden the definition of research to include personal computer-based research products not available in 1976 (*Securities Week,* March 31, 1986, p. 2).

Soft Dollars and Third-Party Payments

There was a boom in soft dollar payments between 1982 and 1984. Based on a 1984 survey of pension funds, *Institutional Investor* (February 1985, p. 66) reported that 13.5 percent of respondents stated that their fund's use of soft dollars had increased dramatically over the past two years, and 31.7 percent answered that it had increased significantly.

An important part of this soft dollar increase consisted of payments to third parties. Many of the services provided by third parties were created in response to technological innovations that have changed the investment world. The third parties often are research and investment advice firms set up by well-known finance academics, high-profile Wall Street securities analysts, former high-level government economists, and the like. They offer an array of computer-based investment analyses that were not previously available from the traditional full-service Wall Street broker-dealers. The third parties thus allow broker-dealers to offer many more research products and services than would be available from the firm's own research department. Indeed, it was estimated in 1985 that institutions spent $400 million for third-party research (*Institutional Investor,* April 1984, pp. 73–80).

A Kink in the Demand for Institutional Brokerage Service

Switching from one brokerage firm to another for transaction services is relatively costless for institutions, since each institution makes transactions through a number of brokers. Firms are therefore reluctant to raise prices for institutions because they fear that the institutions might shift their business to another firm. On the other hand, firms are reluctant to lower prices because they believe that other firms would quickly follow suit. Wall Street has never demonstrated that it can raise commission rates after having cut them (*Institutional Investor,* February 1985, p. 52). This formulation of the pricing problem suggests that institutional pricing can be explained by the kinked demand curve.

The kinked demand curve is illustrated in Figure 10-5. The expectation among businesspersons is that a price reduction, but not a price rise, will be followed.[5] Demand is, therefore relatively inelastic downward. It is elastic upward, however, when a unilateral price rise by a particular firm leads to a contracted share of a constant or slightly smaller market for that firm. The profit-maximizing strategy is generally to maintain prices at the existing level. Large variations in marginal costs will not alter the price at the level of the kink (p*) because there is a discontinuity in the marginal revenue curve, whose length is a function of the difference in the elasticities of the two curves. The main prediction of the kinked demand curve is that prices tend to be rigid in the face of moderate cost-and-demand changes (Scherer 1980, p. 166). But the kinked demand curve is only a theory of price rigidity, not a theory of price determination; it says nothing about how the existing price level is set.

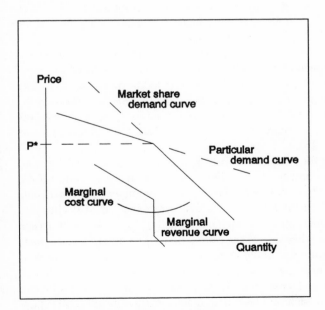

Figure 10-5. The kinked demand curve.

Institutional pricing was characterized by fairly rigorous price competition following deregulation, as shown in Figure 10-1. Commission reductions continued until early 1978, when Donaldson, Lufkin announced that it would stop cutting institutional prices and would raise institutional rates on some transactions. Donaldson, Lufkin had pioneered institutional brokerage services in the 1960s (*Wall Street Journal,* February 6, 1978, p. 7). The prices for institutional firms stablized over the next few months as all firms tacitly agreed to end the extended price cutting. The pricing move by Donaldson, Lufkin thus appeared to have established a kink in the demand curve.

Throughout 1979, 1980, and 1981 there were no press reports of any price increases in institutional pricing. On the retail side, by contrast, there were several rounds of price increases, although there were complaints about institutional firms' inability to raise prices:

While (institution brokerage) desks have tried to negotiate more strongly on commissions, officials complain that they don't get anywhere because the clients hang tight to policy. "They have decided that we should only get paid a certain number of cents per share," said one source. "And they just won't accept the negotiations. They'll just go to the guy across the street if we push!"(*Securities Week,* May 18, 1981, p. 1)

Eight cents appears to have been the kink in the demand curve or a "focal point" for pricing for the larger institutional orders. Focal point pricing occurs when all firms adopt a particular price because it stands out as an "obvious" price and because they believe that their rivals will do the same (Scherer 1980). The use of round sums or reliance on widely publicized data are examples of focal point pricing (Hay and Morris 1979, p. 149). The focal point provides a method of maintaining the kink in the demand curve. The SEC Survey of Commission Charges (discontinued after 1981) could have been used to provide a focal point for pricing by securities firms.

The demand for institutional or large block brokerage services shifted out over this period. In 1977, there were 54,275 large blocks (10,000 or more shares) traded on the NYSE, with an average of 21,813 shares per trade (NYSE *Fact Book* 1978, p. 11). In 1984, there were 433,427 large blocks traded, an increase of almost 700 percent. The average number of shares traded rose to 26,514, a 22 percent increase (NYSE *Fact Book* 1985, p. 15).

The drop in commissions for large blocks from eight to five cents in 1984 suggests economies in handling larger orders. The declining costs for increasingly larger block transactions can be attributed to a number of factors. Telecommunications costs fell, and with a rapidly expanding market, search costs were expected to decline for institutional brokers. With many more potential buyers and sellers, it should be easier to find someone to take the other side of the transaction. In addition, the risk costs associated with block positioning should drop as institutional brokers are able to take advantage of new financial instruments that allow firms to hedge a position.

As demand shifted out and costs fell, large blocks became more profitable, although, profits were taken back by investment managers through soft dollar payments. But following the reduction to five cents in 1984, there were reports of fewer soft dollars in the industry. In some cases, it was reported that soft dollar budgets had been cut back by 50 percent (*Securities Week,* January 7, 1985, pp. 1–2). The decline in commissions per share shown in Figure 10-4 from 1984 to 1988 was accompanied by a decline in soft dollar allocations. It was reported that soft dollar allocations dropped from 22 percent of total commissions in 1987 to 17 percent in 1989 (Greenwich Associates 1990, p. 4). More flexibility in pricing would tend to put pressure on soft dollars.

AN ECONOMIC RATIONALE FOR SOFT DOLLARS

Johnsen and Williams (1991) offer an economic rationale for why soft dollars are used in this industry. The question they address is why research is bundled together with execution rather than being priced and transacted separately in the market. They observe that the entities we call *firms* purposely avoid relying on prices for much of what they do, and indeed, the extent or scope of the firm is determined in part by the transaction costs of using market prices. Within the firm, the agency costs of coordination, monitoring, and control offset these costs. In this context, the provisions of soft dollar research appears to represent a kind of hybrid transaction that occurs somewhere in the gray area between the firm and the market. Johnsen and Williams give two mutually compatible explanations for the persistent use of soft dollars based on transaction and agency costs of optimal portfolio management.

Spillover Costs

Johnsen and Williams's first explanation, referred to as the *spillover cost hypothesis,* assumes that mutual or pension fund shareholders (the shareholders) hire outside fund managers (the manager) to perform wealth-enhancing portfolio transactions. But these transactions require doing research, devising portfolio strategies, finding the best available price, and finding the lowest possible brokerage cost. Managers normally need an independent broker to perform portfolio executions. The broker specializes in discovering better prices, and part of his or her commission is compensation for the search costs incurred and the costs in working the trade to minimize its price impact.

Like those who use brokers in any market, it is efficient for managers to spend some of their resources doing their own research to discover wealth-enhancing portfolio transactions. So, realistically, investment opportunities are produced jointly by the manager and the executing broker. Unless one party's contribution to the total product of the transaction can be easily measured, the optimal arrangement may be for them to share in some way the available residual or benefit of this joint relationship.

In this joint production, one or both parties may purposely or inadvertently impose costs on the other. For example, managers may fail to do the research necessary to package and time the transactions properly to achieve a given quality of execution, and so it will then cost the broker more than necessary to make the trade. Or given some level of research by the manager in packaging and timing the transaction, the broker may fail to work the trade properly, and this will lead to an excessive price impact, which will reduce the profitability of the transaction and the performance of the fund. Since both securities prices and fund performance are noisy, it may take time to measure the relevant values and identify the sources of poor performance.

Soft dollars may therefore be a method by which brokers can simultaneously compensate managers for reducing the spillover costs they generate and share in the residual to their course of dealing. The broker's residual comes in the form of future commissions if past portfolio transactions turn out well, or a loss of commissions if they turn out poorly. The broker has an incentive to reduce whatever spillover costs the manager may impose on him or her, and so the broker allows the manager to pay for brokerages and then gives the manager the kind of research and other services necessary to reduce the spillover costs.

Optimal Employment Contracts

Johnsen and Williams's other explanation is based on *optimal employment contracts*. It is difficult to observe a manager's "performance" because risk is unobservable ex ante and because all securities prices are noisy. Even if shareholders are well informed and participate actively in monitoring their managers, compensation based on salary with the threat of termination for poor performance would probably fail. Instead, shareholders pay managers a percentage based on the net asset value of the fund, in addition to agreeing to pay the brokerage costs.

Some economists argue that most soft dollar arrangements use more research than the shareholders would use if they had to pay for it themselves. Johnsen and Williams note that this conclusion appears correct. But the inference that such arrangements necessarily lead managers to use too much research—that is, to churn the portfolios they manage—is clearly wrong. If anything, fund managers have too little incentive to do research. Wealth-enhancing portfolio transactions require research by the manager, as well as research and execution by the collaborating broker. Managers are called on by shareholders to incur substantial costs to generate portfolio transactions, even though they receive only about 1 percent of any additional shareholder wealth they produce. As with all sharing contracts, without any compensating adjustments, the parties' interests will diverge, and their joint wealth will be less than it might otherwise be.

Managers' engaging in too little research under the prevailing sharing contract illustrates a principal–agent problem. As principals, shareholders have an incentive to subsidize portfolio executions, in part by bearing the cost of portfolio brokerage. Shareholders want the "best" execution and only those portfolio transactions that enhance fund wealth. Just as shareholders have an incentive to subsidize the execution provided by brokers, it appears that they also have an incentive to subsidize research by managers. By tying execution, research, and the manager's labor effort together in a combination that minimizes the spillover costs between the manager and his or her executing brokers, soft dollars may approximate the optimal outcome that equates the marginal social product of portfolio management and its marginal social cost. In the view of Johnsen and Williams, rather than increasing transactions and agency costs, soft dollars may in fact reduce them, thereby benefiting the fund shareholders. They also note the absence of any substantial outcry from fund shareholders, despite the persistent use of soft dollars for more than fifteen years.

NOTES

1. The SEC has not published separate estimates of the concentration of individual and institutional markets.

2. A number of press reports indicate that eight cents a share was the "normal" institutional commission rate until the adjustment to five cents in late 1984 (see, e.g., *Wall Street Journal* February 20, 1985, p. 1; *Securities Week,* November 19, 1984, p. 1).

3. Greenwich Associates (1990, p. v) identifies the difficulties in cost accounting as follows: It is difficult to track in a meaningful way the time an analyst or salesman spends, and it is difficult to account for the value produced by using trading capital. If a broker-dealer has a $25 million research budget, how do you allocate those costs among corporate finance, investment banking, institutional brokerage, and retail brokerage?

4. Section 28(e) provides that an investment manager would not breach a fiduciary duty by paying a brokerage commission "in excess of the amount of commission another member of an exchange, broker, or dealer would have charged for effecting that transaction, if such person determined in good faith that such amount of commission was reasonable in relation to the value of the brokerages and research services provided."

5. This description is based on Hay and Morris (1979).

11

Market Making, Proprietary Trading, and Derivatives

The major dealer markets are the market for U.S. Treasury securities, the market for corporate bonds, the municipal bond market, the OTC (over-the-counter) market for corporate stock, and the market for asset-backed securities, swaps, and derivatives. Dealers in these markets make bid and offer quotes, and take inventory positions in securities. However, differences among securities lead to important differences in the way that dealers carry out their market-making functions (Garbade 1982, pp. 429–30).

In the Treasury market, there are several hundred issues, each on the order of billions of dollars. It is dominated by a small number of primary dealers, and transactions sizes are usually large with small spreads. Since the dealers are quoting similar spreads on a small group of homogeneous securities, this type of dealer market eliminates the need for time-consuming searches for trading partners. In the market for municipal bonds, the market for corporate debt, and the OTC stock market, there are thousands of issues of each type of security. Very few of the issues in each of these markets are large, with relatively few exceeding $500 million. The heterogeneity and relatively small size of municipal bonds and corporate issues of bonds and stock and the type of investor in the instruments have produced some significant differences in the way that dealers operate in each of these markets.

Proprietary trading is an extension of a firm's dealing activities, except that the trading is done for the firm's account rather than a customer's account. It is an important source of revenues for many firms. There is a close relationship among proprietary trading, swaps, and the development of derivatives. The high-tech trading technology and ability to structure hedges to benefit the broker-dealer can also be used to solve customers' problems such as interest rate or currency exposure.

UNITED STATES GOVERNMENT SECURITIES

The Federal Reserve acts as the agent for the Treasury in the sale of bills, notes, and bonds.[1] The amounts of marketable government debt in these instruments are shown in Table 11-1. The thirty-nine U.S. government–authorized primary dealers in government bonds purchase most of the debt, with the major broker-dealers and com-

Table 11-1. Gross Marketable Public Debt of U.S. Treasury, 1980–1991 ($ Billion)

	1980	1981	1982	1983	1984	1985	1986	1987	1988	1989	1990	1991
Bills	216.1	245.0	311.8	343.8	356.8	399.9	426.7	389.5	414.0	430.6	527.4	590.4
Notes	321.6	375.3	465.0	573.4	705.1	812.5	927.5	1,037.9	1,083.6	1,151.5	1,265.2	1,430.8
Bonds	85.4	99.9	104.6	133.7	167.9	211.1	249.8	285.5	307.9	348.2	388.2	435.5

Source: Federal Reserve Bulletin, various issues.

mercial banks that are the primary dealers as the hub of the government securities market. These dealers must put in bids at every Treasury auction and either keep the securities for investment or resell them to other dealers or directly to institutional investors or the public. Salomon is usually the dominant government debt trader; other large government dealers are Merrill Lynch and Lehman Brothers, with Goldman Sachs, Morgan Stanley, and First Boston trading behind them (*Business Week,* August 26, 1991, p. 56). As discussed in Chapter 3, those primary dealers that are broker-dealers account for most of the government securities held by the securities industry.

The Treasury bill market is said to be the most liquid securities market in the world, because the size of a conventional transaction can be around $25 million or $50 million and because the difference between the price that a dealer is willing to pay for an issue and the price at which it is willing to sell the issue is very small, sometimes as low as 1 basis point, or $25 per $1 million face value on a ninety-day bill (Garbade 1982, pp. 13–14). Some federal obligations are listed on the New York Stock Exchange (NYSE), but most are traded over the counter. Although active in the short-term market, the larger dealers and banks do most of their trading in long-term maturities, keeping in constant touch with the owners of existing issues and with potential buyers. Financial institutions, including commercial and Federal Reserve banks, are the dealers' major customers, although they are doing a growing volume of business in bills and certificates with corporations. The market for federal obligations is the largest and most active securities market in the world.

Dealers of Treasury securities often finance close to 100 percent of their collateral value. This high leverage, combined with fluctuating interest rates and the large volume of daily trading, creates a potential for risk taking in this market. For example, between 1982 and 1985, seven secondary government securities dealers failed as a result of taking large gambles on the direction of interest rate changes.

The Government Securities Market as a Cartel

The $2.3 trillion Treasury market may be the world's most sophisticated cartel (*Wall Street Journal,* August 30, 1991, p. A-14). Although the Treasury's practice of limiting its auction to competitive bids from the exclusive club of thirty-nine Fed-licensed "primary dealers" could provide a framework to be used for collusion, in fact, the primary dealers have no special standing in sales; virtually any investor can place competitive bids. But the procedures for bidding through the Fed, which conducts the auctions for the Treasury, are so cumbersome that few outsiders bother. Instead, large mutual and pension funds route their bids through the primary dealers.

Treasury and Fed officials argue that the primary dealers are critical to the system. On their part, the dealers promise that they will bid in almost every auction, thereby eliminating the Treasury's fears that it might hold an auction and have no bidders. However, the market has grown so much in the past two decades with the large U.S. government deficits that concerns about the Fed's ability to sell the debt are not very realistic. Because many buyers are available for the securities sold at each auction, the primary dealers are no longer needed as a backup.

The Possibility of Collusion in the Government Securities Market

Following the admission by Salomon Brothers that the firm had submitted false bids in a Treasury auction, the *Wall Street Journal* stated that collusion and price fixing in the $2.3 trillion Treasury security market have been routine for more than a decade. The *Journal* reported that current and former traders at several prominent Wall Street investment banks said that they regularly shared secrets about the size and price of their bids at the multibillion-dollar government auctions. Interviews conducted by the *Journal* suggested that improper activities are common in the Treasury market and not limited to Salomon Brothers. The market is referred to as a rough-and-tumble world in which usually fierce adversaries share information about their government bids to avoid having to bid too high. The market is so risky that a firm can lose millions of dollars if its bid is even fractionally overpriced. The *Journal* argued that with collusion, dealers ensure that they will get their allotment of notes and bonds that will assure them a profit (*Wall Street Journal,* August 19, 1991, p. A-1).

THE CORPORATE BOND MARKET

The corporate bond secondary market, shown in Table 11-2, is roughly half the size of the total U.S. Treasury market. In the secondary market in corporates, investors contact dealers when they want to buy or sell an issue, and dealers generally transact with their customers as principals rather than as agents. With the exception of new

Table 11.2. Corporate Bonds Outstanding at Year-End, 1983–1991 ($ Billion)

	Nonfinancial Sector	Financial Sector	Total
1983	$ 423.0	$118.6	$ 541.6
1984	496.2	153.0	622.2
1985	542.9	204.5	747.4
1986	669.4	287.4	956.8
1987	748.8	366.3	1,115.1
1988	852.6	331.9	1,184.5
1989	926.9	378.2	1,305.1
1990	947.0	515.0	1,489.0
1991	1,052.6	582.9	1,635.5

Source: Federal Reserve Bulletin, Flow-of-Funds, various issues.

issues and issues of major corporations, trading in most issues of corporate debt is relatively infrequent. But since there are so many debt issues outstanding, it usually is possible to find dozens with similar maturities, coupons, and protection clauses issued by firms of comparable credit risk. An important aspect of being a successful trading firm is knowing which investors own what type of bonds, what they are willing to sell, and what they are looking to buy. In practice, dealers in this market act very much like brokers.

The corporate bond market is not an active market with a large number of bid-and-ask quotes on a variety of bonds.[2] Rather, it is a market of purchase-and-sale interests that have an uncertain potential for an actual trade. Knowledge of those interests is an important determinant of dealer profits and therefore requires an experienced, knowledgeable sales force, more so than for Treasury dealers (Garbade 1982, p. 437).

The relatively high cost of trading corporate bonds resulting from the wide bid–ask spreads, has led to the use of trading mechanisms other than cash purchases and sale. Many transactions in long-term bonds, therefore, are arranged in pairs, in which the dealer and customer *swap* two issues of comparable aggregate value, settling only the difference in cash. Swaps allow an institution, for example, to alter its portfolio in a single transaction and eliminate the need first to sell one issue and then, with the proceeds, to buy another issue. Swaps allow a trader to get out of one issue and acquire another that some third party might be seeking.

In addition, the ability to execute swaps gives a bond dealer a flexibility that is not available to an ordinary broker. The broker must match cash buyer and cash seller for specific issues. But a bond dealer can swap two issues with one investor and then swap out of the newly acquired position with some other investor, thereby entering into transactions foreclosed to brokers. Bond investors often trade large blocks of bonds, and dealers require a substantial capital base to support their inventories. The high degree of interasset substitutability and large capital requirements have led to a corporate bond market dominated by a relatively few large firms, such as Salomon Brothers, Goldman Sachs, and First Boston (Garbade 1982).

THE MUNICIPAL BOND MARKET

Obligations of state and local governments can be classified as general obligations, revenue bonds, and housing authority issues (Garbade 1982). General (''full faith and credit'') obligations are secured by the general taxing power of governmental units such as states, counties, cities, and townships and by special tax districts such as school or water districts. Revenue bonds are issued to finance the provision of particular services on projects such as turnpikes and airports, water and other utilities, and public housing. These debt securities are obligations only of the issuing authority and, unless otherwise provided, are not general obligations of any sponsoring government. Table 11-3 lists the outstanding debt of state and local units over time. As of 1990 the total long-term debt of state and local governments was less than that of corporate issuers.

Municipal bonds (or ''munis'') come to market through a process that is a hybrid

Table 11-3. Outstanding Debt of State and Local Governments, 1980–1990 ($ Billion)

	1980	1981	1982	1983	1984	1985	1986	1987	1988	1989	1990
Long-term debt											
Full faith and credit	149.8	151.8	151.2	163.1	166.9	178.8	190.1	201.1	211.1	224.1	245.1
Nonguaranteed	172.7	196.6	229.1	272.8	318.2	373.0	450.5	483.0	528.2	556.3	596.2
Short-term debt	13.1	15.6	19.0	18.6	20.0	19.6	18.3	17.6	15.7	18.0	19.3

Source: U.S. Department of Commerce, Bureau of the Census, *Governmental Finances,* various issues.

of the unrestricted competition among buyers characterizing Treasury auctions and the negotiated underwritings by a single syndicate of broker-dealers used in most corporate auctions. Issuers of general obligation municipal debt typically advertise for competitive bids for their offerings, just as the Treasury does. Unlike the Treasury, however, municipalities offer new issues on an "all-or-none" basis, so that bidders buy either an entire offering or nothing at all. In practice, this restricts the class of potential bidders to syndicates of broker-dealers and removes retail buyers from the bidding competition. After a syndicate has obtained a new issue, it reoffers the securities on a fixed-price subscription basis, just as in any corporate underwriting.

Municipal securities may also be sold to underwriters on a negotiated basis, in which the issuer negotiates the terms of an issue directly with a single group of broker-dealers. Negotiated underwritings are rare with general-obligation offerings but are more common with nongeneral-obligation issuers like revenue bonds.

Organization of the Secondary Market for Municipals

Many municipal securities have limited markets, and purchasers often hold them until maturity. The secondary market is usually established by the original underwriting banks and broker-dealers who specialize in those securities in the over-the-counter market. Although complete data are not available, the interdealer volume of transactions is known to be substantial, but the total volume of trading is probably much lower than that of new offerings (Dougall and Gaumnity 1986, pp. 205–6).

The market in outstanding municipal securities consists of several overlapping segments. One segment is the dealer activities of large banks and nonbank broker-dealers. Recent offerings, and issues with large outstanding volumes, usually trade quite actively in this market. One step removed from the dealer market are the many broker-dealers that trade a wide variety of smaller issues. These broker-dealers may specialize in securities of issuers in particular geographic areas and often provide specialized financial advice to a limited customer base. Transactions in this market are generally smaller and more costly to complete than are those that can be accommodated in the larger dealer market. Also, there is an extremely thin market in small issues, such as school district bonds and the debt of local governments. Transactions in this segment of the market may depend on word-of-mouth communication of available offerings.

Since there are so many municipal bonds and such a wide variety of coupon rates, most munis are quoted on a yield basis rather than on a price basis. However, those bonds with a large outstanding volume in a single maturity and an active secondary market are traded on a price basis. These munis are called *dollar bonds*.

Bid–ask spreads on munis may vary from 0.25 percent of principal value on an actively traded issue to 5 percent or more of principal value on inactive issues. Dealers do not usually make markets in the latter group, and reported bid-and-offer prices are likely to be brokers' quotes, reflecting the purchase-and-sale interests of investors who have no need to complete a trade expeditiously (Dougall and Gaumnity 1986; Garbade 1982).

THE OTC MARKET IN STOCKS

Before 1971, the information on which dealers were actively making markets in a stock and the prices quoted could be found in the "pink sheets" of the National Quotations Bureau (NQB). These sheets, printed on pink paper, were distributed daily to subscribing brokers and listed the bid-and/or-offer prices submitted to the NQB on the previous afternoon as well as the brokers entering the quotes. A broker handling an order typically called several dealers to get the best price and quantity deal available. This system caused high search costs to find the "best" price and quantity combination available and from time to time resulted in executions away from better (but undiscovered) prices (Garbade 1982, p. 439).

In 1971, the National Association of Securities Dealers (NASD), in response to urging by the U.S. Securities and Exchange Commission (SEC), made available to broker-dealers an automated quotation system called NASDAQ. NASDAQ originally was an electronic, video-screen bulletin board that accelerated the price information to a real-time basis and simultaneously displayed for the searching broker all the dealer quotations for a given stock. In 1982 it was enhanced to include last-sale reporting in National Market System (NMS)[3] stocks and in 1986 to permit the automatic execution of trades up to 1,000 shares. Level 3 service is available only to registered dealers and allows them to enter bid-and-offer quotations on specific stocks in the system. All quotes are firm for up to quantities of 1,000, 500, and 200, depending on the stock. The quotes, together with a legend identifying the stock and dealer, appear within a second or two on the video screens of thousands of broker-dealer subscribers. Level 2 service also permits the display of a complete range of dealer bids and offerings on a given stock, arranged in order of decreasing bids and increasing offers, with the name of each dealer next to the dealer's quote. Level 2 service is available to the public as well as brokers and institutional investors. Level 1 subscribers can access the best bid-and-offer price for each issue. These subscribers number about 200,000 worldwide and include registered representatives in branch offices of broker-dealer firms.

A trade in a NASDAQ security starts with a customer's call. To give the customer current trade information on the stock, the registered representative queries his or her desktop terminal by keying in the stock's NASDAQ symbol. The Level 1 terminal displays the best bid-and-offer quote drawn from all competing market makers for that security (the inside market). The terminal also displays the daily high, low, and last-sale prices, as well as the daily cumulative volume.[4]

The registered representative then directs the order to the firm's trading department. There the order is handled in one of two ways. First, if the firm with the customer's order makes a market in the security, it will sell the stock to the customer from its own inventory at the best bid or offer on the NASDAQ, plus a retail markup or minus a retail markdown, normally calculated on the same basis as a retail commission is. These "internalized" orders account for about half of all retail orders in NASDAQ stocks. If the firm is not a market maker in the security, the trader will query the Level 2 or Level 3 NASDAQ service for current quotes and other information. The terminal displays each of the bid-and-ask quotations of all market makers in the stocks, with the best quotation ranked first.

The Levels 2 and 3 terminals also show the market makers participating in the NASD's Small Order Execution System (SOES). SOES provides automatic execution, at the best quoted bid or offer price, of trades up to 1,000, 500, or 200 shares, depending on the security. If the order falls within SOES parameters, the trader may execute the order automatically through SOES. On the other hand, if the order is large and exceeds the SOES parameters, the trader may execute the transaction by telephone or enter the order in another automated system called Selectnet, which broadcasts the order to all market makers. In all non-SOES transactions, market makers are governed by a "firm quote" rule requiring them to buy or sell at least the SOES order size number of shares at their quoted prices.

The Cost Structure in NASDAQ Market Making

Ho and Macris (1984) examined market structure and performance in the NASDAQ dealer market and classified costs incurred by market makers into three types: variable costs, inventory costs, and fixed costs. Variable costs are those costs that the market maker must bear for each trade, including clearing and paperwork costs. If the market maker clears his or her own trades, then clearing costs may be viewed as either fixed or variable costs, because costs of in-house clearing consist of salary expenses, which are usually independent of trading volume. When trading volume exceeds normal levels, the firm may seek additional clearing capacity and therefore raise its costs.

The cost of carrying inventory is another significant variable cost. The ability of a market maker to carry inventory positions is directly related to the trading firm's capitalization. Inventory costs have three components. First, while holding inventory, in either a long or a short position, there may be unanticipated changes in price level, and so there is a price risk for the market maker. Second, when the dealer borrows at a rate higher than the normal rate of interest, the dealer will pay for the financing costs. Third, when offering firm quotes to the transacting public, the market maker is exposed to traders and investors who may have better information about the issuer than the market maker does and so can trade against the market maker. Trades by investors motivated by knowledge superior to the market maker's will cause the market maker to incur additional costs.

A variety of fixed overhead costs, such as rent, salary, and equipment rental, are also associated with market making. In order to control many of these costs, some OTC firms that specialize in market making have moved to New Jersey, to avoid a New York City security excise tax. But even after the tax was repealed, most of them remained in New Jersey. Large wholesale OTC market makers, including Herzog Heine Geduld, have invested millions of dollars in computerized order systems, and to keep these systems operating at efficient capacity levels, these firms and some other non-NASDAQ OTC market makers have paid for retail order flow directed by discount brokers.

The Structure of the Dealer Market

In the NASDAQ system, each dealer may choose to trade in any NASDAQ stock; there is no limit on the number of stocks in which a dealer may make a market. The large full-line firms make markets in many NASDAQ stocks: In 1985, Shearson Lehman made markets in nearly 1,700 OTC stocks, and Merrill Lynch and Dean Witter made markets in slightly more than 1,000 issues each (*Wall Street Journal,* January 11, 1985, p. 8). Specialty OTC dealer firms such as Troster Singer and Herzog Heine Geduld make markets in as many, if not more, OTC stocks than do the national full-line firms (*Fortune,* June 24, 1985, p. 85).

But since OTC stocks are not always close substitutes for one another, a dealer with limited capital can make a living by making markets even in a relatively narrow range of stocks, and so there are many relatively small OTC dealers. This is quite different from the corporate bond market, which is dominated by perhaps five broker-dealers trading in a full line of corporate debt securities, although the OTC dealers often concentrate their trading in particular industry groups or geographic areas (Garbade 1982, p. 438).

For the market in each stock, there is no limit to the number of market makers registered for the stock. Table 11-4 shows the number of NASDAQ securities and market makers from 1978 to 1991. Market structure and performance are determined by competition among the dealers to capture order flow. Unlike the NYSE, the NASD does not assign market-making responsibilities for particular stocks to certain firms, and so the number of market makers in a stock is determined strictly by economic forces. Market makers could differ significantly from one another in their capitalization and trading portfolios' size and composition. Some firms commit significant amounts of capital to market making by trading a large number of stocks, as we discussed earlier. Others may trade only a few stocks. But the capital committed to a particular stock and the trading strategies of a market maker must be competitive with those of other market makers, because there are few economies of scale in trading and portfolio diversification is a secondary consideration. Therefore, each dealer must reach his or her optimal capitalization and pricing strategy for a specific stock. The dealer's optimal decisions depend more on the stock's characteristics than on the firm's characteristics. For this reason, Ho and Macris (1984) argue that it is useful to view the dealers in each stock as being identical, and therefore the number of market makers for a stock becomes a meaningful measure of market structure.

Ho and Macris also show that a stock's trading volume determines the number of

Table 11-4. NASDAQ Securities and Market Makers, 1981–1991

Year	Number of Securities	Active Market Makers	Market-Making Positions	Average Number of Market Makers per Security
1981	3,687	420	26,935	7.4
1982	3,664	407	27,734	7.6
1983	4,467	441	32,923	7.4
1984	4,728	473	38,820	8.2
1985	4,784	500	40,093	8.4
1986	5,189	526	41,312	8.0
1987	5,537	545	41,397	7.5
1988	5,144	570	48,370	9.4
1989	4,963	458	49,670	10.0
1990	4,706	421	44,243	9.4
1991	4,684	425	47,272	10.1

Note: Compared with the average of 10.1 market makers for each NASDAQ issue in 1991, each NASDAQ National Market System issue had an average of 11.7 market markers.

Source: National Association of Securities Dealers (1992a).

market makers, which in turn specifies the amount of capital committed to market making. The larger the trading volume is, the larger will be the amount of capital committed to provide liquidity to the stock. When there are more dealers competing for the order flow, each dealer's pricing strategy (bid-and-ask quotes) will be affected, which then will influence the market bid–ask spread. Table 11-5 gives the number of market makers per stock based on the average market value of the stock for both NASDAQ/NMS and total NASDAQ. As Ho and Macris predicted, the higher the capitalization of the security was, the more market makers there were.

Table 11.5. Market-Value Distribution According to Number of Market Makers, 1991

Market Makers	NASDAQ/NMS		Total NASDAQ	
	Number of Issues	Average Market Value ($ Thousand)	Number of Issues	Average Market Value ($ Thousand)
Fewer than 3	100	$ 14,147	323	$ 9,398
3–5	456	44,304	1,049	24,735
6–10	894	80,689	1,528	50,990
11–15	609	149,639	978	99,518
16–20	309	235,631	444	174,093
21–25	133	388,798	173	305,776
26 or more	159	1,135,652	189	979,003

Note: Each NASDAQ security must have at least two market makers before it can enter the NASDAQ system. This prerequisite preserves the competitive environment that is the hallmark of NASDAQ's multiple market-maker system. A strong, positive relationship exists between the size of an issue, as measured by market capitalization, and the number of active market makers.

Source: National Association of Securities Dealers (1992a).

PROPRIETARY TRADING

The proprietary trader for a broker-dealer is a combination of market maker and investor. This trader has all the dealer's advantages, such as greater leverage and access to the high-tech computerized workstations that provide on-line data, pricing information, and the ability to execute trades. Proprietary trading encompasses a wide variety of transactions. A proprietary trader may keep a position for days, weeks, and sometimes months while trying to exploit a technical aberration in the market or speculating on the future of interest rates.[5]

Proprietary trading successes can come from many areas. Salomon was reported to have realized huge returns arbitraging between Japanese futures markets and Japanese government bonds. The firm also made a big bet on the direction of U.S. interest rates in 1990, and it was right on the mark. Goldman Sachs was reported to have taken advantage of volatility in bank bonds, reflecting credit concerns about banks. And Lehman did well going long in two-year French governments against a short in U.S. Treasuries. Proprietary traders use leverage to make money from relatively small price movements. The mechanics of the bond–repurchase–agreement market are such that a dealer need put up virtually no capital to borrow bonds. Here, the return on capital is a nearly meaningless yardstick. Rather, firms keep score with a measure of return on risk—that is, their anticipated profits compared with their maximum potential loss.

Some of the ideas that proprietary traders used ten years ago can now be found in introductory college finance textbooks. Many of the original concepts are so well known and the tools to execute them so readily available that they are part of every trader's daily routine. Accordingly, many of the market aberrations or inefficiencies that were the source of traders' profits have disappeared.

Whether it is because they had poorly constructed models or just bad luck, many of the firms that entered proprietary trading pulled back after getting burned. In the mid-1980s, dozens of regional firms set up proprietary bond-trading operations. But in 1987, a year marked by volatile interest rates and a stock market crash, many firms found that the business contained more risk than they were able to absorb. Consequently, proprietary trading is now concentrated in some of the firms in the oligopoly group that are comfortable with the high risk accompanying this type of trading. For example, Salomon lost $90 million in the fourth quarter of 1990, mostly from trading, but kept right on going. However, Salomon points out that the quarterly earnings reports based on a mark-to-market of the trading book substantially overstates the volatility of profits from proprietary trading. Since many of the trades are on the books for months, the results of this business are more stable when viewed from a long-term perspective than from a day-to-day or month-to-month perspective.

For future profit opportunities, traders see promise outside the United States, where markets may be less sophisticated or less liquid. The rise of derivative markets in other countries has opened up related arbitrage strategies as well; that is, inefficiencies provide profit opportunities for as long as they remain inefficiencies. Some inefficiencies result from the difficulty of executing trades in a particular market. For example, in many markets it is difficult to borrow bonds in order to sell them short, a necessary tactic for, among other things, futures arbitrages. One of the reasons *Institutional Investor* stated that Salomon continues to do well in proprietary trading is that the firm invested in back-office capabilities outside the United States. Salomon's trade arbitraging of the futures market for Japanese government bonds was profitable because it was one of the few firms in Japan that could borrow the bonds.

Currently, the most lucrative and most complex proprietary trading is in options and related products, because they are much harder to value than bonds are. If there are no credit problems, a bond represents a series of payments that are certain to take place. An option, however, represents one or more payments that might take place. To value the option, one thus must make assumptions about the possibility of future events. The Black–Scholes option-pricing model, still used by most options traders, assumes that the direction of change is unpredictable. Changing that assumption by betting that prices will stay within a certain range, for example, can lead to far different values for options and thus to spread-trading possibilities.

Many traders do not buy options because option prices are out of line with true values based on the option-pricing formulas. Rather, they simply buy options because they want leverage speculation or hedging protection. In addition, the complexity of options pricing is a barrier that keeps some traders from getting involved with options.

An Example of Computer-Based Trading

Gary Weiss of *Business Week* described how computer-based trading systems operate using a popular options-trading system. Using a theoretical capital commitment of $10,000 and Option Vue VI software, Weiss employed an options-trading strategy based on Standard & Poor's 100 stock index, the OEX. On April 24, 1991, the OEX closed at 362⅞. Like the far more sophisticated options software used by the major broker-dealers, programs such as Option-Vue combine pricing models with current pricing data to determine whether the options are fairly valued. Using historical volatility data, computer programs determine which options are overpriced and underpriced and then recommend options strategies. For Weiss, the Option Vue churned out a dozen such strategies. All were ''straddles''—the purchase and/or sale of puts or calls of the same expiration month aimed at locking in a riskless profit. Along with each straddle were projections of associated risk and return.

Of the twelve strategies, only four were profitable, but the best recommendation was a standout. The first recommendation was the purchase of 90 May 355 calls at 8⅛ and the sale of 90 May 335 calls at 27⅞. By the close of trading six days later on April 30, the 355 calls were worth 5⅝, a loss of 3¼ and a dollar loss of $325 times 90, or $29,250. But that loss was more than offset by the 5⅞ gain—$572.50 times 90, or $51,525—on the 335 calls. Weiss's theoretical profit was $22,275, excluding commissions (*Business Week,* June 10, 1991, p. 86).

INTEREST RATE AND CURRENCY SWAPS

Unlike futures and options, which have been around in various forms for a long time, financial swaps are a relatively new idea. The first of these swaps occurred in

1981. By 1983, the amount of swaps outstanding had risen to $3 billion; by 1986, to $300 billion; and by 1988, to over $1 trillion. In 1985, the International Swap Dealers Association was formed to standardize documentation and procedures in this rapidly growing market. Swaps are widely used by broker-dealers, commercial banks, savings and loan associations, government agencies, and corporations. The dominant types of swaps are interest rate swaps (about 80 percent of the total) and currency swaps.[6]

Swaps can be thought of as bundles of forward transactions. However, there are problems in arranging these transactions directly. First, it may be difficult to find suitable partners, and consequently, it may be difficult to arrange a good deal. Then there is the problem of credit risk. If you are a fixed-rate player and interest rates increase, your partner to the swap may default on the agreement, leaving you with a loss. That is, the swap is a hedge only as long as there is confidence that the promised payment will be made.

Swap intermediaries make a market in swaps and are ready to provide swaps to fixed-rate and floating-rate customers at any time at their advertised rates. That is, swap intermediaries do not wait to match up individual fixed- and floating-rate players. Parties to swaps, just like parties to futures and options contracts, neither know nor need to know who ultimately takes the other side of a transaction. From the customer's point of view, the deal is with the intermediary. The intermediaries also offer a ''secondary market'' in swaps.

Because intermediaries—broker-dealers and others—make a market in swaps, their commitments to fixed-rate and floating-rate payers are unlikely to match exactly at all times. For example, if the amount of commitment to floating-rate payers exceeds the commitment to fixed-rate payers, then the intermediary itself will be committed to paying a fixed rate in exchange for a floating rate on the difference. If interest rates fall, the intermediary will take a loss; if they rise, it will make a profit. However, the intermediary does have the ability to hedge its open position in swaps and futures or options.

Swaps have opened up certain financial markets to those who would not normally have access to them. For example, a small firm that would not normally be able to borrow in direct financial markets may be able to ''swap into'' these markets. Firms or banks that would not normally be able to borrow in Japan or Germany can now do so via currency swaps. Borrowers and lenders can now more easily shop around worldwide for the best deals.

DERIVATIVES

For broker-dealers, the new derivative securities they have constructed transform part of their equity and debt business into a business with the far more attractive characteristics of swaps trading.[7] The private nature of the deals and their many variations minimize some elements of competition by erecting some barriers to entry into the derivative business. Also, dealers almost always act as principals rather than agents so that they can profit from trading opportunities. However, the broker-dealers are also committing themselves to contracts as long as ten years on markets that can become quite volatile. Traders argue that they have sophisticated models to hedge their risks. But if the hedges fail, the broker-dealers and their customers may have severe problems.

The traders that are running the books that include the derivative commitments must at the same time hedge the firm's exposure to volatile markets and also try to exploit lucrative arbitrage opportunities. Most broker-dealers centralize their trading in one worldwide book. Using computer models developed for the swaps market, they analyze their aggregate positions and project what would happen to them under various market conditions. They then use this information to construct hedges, typically with listed options or futures or by buying or selling short the actual stock. In general, these are "dynamic hedges" in which traders adjust their positions as the market changes. Because hedging long-term derivatives with short-term options and futures can be precarious positioning, the key to success in the derivatives business is to build such a broad book that customers' transactions will offset one another. Then listed futures and options need be used only to hedge the residual risk.

The advantage of a global book is that derivative positions can create trading opportunities for broker-dealers in the worldwide equities business; that is, derivatives provide positions to trade against the cash market. If, for example, a dealer owns a put on a particular stock—as part of its market making for customers' selling orders—buying the security long will offset the put's position. A broker in that situation can then be much more aggressive in bidding for a block of that stock than can another dealer who would have to go out and find the other side. According to *Institutional Investor,* dealers state that as much as half the profits from a derivative business come from this sort of trading rather than from the initial bid–ask spread.

MARKET MAKING AND CONTESTABILITY

Entry barriers to OTC market making and the municipal bond market are low; and so many firms maintain proprietary positions or firm trading accounts. Becoming a primary dealer in the government bond market is limited to relatively large firms, although smaller firms can become secondary dealers. With the large number of "bought" deals in the corporate bond–underwriting business, market making in the aftermath is generally limited to those firms that underwrote the initial offering. Market making in asset-backed securities initially was concentrated in the hands of those firms that had originated the business. As asset-backed securities have become more of a commodity, many regional firms are participating in syndicates of asset-backed securities and thus are becoming market makers in the product. The creation and trading of derivatives is mainly in the hands of firms in the oligopoly group. But some regional firms have entered this business.

In those lines of business with easy entry and exit, the market is contestable, and the properties of the competitive market are expected to prevail: Prices equals marginal cost. In those market-making areas into which entry is not easy—corporate bonds and the derivatives area—strategic behavior is observed.

It could be argued that the emergence of the "bought" deal in corporate bond underwriting was a strategic response to the opportunity provided by Rule 415. Alternatively, the bought deal might provide a more efficient way to distribute securities if the time restrictions on these deals make cumbersome the assembly of a large syndicate. The derivative business is a relatively new one for broker-dealers, and it appears that firms' efforts are directed more toward learning the business than erecting barriers to entry for firms not already in this line of business.

CONCLUSION

The wide breath of the dealer business provide many opportunities for broker-dealers. Entry is relatively easy into some parts of this business. Chapter 9 stated that economies of scope are not strong in the market-making, brokerage, and underwriting businesses. The fact that some large firms are primarily OTC market makers, such as Troster Singer and Herzog Heine Geduld, is evidence that economies of scope are not important to the OTC line. But for newer lines of business, such as swaps, derivatives, junk bonds, and asset-backed securities, economies of scope between market making and underwriting may be important. Broker-dealers most likely will have to provide trading support to maintain liquidity for their underwriting issues. The fact that the large OTC market makers are willing to pay for order flow suggests that there are some relevant economies of scale in this line of business.

With new instruments, such as asset-backed securities, early entrants have been able to earn large profits by making markets in the new securities. As more firms enter the new line, profits will decline to normal levels. In addition, the high profits available in a new line from both underwriting and market making provide incentives for developing new products.

NOTES

1. Treasury bills range in maturity from three months to one year. Treasury notes and bonds are available with maturities from one to ten years. Treasury bonds have original maturities ranging from ten to thirty years. Other types of U.S. government debt (such as savings bonds) are generally not considered marketable (Dougall and Gaumnitz 1986, pp. 174–75).

2. In addition to the market for publicly issued corporate debt, there is a sizable matket for privately placed corporate debt. The size of this market and the restrictions on trading these issues are described in Garbade (1982).

3. National market System stocks are the most actively traded issues in the OTC market. More detailed information is published in newspaper stock tables about NMS stocks than about other OTC stocks.

4. At the end of 1991, there were 4,684 securities in the NASDAQ system, and of these, 3,045 were carried in NASDAQ/NMS. Beyond the securities listed on NASDAQ, there were an estimated 45,000 to 50,000 non-NASDAQ OTC stocks traded in the "pink sheet" market. The existing pink sheet market is composed of stocks that are too thinly traded to be considered for listing on NASDAQ (National Association of Securities Dealers (1992).

5. This section is based on *Institutional Investor,* April 1991, p. 36.

6. This section is based on Kohn (1991), chap. 13.

7. This section is based on *Institutional Investor,* August 1990, pp. 54–61.

12

Investment Banking

The dynamic competition among broker-dealers is most apparent in investment banking. In the 1980s, market areas of enormous profitability were developed by the large full-line and investment-banking firms. In the areas of mergers and acquisitions, mortgage- and asset-backed securities, and junk or high-yield bonds, these dominant firms quickly captured and fortified large market share positions. In addition, Rule 415 changed the nature of the traditional underwriting syndicate, giving advantages to the large, better-capitalized investment banks.

This chapter examines investment banking using a somewhat self-contained structure–conduct–performance analysis of this industry group within the larger broker-dealer industry. The investment bankers have been the subject of more industry analysis than has the overall broker-dealer industry. Pugel and White (1984) studied the investment-banking industry using the structure–conduct–performance paradigm in a consideration of allowing commercial bank affiliates to underwrite corporate securities. Rogowski and Sorensen (1985) considered the impact of shelf registration on the structure and performance of the investment-banking industry. Hayes, Spence, and Marks (1983) analyzed the industry in depth and used logit analysis to look at the characteristics that attract specific clients and investment bankers to one another. Auerbach and Hayes (1986) examined the impact of Rule 415 on due diligence examinations by underwriters. Eccles and Crane (1988) studied the strategic and management issues facing investment bankers. And Hayes and Hubbard (1990) looked at the state of global investment banking in the late 1980s.

THE UNDERWRITING FUNCTION

We will begin with underwriting, which encompasses three major activities: origination, risk bearing, and distribution. Origination requires decisions about the type (e.g., debt, equity), quantity, price, timing, and other features of the new securities issue and the determination of the method of distribution. Risk bearing comes into play when the issue is a *firm-commitment* offering, in which the underwriter buys the securities from the issuer at a fixed price and resells them to the public. It is by far the most common form of underwriting. If the price of the securities falls before they can be resold, the underwriter will suffer a loss, thus the risk associated with this activity. Occasionally, underwriters suffer substantial losses due to abrupt declines in some underwritten offerings.[1]

An alternative offering approach that eliminates most of the risks of underwriting is the *best-effort* offering, in which the underwriters do not buy the securities but use the firm's "best efforts" to sell the entire offering for the issuer. In this approach, the risk of the offering is shifted back to the issuers, and any unsold portion of the offering is returned to the issuer.

The issuer has the choice of two offering methods, a negotiated or a competitive-bid offering. In a negotiated underwriting, the issuer chooses a lead manager and normally selects the comanager. Often each bidder has a potential syndicate largely in place, which has traditionally been used in order to spread the risk and distribute the issue. The lead manager(s) earns an additional fee for controlling the syndicate and "running the books." In a competitive-bid underwriting, the issuer frequently designs the issue and collects bids from various underwriters. The underwriters then bid for the issue as either the lead manager or one of a group of comanagers, again with each bidder often having a potential syndicate lined up. Public utilities are often required by federal or state regulators to issue securities through the competitive-bid process (Pugel and White 1984, pp. 96–98).

The syndicate form emerged in the first part of this century, and by the time the basic securities laws were being written in the 1930s, it was an established way of doing business. The Exchange Act of 1934 did not address the syndicate system, but subsequently the U.S. Securities and Exchange Commission (SEC) wrote rules that recognized the existence of syndicates. The most important of these rules allows a syndicate, when making an offering of a company's common stock, to "stabilize" the price of stock that the company already has on the market, so that the new stock can be sold at a roughly equal price. The underwriters do this by standing ready to buy stock being sold into the market. Later, both the SEC and a federal court expressed their views—without issuing legal rulings—that the syndicate form did not violate the Sherman Act. In 1953, the court found it important that the syndicates were limited in scope, duration, and purpose.

ELASTICITY OF DEMAND FOR UNDERWRITING SERVICES

Issuers have a number of alternatives to raising funds through a public offering through an underwriter. They can privately place securities with an institution. Insurance companies, for example, are large purchasers of corporate bonds in the private placement market. These offerings are not registered with the SEC and have significant resale restrictions. Both broker-dealers and commercial bankers assist in private placements. As discussed in Chapter 3, the development of screen-based information systems by the National Association of Securities Dealers (NASD) and the American Stock Exchange (ASE) enables more offerings to be shifted to the private placement market and away from traditional underwritten offerings.

Issuers can raise funds from commercial bank loans or from internal sources such as retained earnings. Or issuers can sell their securities directly using rights or warrants offerings. Some corporate issuers have conducted auctions of bond issues without any underwriting intermediary. Since 1977 or so, issuers have significantly built up their in-house financial staffs, who have been issuing their own corporate paper, speculating in foreign-exchange markets, and setting up their own credit subsidiaries such as IBM Credit and Xerox Credit. This expertise has meant that issuers are less likely to rely on investment bankers for financial services that they can perform themselves. That is why large corporate issuers aggressively lobbied the SEC for Rule 415 to give them more flexibility to operate in a volatile financial environment (*Institutional Investor*, June 1982, pp. 284–306).

Given the existence of close, but not perfect, substitutes, Pugel and White argue that there is some degree of price elasticity of demand for the services of the underwriters of publicly offered securities, which would limit the exercise of market power by investment bankers. Smith (1977), on the other hand, suggests that issuers often use underwritten offerings even when other methods of raising funds are significantly less expensive,[2] thus implying that other important factors enter the decision, so that demand might be relatively inelastic. Developments that have occurred since these articles were written also seem to have reduced the market power of individual investment bankers. Clients now appear to be more interested in pursuing suggestions for innovative financing approaches and more willing to shop for innovations. The potential for dramatic expansion of the private placement market also has limited the market power of investment bankers, especially with more success by commercial bankers in this area.

ENTRY AND CONTESTABILITY IN INVESTMENT BANKING

Entry into Investment Banking

There are at least three levels of entry in the investment-banking or underwriting business: entry into the managing underwriter status for small ($10 million and under) and medium-size ($10 million to $50 million) offerings; entry as a syndicate member into an offering syndicate run by a national managing underwriter; and entry into the ranks of the national managing underwriters.

Small issues ($10 million and under) are generally handled by regional broker-dealers. For example, eight-seven of the eighty-nine small issues of common stock offered between April 1979 and September 1980 were managed by regional firms (U.S. Securities and Exchange Commission 1981a, p. 43). Many of the broker-dealers that handled these offerings were relatively recently formed firms, and many of the small issuers were "best-efforts" offerings in which the broker-dealer did not take a position in the stock. The offerings for many of these small issues did not involve the formation of a syndicate.

The entry into the small offerings sector of the underwriting business does not appear to be characterized by substantial barriers. There are no SEC capital requirements that specifically apply to underwriting. Since many of the offerings are best-efforts offerings, the broker-dealer does not put his or her capital at risk, and therefore there is no substantial capital barrier. In addition, many of the issuers in the $10 million-and-under market are initial offerings for a firm—the time that the firm "goes public." Therefore, there is no previous relationship with an investment banker that would serve as a barrier. Although the capital requirements are low, an underwriter must have some "know-how" or experience in the industry in order to be successful. But given the large number of trained people in the industry, many people have the required know-how to underwrite small issues. We could thus conclude that the barriers to entering the underwriting business at a relatively small scale are low.

As the offering size increases, however, the barriers to entry also become more formidable. Offerings in the $10 million to $50 million range are generally managed by regional broker-dealers with experience in underwriting. Capital is put at risk by the underwriter in these offerings, and a syndicate will probably be formed to distribute the offerings. The underwriter often has some relationship with the issuer based on a previous offering. In order to enter this area of the market, a broker-dealer must have a proven track record as a successful underwriter and also enough capital to take down a significant portion of the offering.

Entry into a syndicate run by a national managing underwriter for a large (e.g., Fortune 500) issuer generally requires some experience as a successful regional underwriter. Also required is enough capital to take a small position in a larger offering. The relationship with the issuer is maintained by the national managing underwriter.

Entry into the ranks of the national managing underwriters is more difficult than entry into any area of the securities industry. A firm must have substantial capital to enable it to take a large position in offerings with total values in the hundreds of millions of dollars. A managing underwriter must have the confidence of the issuer that it can successfully bring to the market the right type of issue (debt, equity, etc.) at the right time and at the right price. The managing underwriter must also be able to put together and lead a syndicate of fifty or more underwriters, run the books of the syndicate, and ensure that the members live up to the terms of the syndication agreement.

The introduction of shelf registration has raised the amount of capital required to enter the managing underwriter business. Rule 415 has resulted in more "bought deals," especially in the bond market. Bought deals require enough capital to take down the entire offering. The nonsyndicated share of the value of U.S. debt underwriting rose from 1 percent and 2 percent in 1980 and 1981, respectively, to 82 percent and 87 percent in 1988 and 1989, respectively (Securities Industry Association, *Trends,* May 31, 1990, p. 21). Nevertheless, even with shelf regulation, relative position within the ranks of the national managing underwriters is vigorously contested and used as a selling point in negotiations with prospective issuers.

Contestability in Investment Banking

The small offerings area (under $10 million) of the market has the characteristics associated with a contestable market—low entry barriers and easy exit. One constraint on entry to this part of the business is the volatility in the number of initial public offerings (IPOs), and many of the small offerings in the United States are IPOs. As Table 12-1 shows, these offerings dropped from 481 in 1972 to 6 in 1975.

Table 12-1. Annual Total of Initial Public
Offerings, 1972–1988

	Number of Issues	Dollar Amount ($ Million)
1972	481	$ 1,973
1973	83	290
1974	12	37
1975	6	33
1976	21	127
1977	33	96
1978	41	176
1979	81	506
1980	153	1,458
1981	355	3,180
1982	124	1,351
1983	686	12,416
1984	353	3,720
1985	357	8,508
1986	725	22,034
1987	548	23,499
1988	290	23,811

Source: 1972–1978: U.S. Securities and Exchange
Commission (1980), p. 23; 1979–1988: Securities
Industry Association, *Securities Industry Yearbook,* var-
ious issues.

In the 1980s, offerings peaked at 725 in 1986 and fell to 290 in 1988. Firms thus
enter and exit this part of the business in response to the level of IPO activity.

As the offering size becomes larger, entry barriers to participation in syndicates
and managing underwritings appear. A firm that aspires to be a national managing
underwriter must have a certain size and stature in the investment community. There
are also strong ties between investment bankers and clients that are often based on
decades of cooperation and are anchored in personal relationships. There are cost
savings associated with ongoing relationships between the corporation issuer clients
and their investment bankers. The underwriter can more easily meet the "due diligence" requirements of the securities laws than a competitor can because of the
former's familiarity with the issuer. There is no learning curve experience necessary
in getting to know the issuer and its management.

National managing underwriting clearly does not have the characteristics of easy
entry and exit associated with contestable markets; that is, a small firm cannot make
a "hit and run" entry into underwriting an offering for a large issuer. On the other
hand, there is vigorous or potential competition for each offering from each issuer,
with a considerable shifting of positions among investment bankers through the
1970s and into the 1980s. The importance of retail distribution capabilities has enabled firms that have had a predominantly retail business to participate in more underwritings as a manager or comanager. Issuers have become more performance oriented in evaluating their investment-banking relationship, and they have broadened
their experience with different underwriters beyond their traditional one, by allowing

other underwriters to comanage deals. (This greater use of comanagers is also attributed to the greater offering sizes.) All this may suggest that the national managing underwriter business is characterized by substantial barriers to entry. However, some firms have successfully surmounted those barriers and provide aggressive competition for established firms.

LACK OF DIVERSIFICATION BY LARGE INVESTMENT BANKERS INTO RETAIL BROKERAGE

Following the introduction of competitive commission rates, some observers predicted a trend toward the acquisition of more retail distribution capability by traditional investment bankers, but this did not happen. The finding of diseconomies of scope for large firms explains why this trend did not emerge, and so the strategy pursued by the traditional investment-banking houses (e.g., Morgan Stanley, Goldman Sachs, Salomon Brothers, First Boston) of remaining aloof from the broad-based retail business has been a sound one to date.

CONCENTRATION TRENDS IN UNDERWRITING

Table 12-2 shows the trends in concentration in the management of publicly offered corporate securities, from 1934 to 1990. The measure of concentration used in this

Table 12-2. Concentration in the Management of Publicly Offered Corporate Securities, 1934–1990

Period	Concentration Ratios			
	One Firm	Three Firms	Five Firms	Ten Firms
1934–1938[a]	25	43	53	69
1947–1949[a]	24	52	60	74
1952[a]	15	40	51	71
1960–1969[a]	11	28	40	61
1975[a]	16	38	54	76
1978[a]	11	31	46	70
1981[a]	13	35	53	74
1983[a]	19	42	57	79
1984[b]	15	35	51	71
1985[b]	13	33	51	71
1986[c]	18	44	70	89
1987[c]	15	41	64	86
1988[c]	15	40	61	87
1989[c]	15	41	61	88
1990[c]	18	41	61	87

[a]Proportionate credit given to comanagers.

[b]Credit given to each underwriter for its commitment in each offering.

[c]Credit given to the lead (book) manager for the issue.

Sources: 1934–1983; Pugel and White (1985); 1984–1990: *Investment Dealers Digest,* various issues.

table is the share of dollar volume of new issues managed or comanaged by the large investment banks.[3]

Auerbach and Hayes (1986) examined concentration data to determine whether shelf registration had made a discernable difference in the degree of concentration in the securities-underwriting sector as a whole. Based on data from Securities Data Company, they found that the top fifteen investment bankers underwrote 93 percent of all public offerings of new securities in 1981, the last full year before shelf registration. During 1982, they underwrote 95 percent; in 1983, 82 percent, an aberrational year in volume; and in 1984, 96 percent under the permanent rule. The results before and after Rule 415, comparing 1979–1982 with 1984, showed little change in market share going to the top four or the top eight houses. In their judgment, the basic competitive structure of the underwriting industry has not been altered by the introduction of shelf registrations, but, there has been some shift in position among the leading investment banks and some gains and losses in client relationships as a consequence.

STABILITY OF LEADING POSITIONS

Scherer (1980) argues that relying on concentration ratios alone to measure the intensity of competition may be misleading. Concentration ratios are a static index, characterizing the market structure for a single typically short time interval. But when the leading sellers in an industry turn over often, high concentration ratios may conceal the intensity of competition, for two reasons. First, the shares of industry leaders, and therefore the concentration ratio, will be lower when computed on, say, a five-year basis than when the shares of leaders are identified for any shorter interval. Second, a rapid turnover suggests dynamic competition, which may be present even when concentration ratios imply the absence of competition in a static, structured sense.

Tables 12-3 and 12-4 show a transition matrix of leading underwriters from 1982 to 1991 for all corporate securities and municipal securities. With 1982 as the base year, both matricies show a substantial turnover in positions from year to year among the leading firms, a finding suggesting that the industry is more dynamically competitive than the concentration numbers alone imply.

PRICES

Pugel and White assembled evidence to determine whether prices approximate long-term marginal costs in investment banking. Based on a review of the research, they pointed to a number of patterns known to hold generally for underwriting fees. The research demonstrates that spreads tend to be smaller for debt than for equity issues, well-known companies than for initial public offerings of relatively unknown companies, large issues (in dollar size) than for small ones, and competitive underwritings than for negotiated underwritings for public utility issues.

Pugel and White observed that these patterns, with the possible exception of the

Table 12-3. Transition Matrix for Corporate Underwriters, 1982–1991

1982	1983	1984	1985	1986	1987	1988	1989	1990	1991
1	2	2	2	2	2	1	1	1	1
2	1	5	5	5	5	4	4	4	4
3	4	1	1	3	4	2	5	5	6
4	5	9	4	1	1	5	2	2	5
5	9	4	9	9	3	6	3	3	8
6	3	3	3	4	9	3	6	8	3
7	6	6	6	6	6	7	19	6	2
8	8	8	8	8	8	15	9	19	19
9	12	15	7	7	19	19	15	15	15
10	10	10	11	19	15	8	8	22	22

Source: Institutional Investor, various issues.

last comparison, appear to be roughly consistent with the cost factors. That is, the specific patterns seem to correlate with the likely cost differences of varying kinds of issues and issuers. They believe, however, that this consistency with the cost patterns does not imply that fees bear the close reflection of cost differentials that would be expected in a competitive industry. They cited a paper by Giddy (1985) indicating that the likelihood of underwriters' experiencing a loss on equity issues is quite small. This evidence raises the question of whether the relative costs of underwriting equity issues are as great as the spread differential indicates (spreads of around 3 percent to 4 percent for equity versus around ⅞ percent for bonds). In addition, the relative stability over time of at least some spreads—a spread of ⅞ percent on high-quality, long-term corporate bonds has apparently persisted for a number of decades—is not likely to be consistent with cost-based pricing. Pugel and White used two studies of public-utility securities flotations showing that issuers' costs are significantly lower when an issuer can attract three or more underwriters to bid for the opportunity to underwrite its issue. Thus spread differentials may be due to differences in competitive vigor rather than to cost differentials.

Pugel and White conducted their own empirical examination of underwriter pric-

Table 12-4. Transition Matrix for Municipal Bond Underwriting, 1982–1991

1982	1983	1984	1985	1986	1987	1988	1989	1990	1991
1	1	1	1	5	1	1	3	1	3
2	2	2	2	3	3	3	1	3	1
3	5	5	7	1	6	9	9	7	9
4	3	6	8	6	5	7	6	9	7
5	4	8	2	9	7	6	7	6	6
6	8	3	5	7	4	4	4	4	17
7	6	9	9	2	9	14	14	17	4
8	9	4	6	4	2	20	17	14	14
9	10	7	4	9	*	17	12	20	20
10	7	14	20	12	*	*	22	*	*

*Below 25 in 1982.

Source: Institutional Investor, various issues.

ing by studying spreads on IPOs. They found that if the underwriter of an IPO was one of the leading national underwriters (e.g., a member of the oligopoly group), the spread would tend to be 10 percent smaller than if the underwriter was a smaller, regional firm. They offered two possible explanations for this finding. The first is that if an IPO issuer can attract the attention of a leading underwriter, the issuer probably can create a more competitive environment for underwriting the issue. This added competition would then cause the price (spread) of the underwriting services to be lower.

The other explanation is that the leading underwriters are selecting particular IPOs that are less risky or have other lower-cost attributes than the remaining IPOs in the sample. Pugel and White were unable to distinguish between these two explanations. But to the extent that the former is valid, the results indicate that at least for the IPOs, more vigorous competition yields lower IPO prices, with the benefits accruing to IPO issuers.

IMPACT OF RULE 415 ON UNDERWRITING

At the hearings conducted by the SEC on Rule 415, many of the participants argued that the rule change would significantly alter the underwriting process. Rogowski and Sorensen (1985) reviewed the arguments.

The *proponents* of the rule contended that it would reduce the regulatory costs of an offering, increase the issuers' flexibility, enable them to sell securities at the right time, and strengthen underwriting competition. The consensus among the issuers was that shelf registration would reduce registration requirements and lower borrowing costs. Rule 415 was expected to reduce underwriter returns, and a shelf registration would be expected to increase the number of underwriters bidding for an issue. Intensified competition would invariably lead to lower profit margins for underwriters.

Also under Rule 415, issuers may find it cost effective to make many small offerings through various underwriters. Before Rule 415, issuers made infrequent trips to the market with large offerings managed by the firm's "traditional" underwriter. Shelf offerings do not require the preparation or distribution of a detailed prospectus; multiple offerings may be made from a single registration statement. Costs would be lower because of the savings in the preparation of additional registration statements as well as the cost of printing and distributing documents. Issuers would not incur the costs of high-priced underwriting professionals spending "a night at the printers."

The *opponents* argued that underwriters may not be able to discharge adequately their traditional due-diligence responsibilities, owing to the uncertainty surrounding the timing of the shelf offering and the speed with which a shelf offering can be made. Also, the intensification of the bidding among underwriters should result in higher spreads in shelf offerings as a premium for protection against potential lawsuits or the tarnishing of an underwriter's reputation arising out of possibly inadequate due diligence. In addition, issuers who insist on shelf registration may offer less to compensate underwriters for bearing any uncertainty arising out of inadequate due diligence. Any impairment of the quality and timeliness of financial disclosure and the ability of underwriters to discharge their due-diligence duties would erode investors' confidence and lessen capital formation.

The Effect of Rule 415 on Returns to Investment Bankers

Using a sample of 400 industrial bonds issued between January 1981 and October 1983, Rogowski and Sorensen analyzed underwriter spreads before and after shelf registration. They found that returns to investment banking on a risk-adjusted basis may have declined because of Rule 415. Direct or implied competition may have induced investment bankers to price new issues more aggressively, or it may have intensified the search for those investors willing to pay the highest price for the issue. Consequently, their evidence somewhat corroborates the prediction that returns to investment banking would decline because of Rule 415. Rogowski and Sorensen, however, found the due-diligence issue difficult to assess, as measurement problems made any inferences suspect.

The Effect of Shelf Registration on Regional Broker-Dealers

Some observers suggested that shelf registration would have adverse consequences for regional broker-dealers. The NASD argued that the shortened time for transactions with shelf registrations would make it difficult for a managing underwriter to use a syndicate to achieve an orderly distribution of securities. Although shelf registration would not stop the use of traditional syndicates, the NASD contended that the constraints caused by shelf registration were such that it would often be impractical to use such a syndicate.

Others argued that changes (declines) in regional broker-dealers' revenues from underwriting could have widespread consequences. Shelf registration could lead to a reduction in the support of small and developing companies that rely on regional broker-dealers for underwriting and might force regionals to sell out to larger firms, thus intensifying industry concentration. The resulting smaller syndicates might also increase the risk of underwriting, since the risk would be borne by a few large firms rather than being shared by many firms.

Poulsen and Marr (1987) examined this issue empirically, considering whether a sample of 124 broker-dealers were receiving less, the same, or more underwriting revenues than they had before shelf registration, after adjusting through regression analysis for certain market factors such as overall business financing. They based their analysis on FOCUS data for these firms from the first quarter of 1977 through the fourth quarter of 1985. They found that on average, the largest broker-dealers experienced significant increases in their underwriting revenues relative to total business financing following the adoption of shelf registration, whereas smaller firms experienced no significant changes. At the same time, total underwriting revenues were increasing as a fraction of total business financing. This evidence suggests that in addition to shelf registration, other factors, such as the greater use of noninvestment-grade debt and municipal securities and increased merger and acquisition activity in the 1980s, may have influenced the investment-banking side of the business.

Poulsen and Marr concluded that their evidence does not point to the demise of regional broker-dealers, and they found no statistically significant change in regional broker-dealers' underwriting revenues. In addition, they reported press accounts suggesting that regional firms are finding new products to sell to their customers, such as certificates of deposit and mortgage-backed securities. Regional firms are also marketing their strong retail bases to major underwriters in order to be included in more syndicates. Poulsen and Marr (1987, p. 27) conclude that those who argue that regional broker-dealers would be seriously hurt by shelf registration underestimated the competitive strength of these firms.

KEY INVESTMENT-BANKING LINES IN THE 1980s

Mergers and Acquisitions

Mergers and acquisitions (M&A) became an enormously profitable business for investment bankers in the 1980s. Mergers and acquisitions activity rose from an annual figure of $50 billion to $80 billion in the early 1980s to peak at $265 billion in 1988, as shown in Table 12-5. Much of this growth was fueled by leveraged buyouts (LBOs) and foreign investment in U.S. firms. In late 1989, however, the domestic M&A market weakened, reflecting a souring junk bond market. (By 1984, junk bonds had become an important source of financing for M&A activity.)

The first separate mergers and acquisitions unit in a broker-dealer was started by Morgan Stanley in 1972. Mergers and acquisitions groups within a firm are generally small, not exceeding 200 to 300 people. Traditional M&A services included giving advice on proposed mergers or tender offers, structuring and managing the deals, and providing takeover defense strategies. Investment bankers traditionally have provided expertise but no capital. More recently, however, investment bankers have been lending their own money as "bridge loans" in order to make some deals work.

Mergers and acquisitions professionals engage in intense, sometimes short-term work to bring off a deal. For example, a team of fifteen First Boston M&A staffers put in 100-hour weeks for four weeks to consummate a deal and were rewarded with

Table 12-5. Mergers and Acquisitions, 1981–1991 ($ Billion)

	Leverage Buyouts	Foreign Buyers	All Others	Total
1981	$ 3	—	$ 80	$ 83
1982	4	—	50	54
1983	5	—	69	74
1984	19	$ 8	96	123
1985	20	18	142	180
1986	45	25	105	175
1987	36	42	91	169
1988	47	60	158	265
1989	61	52	117	230
1990	18	46	103	167
1991	4	23	72	99

Source: Securities Industry Association, *Fact Book* (1992), p. 18.

$8 million in fees (*Fortune,* January 20, 1986, pp. 22–23). In order to prepare for these short bursts of intense activity, M&A groups construct extensive data bases that analyze potential takeover or merger candidates, and they also have developed various strategies to be used in different types of merger and takeover battles.

The mergers and acquisitions business is highly concentrated. Statistics cited by *Fortune* show that for the more than 400 U.S. deals valued at $100 million or more in 1985, corporations hired one of the top three investment-banking firms in 35 percent of the deals and one of the top seven firms in 57 percent of them. Commercial banks, on the other hand, have not made substantial inroads in the mergers and acquisitions business. For years, banks have offered merger assistance, sometimes at cut rates, but have rarely challenged the broker-dealers in this area (*Fortune,* January 20, 1986, pp. 18–23).

Mergers and acquisitions fees generate enormous revenues for each M&A employee. *Fortune* reported M&A fees collected by securities firms for the fifty largest deals in 1988: Goldman Sachs led all firms with $172.6 million in fees for managing or comanaging fourteen of the fifty deals for which *Fortune* reported fees. With billions of dollars at stake in the deals, principals in the merger market are willing to pay high fees for the unique know-how of experienced investment bankers. As a percentage of the deal, the fees are relatively small. For example, Goldman's fees, on average, represent only 0.28 percent of the deals.

The enormous power of mergers and acquisition professionals has resulted in friction between M&A specialists and other firm members. For instance, in 1987 the M&A department at First Boston brought in $350 million in fees with a department that consisted of only 170 of the firm's 5,500 employees. On the other hand, First Boston's net income for the entire firm in 1987 was $108.9 million, reflecting the October collapse of the stock market (*Business Week,* February 15, 1988, p. 90). This disparate performance led to tension at First Boston, especially between the "star" M&A professionals and the rest of the firm's management. The result was a split as the top M&A professionals left the firm. Bruce Wasserstein and Joseph R. Perella, the leaders of the M&A group at First Boston, resigned in early 1988 to start their own merchant-banking firm—Wasserstein Perella Group, Inc.

Mortgage-backed Securities

Until 1980, it was common for mortgage lenders to keep in their own portfolios the mortgages they originated. Now, however, mortgages are being "securitized"— assembled into pools and transformed into bondlike tradable securities. Securitization allows banks and thrifts that originate mortgages to achieve the desired changes in their balance sheets. Thrifts especially suffered during the 1980s when they were holding low-yield mortgages while being forced by market conditions to pay higher and higher interest rates to depositors. Selling off the mortgages, however, allows the thrifts and banks to free up capital for new investments (*Wall Street Journal,* August 17, 1988, p. 1).

Large insurance companies and pension funds are large purchasers of mortgage securities, as many mortgage securities carry triple-A credit ratings and yield a full percentage point more interest than comparable bonds do. They now account for 25 percent of some institutions' portfolios. The most important breakthrough in the securitization of mortgages came in 1983 with the collateralized mortgage obligation (CMO). By allowing investors to choose whether they want a piece of the early, middle, or late maturities in a single pool of mortgages, the CMO solves the most difficult problem associated with mortgage securities: their uncertain life span and their unpredictable mix of principal and interest payments every month. The breakthrough came when the investment bankers began looking at mortgages as a process—a stream of surprises when people pay off their mortgages ahead of schedule—rather than as a single entity with a fixed thirty-year life. Cash flows could be managed so that all investors would get their share of interest payments but principal payments would go to investors holding the shortest-maturity bonds (*Business Week*, June 11, 1984, p. 140).[4]

Mortgage-backed securities became an immediate success; the volume of collateralized mortgage obligations, mortgage-backed bonds, and mortgage passthroughs increased from $74 billion in 1984 to $317 billion in 1986. Lewis S. Ranieri, who was head of the mortgage products group at Salomon Brothers, is credited by *Business Week* with creating the CMO, whereas *Institutional Investor* gives that honor to First Boston. Ranieri's 135-person group was credited with bringing in 40 percent of Salomon Brothers' $500 million profit in 1983, more than for any other department in Salomon's history.[5] Because of the high profits produced in mortgage securities, competitors attempted to enter this business by hiring away experienced mortgaged-backed securities professionals from firms already in the business. It was reported that top professionals were courted with a guaranteed annual compensation of $1 million or more, plus sizable partnership interests.

Junk, or High-Yield, Bonds

Junk bonds—or, as their proponents prefer, high-yield, low-rate debt—became an important new market in the 1980s. The credit for creating this market goes to Michael Milken of Drexel Burnham Lambert (Lehman Brothers is credited with issuing the first high-yield, high-risk bond.) Drexel Burnham Lambert was formed in 1973, the product of a merger of Burnham and Co. of New York and an old-line Philadelphia firm, Drexel, Firestone, Inc. A medium-size firm with successful securities and commodities operations, Drexel Burnham Lambert was never an investment-banking powerhouse until it discovered the potential of junk bonds (*Wall Street Journal*, December 13, 1985, pp. 1–13).

A junk bond is usually defined as any bond that is rated below investment grade by the bond-rating agencies (Standard & Poor's and Moody's) and that carries an above-average yield because of a below–investment grade rating.[6] Forerunners of junk bonds were the bonds of investment-grade companies that ran into trouble and found their bond rating falling from investment grade to below investment grade. Typically, the price of these "fallen angel" bonds would drop significantly with the downgrading. Milken, working in the bond department at Drexel, analyzed the performance of these bonds and found that the rate of default, even among the lowest-rated issuers, was very small. So investors could buy these bonds at large discounts to face value and profit if the company's condition improved.

Traditionally, only the most creditworthy (e.g., Fortune 500) corporations had access to the corporate bond market. Beginning in about 1977, Milken and Drexel realized that some not-so-prestigious companies wanted to issue bonds but could not qualify for investment-grade ratings. Drexel also had client institutions that wanted high-yield corporate debt, and accordingly, the firm soon was placing securities that were junk bonds from the outset.

Milken argued that a significant number of companies that were not rated investment grade would be able to meet their debt payments if they had sufficient cash flow (*Wall Street Journal,* December 13, 1987, p. 13; *Business Week,* July 7, 1986, p. 60). He managed to convince a number of institutional investors, including some mainstream institutions—such as Massachusetts Mutual Life Insurance, Kemper, and Prudential Insurance—that the additional return was worth the additional risk of these "junk" bonds. Milken assured his investors that he would always be there with a bid when they wanted to sell, and Drexel carried inventories of junk bonds that at times reached $2 billion. John H. Gutfreund, chief executive officer of Saloman Brothers, noted that Drexel had created an investment banking syndicate that existed completely outside the traditional investment banking industry (*Business Week,* July 7, 1986, p. 57).

In late 1983, Drexel devised a strategy to use the firm's growing financing capacity to further penetrate the mergers and acquisitions business, then dominated by Morgan Stanley, Goldman Sachs, and First Boston. The answer was the marriage of junk bond financing and hostile takeover bids, which enabled Drexel to become a force in mergers and acquisitions (*Wall Street Journal,* December 13, 1985, p. 13).

By 1985, Drexel's junk bond sales and trading group consisted of 150 persons and was reported to have generated 25 percent of the firm's total revenues of $2.5 billion and an even higher percentage of its earnings. Building on the strength of its junk bond–trading operation, the firm had started to diversified into and improved its position in various other lines of business. Starting from scratch, it built a mortgage-backed securities–trading operation of 280 people in two years, and by 1986 the group ranked in the industry's top five. The firm also climbed from fifteenth to eighth in U.S. government securities trading and from thirtieth to tenth in municipal bond underwriting.

Proponents of the junk bond market believe that this type of financing allowed firms to borrow more money, often at a lower cost and with fewer restrictions, than they could by borrowing from a bank or an insurance company. It is said that Drexel did to the small corporate loan what Salomon Brothers did to the mortgage—turn it into a publicly traded security. Drexel also had an enormous impact on the banking industry by taking a large chunk out of the loan market, which added to pressure on the banks to lend to credits of lower and lower quality.

STRATEGIC MAPPING IN INVESTMENT BANKING

Eccles and Crane (1988) identified the dimensions of strategy along which the top twenty investment bankers compete, using the mapping approach developed by Porter (1980) to discover the strategic groups to which the firms belong. A strategic group is a group of firms in an industry that follow the same or similar strategies.

Firms within the same strategic group are especially competitive with one another because they generally seek the same customer base and use the same strategies. Each group, however, attempts to create mobility barriers between it and the other groups that would make it difficult for firms outside the group to compete successfully against its members.

Strategy can be defined along four dimensions. The first relates to customers served. Some investment banks target large, relatively sophisticated companies that go frequently to the capital market. Others target medium-size companies that are less active, and still others focus on small, emerging companies.

The second strategy dimension concerns the firm's lines of business and the emphasis it places on each. Investment-banking firms include all types of product mixes. Such firms may choose to be full-line firms or to maintain an investment-banking focus, to be a niche player, to provide a mix of broker and dealer services, or to provide only brokerage, market-making, or other unitary services. Eccles and Crane, writing in 1987, suggested that some firms had developed enough strength in one or a few products to appear to have a more focused strategy but were actively attempting to diversify, such as Drexel Burnham Lambert, the dominant firm in junk bonds at the time.

Distribution capacity is the third dimension of strategy, indicated by the size of each firm's retail distribution network. Merrill Lynch and Shearson Lehman used their retail distribution networks to achieve the status of ''special bracket firms'' in underwriting,[7] and Paine Webber and Smith Barney also used their retail brokerage network as a competitive weapon to expand their underwriting business.

The fourth dimension concerns the amount of capital that firms committed to capital-intensive businesses including principal positions, bridge loans, equity investments, swaps, and trading. Until the 1980s, capital was at risk in the underwriting of securities, but this risk was tightly controlled and shared with other firms in the syndicate. Investment banking then became riskier with more ''bought'' offerings and the use of capital to gain an advantage in M&A deals by engaging in the merchant-banking activities of bridge loans and equity investments.

Eccles and Crane also discovered barriers to mobility into different groups. Some are natural groupings, such as the special-bracket firms and other categories used in tombstone advertisements, with mobility barriers that make it difficult to move up in the standings. They also point out that large corporate issuers tend to use investment banks that have large corporate finance staffs. There also are barriers along the product diversification dimension: Product expertise must be developed or acquired, and many firms attempting to diversify their products do so by building up secondary trading capabilities in the new product in order to learn about the market.

Strategic Groups

Eccles and Crane limited their strategic mapping to two dimensions, product diversification and the number of deals done. The diversification measure used for each firm was based on its market share, according to the number of deals it did between 1984 and 1986 in each of twelve product categories (e.g., common stock, tax-exempt bonds, investment-grade bonds, initial public offerings). They identified four strategic groups.[8]

Group I is defined mainly by the number of deals done and is made up of First Boston, Goldman Sachs, Merrill Lynch, and Salomon Brothers. These firms were primary bankers for very active users of investment-banking services. All were among the most diversified, and each accounted for a major share of the volume of securities underwritten.

Group II consists of Shearson Lehman and Morgan Stanley. These two firms were even more diversified than those in the first group, reflecting strength in all product areas, even their weakest ones. Although customers of both firms had about the same level of investment-banking activity, there was a significant difference in their customer bases. Morgan Stanley had a much better penetration of large customers, and Shearson's customers were smaller on average because they included more middle-market customers.

Group III firms (Bear, Stearns; Dean Witter; Drexel Burnham Lambert; E. F. Hutton; Kidder Peabody; Paine Webber; Prudential-Bache; and Smith Barney) were less diversified firms that largely served middle-market companies. In 1987, most of the firms in this group were attempting to move into Group I or Group II. They were conducting aggressive calling efforts to obtain business with large issuers, and they were also attempting to improve their market shares, particularly in their weaker product areas that would increase their diversification.

Group IV firms (Alex. Brown; Dillon, Read; Donaldson, Lufkin & Jenrette; L. F. Rothschild; and Lazard Frères) are what are known as *niche firms,* those with a low degree of diversification. Lazard and Dillon, strong in M&A, serve both very large and middle-market customers. Alex. Brown, Donaldson, Lufkin & Jenrette, and L. F. Rothschild concentrate more on middle-market companies and were especially strong in initial public offerings and other common stock offerings.

The strategy of these firms emphasizes high-margin, value-added products while ignoring the low-margin commodity ones. Implicit in these strategies was the belief that the value-added services could be sold to customers without also having to meet their needs in commodity products. Individuals in these firms spoke to Eccles and Crane about needing to have the courage to say no to particular types of deals and to take the risk of another firm using a low-margin deal as a prelude to a broader relationship.

STRATEGY VERSUS CONTESTABILITY IN INVESTMENT BANKING

The Eccles and Crane (1988) model of strategic groups appears to be more applicable to investment banking than does the contestability model of Baumol, Panzar, and Willig (1982). Although entry into low-level participation in many investment-banking lines is possible for many small and mid-size firms, entry into the business of managing underwriter for a major client is quite difficult. Movement from one strategic group to another is also blocked by mobility barriers. Eccles and Crane believe that a firm's reputation provides this mobility barrier. Reputation can limit the ability of firms in Groups III and IV to hire the experienced personnel they need to diversify and get business with large customers. This reinforces any misgivings that customers might have about moving from a Group I firm to a Group IV firm out of concern for the Group IV firm's investment-banking or distribution capabilities.

The dimensions along which firms seek to differentiate by establishing a particular reputation are often general and difficult to measure, such as "quality people," "commitment to relationships," and "teamwork and communication." Whether based on real or imagined qualities, these groups have staying power, as some have tried for years to move into a higher-level group and have met with only limited success.

Despite limited mobility, there is fierce competition for the leadership position in each line of business. Leadership positions also vary from year to year. So even though this part of the industry cannot be classified as contestable, I have not seen any evidence that it is characterized by collusion. The barriers to entry to various groups do, however, allow some firms to earn above-normal profits in some lines over some periods of time.

CONCLUSION

Investment banking has always been a highly profitable but risky business for securities firms. Before Rule 415 was enacted, underwriting was very profitable, especially for the leading firms. Some of the profits were the result of entry barriers into the ranks of the top underwriters. But with Rule 415, the profitability of underwriting traditional corporate issues has declined, although new, highly profitable lines of business were introduced in the 1980s. Now, in the mid-1990s, the high-profit lines of the 1980s are not quite as profitable, although, there are always opportunities for securities firms, because of the ever-changing market conditions. For example, the opening of Eastern Europe may provide an area in which the ability of Wall Street firms to develop new products might be put to good use. As the Eastern European countries introduce more market-oriented approaches to economic management, there may be a need for unique securities instruments that would be compatible with the types of ownership that will emerge in these countries.

NOTES

1. An underwriting syndicate lost $130 million in a British Petroleum issue that fell apart following the stock market crash of October 1987 (see Chapter 5).

2. As discussed in Chapter 7, Baron (1982) contends that investment bankers are used by issuers because the bankers are better informed about capital markets and can distribute the issue better than the issuer can.

3. Hayes, Spence, and Marks (1983) tested statistically for the significant trends in concentration between 1972 and 1977 and found significant increasing concentration for debt underwriting but not for equity underwriting.

4. For a description of the construction of a specific mortgage pool and the bond payment structure, see *Wall Street Journal*, August 17, 1988, p. 12.

5. Another Salomon employee, Robert Dall, is credited with developing in 1977 the first mortgage-backed security with the first private sector pass-through for the Bank of America. First Boston's Dexter Senft is credited with an important conceptual breakthrough in 1977, a way of measuring real

returns on mortgage securities, which he called the *honest-to-God yield* (*Business Week,* June 11, 1984, p. 140; *Institutional Investor,* March 1984, p. 90).

6. Investment-grade bonds are considered those rated BBB-/Baa3 or higher (Altman and Nammacher 1987, p. 26).

7. Hayes, Spence, and Marks (1983, p. 26) refer to Morgan Stanley, First Boston, Merrill Lynch, Salomon Brothers, Goldman Sachs, and Shearson Lehman as "special bracket" or apex firms. A firm's relative position in the investment-banking business is determined largely by its access to lucrative future business as well as to substantial current income. Standing was indicated not only by the frequency with which firms managed or comanaged a major syndicate but also by the frequency of its participation in syndicates managed by others, and the status and prestige following from them. A firm's standing among investment bankers was expressed in "tombstone" ads that appeared in the financial press. The ads divided syndicate members into several categories or "brackets."

8. For the mapping, see Eccles and Crane (1988), fig. 5.2, p. 104.

13

Competition Through Innovation

The previous chapters in this book show that concentration has increased in the securities industry over the last twenty years. Mergers can explain some, but not all, of this increase. Economies of scale do not provide an answer. What, then, is the cause? This chapter suggests that competition through innovation is at least partially responsible.

We will develop a general model of innovation rivalry in this chapter in which firms assume one of three roles: (1) innovation leader, (2) fast second, or (3) slow follower. Some firms prefer (or must accept) being fast seconds; that is, they rapidly follow an innovation with an imitative product or service. Others are slow to follow any innovation and therefore tend to lose market share to the innovators and fast seconds. If the same firms continue to act as slow followers and if there are a number of innovations in an industry, the industry will become more concentrated.

The strategic choice that a firm makes as to whether to be an innovator, a fast second, or a slow follower depends on the profit potential for the firm associated with each of these roles. In our model, luck plays a very small role in innovation. Firms choose to be innovators because of their market position, their ability to develop new products, their costs of replacing old products, and their perception of how quickly they can penetrate the competition's customer base. Empirical research supports the implications of this model for broker-dealers.

THE LINKS BETWEEN MARKET STRUCTURE AND INNOVATION

The Schumpeterian view is that monopoly power is conducive to innovation, since larger firms with monopoly power have more incentive to innovate. Firms that have monopoly power can support research and development (R&D) efforts to use the new products to defend their market position. The empirical evidence as to whether or not innovation increases concentration, however, is mixed.

Some studies show that innovation does increase concentration. Mansfield (1968) examined empirically whether successful innovators grow faster than their competitors do. He found that they do grow faster than their competitors but that their advantage usually disappears over time. Phillips (1971) proposed that in an industry in which there are few opportunities for major technological advance and there are significant and long-run advantages to a firm that innovates first, a high degree of concentration is likely. Nelson and Winter (1978, 1982) used simulation to show that the development of concentration in their hypothetical model industry was significantly affected by the rate of growth of potential or latent productivity, the effectiveness of technological imitation efforts, and the extent to which firms restrain investment in response to perceived market power.

Other studies suggest that concentration is reduced through innovation competition. Geroski (1989) found a strong tendency for concentration to fall during the 1970s with more vigorous innovative activity, based on data for British firms. Mukhopadhyay (1985) demonstrated that U.S. industries with innovation competition had falling concentration levels. Lunn (1986) saw that U.S. market concentration tended to fall when innovation competition was primarily through the development of new products.

Based on their review of the research, Scherer and Ross (1990, p. 651) observed that existing evidence favored the conclusion that innovation under late-twentieth-century conditions has tended to be more concentration reducing than the opposite. The model we develop in this chapter suggests that effects of innovation on concentration vary considerably depending on the basic parameters of the industry that affect the innovation decision. Innovation may increase concentration in one industry and decrease it in another.

MODEL DEVELOPMENT

The objective of a study by Scherer (1967) was to predict the market structure condition most conducive to rapid technological progress. He focused on a duopoly characterized by intense innovation rivalry. This chapter extends Scherer's work by considering the situation in which the innovation replaces an existing product and models two effects: (1) the penetration of the potential market for the new product by the innovator, the fast second, and the slow follower; and (2) the shift to the left of the demand for the existing product. By explicitly examining the reduction of the existing market, we can show that the hesitancy by the slow followers in introducing the new product can alter industry concentration in favor of the innovators and fast seconds.

The essential component of any innovation model must be a potential for profits, caused by entry barriers, imitation lags, or other imperfections. We start by allowing the cash flows that can be attained from the sale of a new product to be estimated at V per year. Future returns are discounted to present value at the opportunity cost of capital r. In addition, the profit-making potential of a new product is likely to decline over time owing to exogenous technological obsolescence at a rate of 100 $\times$ g percent per year. The discounted cash-flow potential for year t will therefore be $V(t)e^{-pt}$, with $p = r + g$.

Innovator's Gains

An innovator will not realize all of this cash-flow potential, for two main reasons. First, new markets must be cultivated and won. It takes time to overcome consumers' resistance to change and develop the market's full potential. Second, imitation by fast seconds and slow followers will deprive the innovator of some cash flows. It is assumed that the innovation will gradually penetrate the innovator's own share of the market for the existing product that is replaced by the innovation and also capture some of the remaining market that is in the hands of the innovator's competitors. The gradual penetration of the innovator's *own market share* can be represented by the innovator's discounted total cash-flow realization in the absence of imitation:

$$V_{I0} = \int_0^\infty S_I \, (1 - e^{-a_0 t}) \, V(t) e^{-pt} \tag{13-1}$$

where $V(t) = (P(t)\text{-}D\text{-}C\text{-}E\text{-}r_0\text{-}r_I S_I)$

$a_0 =$ penetration coefficient
$P(t) =$ product price
$D =$ research and development costs
$E =$ market education costs
$C =$ all other costs
$r_0 =$ fixed component of replacement costs
$r_I =$ variable component of replacement costs related to market share
$S =$ market share

(The subscript I identifies the variables of the innovator; F identifies the variables of the fast-second firm or firms; and S identifies the variables associated with the slow follower.)

An innovator will not introduce a new product unless the discounted cash-flow potentital from that product exceeds the costs of developing and marketing it. These costs include research and development costs *(D)*, which encompass regulatory approval costs if necessary. Another important cost is the cost of replacing the existing product line when applicable. This cost includes the expense of retaining personnel and scrapping the plant and equipment dedicated to the old product. Replacement costs have two components: (1) r_0 represents the fixed costs of replacement, and (2) $r_I S_I$ represents the replacement costs that are a function of the firm's market share. A large firm would be forced to scrap a larger plant than a smaller firm would.

A third element of expense incurred by an innovator is the expense of educating customers about the characteristics and uses of the product *(E)*. In financial services, this is an important element of cost. Other remaining elements of cost are denoted as *C*.

The Decision to Innovate

The decision to innovate is related to the trade-off between the cost of innovation and the quasi-rents that can be earned by innovating.[1] The innovator calculates the return to innovating given the likelihood of fast seconds and slow followers. The innovator is motivated by the opportunity to draw customers away from the slow followers. Firms are innovators because they have an advantage in one or more parameters of the model. For example, an innovator may have a more efficient R&D staff, or a firm might be more efficient at educating customers. The firm's culture may encourage innovative ideas, or the firm may have a marketing ability that enables it to move rapidly and penetrate the market share of slow followers. The innovator's replacement costs may be lower than that of its competitors.

The innovator may have a market-share advantage. That is, the firm may be large enough to handle the demands of new customers without expanding the organization. With a larger customer base, the R&D costs can be spread over a larger number of customers. Or a firm may have an advantage in jointly producing the innovation with another product. Any one or a combination of these elements might give a firm an advantage in innovation competition. Innovation is thus strongly influenced by the firm's structural characteristics. But the structure condusive to innovation must be accompanied by a strategic commitment to innovate. That is, some firms may have the structural characteristics necessary to be a consistent innovator yet not act like an innovator. Both the structural characteristics and a strategic commitment to innovate are found in those firms that are consistent innovators.

Strategic Elements in Decision Making by Innovators, Fast Seconds, and Slow Followers

Structural characteristics of the market play an important role in determining which firm innovates. Once an innovator is introduced, however, strategic considerations are important to the innovator, fast seconds, and slow followers. As a strategic matter, firms that are fast seconds will quickly follow innovations by introducing an imitative product. Firms that are fast seconds probably also possess some advantages relative to the slow followers in the innovative game.

Slow followers may be at a disadvantage to the innovator and fast seconds because of their firms' configurations. However, there are strategic reasons for firms to choose to be slow followers: They may be uncertain of the success of an innovation. With the multitude of new products and services introduced by broker-dealers over the past twenty years,[2] it is reasonable to delay imitation until there is some certainty that the product will have a market. Or firms that are slow followers may not have a full-time product development staff. Also, the cost of product development may exceed the potential quasi rents for the product. Finally, if the slow follower is slow to imitate, the firm can piggyback on the expense of educating the market about the new product that would be borne by innovators.

At some time after the innovation, however, the slow followers will decide that the costs of imitating have fallen enough and/or the loss of their customers to the innovators and fast seconds is sufficient that they should imitate.

Operation of the Model

The innovation is introduced at $t = 0$, and a_0 is a "penetration coefficient" indicating the proportion of the unexploited cash-flow potential captured each year. The value of a_0 depends on the receptiveness of customers to new products and on the degree of qualitative superiority that the new product has over existing substitutes, the amount of sales promotion effort put forth, and the like.

In our model we assume that the innovator will gradually penetrate the share of the market in the hands of its competitors until the competitors follow the leader by imitating the product. The imitation will occur at T_F for the fast second(s) (one or more firms may act as fast seconds) and at T_S for the slow followers After the fast seconds imitate, their market share S_F, will be out of the reach of the innovator, and after the slow followers imitate, the share of the market left in the hands of the slow followers will be out of the reach of the innovator and the fast seconds.

Additional assumptions must be made regarding the reactions of the customers of the fast-seconds and slow-follower firms to the product innovation. These assumptions relate to switching costs in this product market. These costs may be small, as in the case of switching from one money market product to another, or they might entail sizable transaction and capital losses, as in the switch from one long-term capital asset to another. In our study the switching costs are assumed to be moderate. We also assume that the customers of fast-second firms know that their firm will follow any innovation rapidly, and so they will not switch to the innovative firm. The customers of the slow followers, on the other hand, know that their firms will not have the innovation available soon, and so some will switch to a firm that does.

We also assume that neither the innovators nor the fast seconds lose their customers to competitors for the new product because of switching costs. However, the share of the slow followers' market is up for grabs until they follow the innovation with a product of their own. After they introduce their version of the innovation, the slow followers retain their share of the market, and their customers will cease switching.

Assume that the innovator initially penetrates the potential share of the product market in the hands of the slow follower (S_S) at the rate a_1. Like a_0, a_1 depends on the receptiveness of customers to new products, and so forth. The penetration continues at this rate until the fast second(s) imitate at T_F. Then the innovator's penetration of S_S falls off to a_2 until the slow followers imitate. After the slow followers imitate at T_S, penetration of their market share by both the innovator and fast seconds ceases.

For the innovator, the discounted streams of quasi rent captured from the slow followers is equal to the portion captured between the time of innovation (0) and the time that the fast seconds introduce their innovation (T_F).

$$V_{I1} = \int_0^{T_F} S_s \left[1.0 - e^{-a_1 t} \right] V e^{-\rho t} dt \qquad (13\text{-}2)$$

Let us define the share of the slow followers' market captured by the innovator before the imitation by the fast seconds as

$$S_{I0} = \int_0^{T_F} S_s \left[1.0 - e^{-a_1 t} \right] \qquad (13\text{-}3)$$

The quasi-rent stream captured after the fast seconds imitate but before the slow followers imitate is

$$V_{I2} = \int_{T_F}^{T_S} [S_s - S_{I0}] [1.0 - e^{-a_2 (t - T_F)}] V e^{-pt} dt \qquad (13\text{-}4)$$

We also define the share of the slow followers' market captured by the innovator between the time that the fast second(s) imitate and the slow followers imitate as

$$S_{I1} = \int_{T_F}^{T_S} [S_s - S_{I0}] [1.0 - e^{-a_2 (t - T_F)}] \qquad (13\text{-}5)$$

Following Baldwin and Childs (1969), if a new product is a substitute for an established product, the demand curve for the latter will be shifted to the left. The following is the present value of the quasi-rent loss to the innovator caused by the leftward shift over time of the demand for the innovator's established product:

$$C_I = \int_0^\infty S_I [1.0 - e^{-h_0 t}] G e^{-pt} dt \qquad (13\text{-}6)$$

where

G = total quasi-rent per period earned by all competitors in the established markets

S_I = innovator's share of established markets

h_0 = instantaneous rate at which quasi-rents per period for innovator's established products are reduced ($h_0 = a_0$)

It is assumed that over time the new product completely replaces the existing product. Combining all the elements of the revenue stream for the innovator gives us the following:

$$V_I = V_{I0} + V_{I1} + V_{I2} - C_I \qquad (13\text{-}7)$$

Where V_I is the present value of the quasi-rents that the innovator earns over the life of the product.

Fast-Seconds' Quasi-Rents
The fast seconds' quasi-rents from their own customers are

$$V_{F0} = \int_{T_F}^\infty S_F [1.0 - e^{-b_0(t - T_F)}] V e^{-pt} dt \qquad (13\text{-}8)$$

and their share of quasi-rents captured from the slow followers are equal to

$$V_{F1} = \int_{T_F}^{T_S} [S_s - S_{I0}] [1.0 - e^{-b_1(t - T_F)}] Ve^{-p't}dt \tag{13-9}$$

with b_1 as the rate at which the fast seconds penetrate the slow followers' market share.

The loss to the fast seconds caused by the leftward shift over time of their demand for their displaced product is

$$C_F = \int_{T_F}^{\infty} S_F (1.0 - e^{-m_0(t - T_F)}) Ge^{-p't}dt \tag{13-10}$$

Therefore, the complete function for the fast seconds is

$$V_F = V_{F0} + V_{F1} - C_F \tag{13-11}$$

We also define the share of the slow followers' market share captured by the fast seconds as

$$S_{F0} = \int_{T_F}^{T_S} (S_s - S_{I0}) [1.0 - e^{-a_2(t - T_F)}] \tag{13-12}$$

Slow Followers' Qusai-Rents
Following the same logic, the complete function for the slow follower is

$$V_S = V_{SI} - C_{S0} - C_{S1} - C_{S2} \tag{13-13}$$

Where C_{S0}, C_{S1}, and C_{S2} represent the reduction in benefits from the old product that the slow followers experience after the innovation, the fast seconds' imitation, and their own imitation, respectively. The expression for each value is

$$V_{SI} = \int_{T_S}^{\infty} [S_s - S_{I0} - S_{I1} - S_{F0}] [1.0 - e^{-d_0(t - T_S)}] Ve^{-p't}dt \tag{13-14}$$

$$C_{S0} = \int_{0}^{T_F} S_s [1.0 - e^{-n_0 t}] Ge^{-p't}dt \tag{13-15}$$

$$C_{S1} = \int_{T_F}^{T_S} [S_s - S_{I0}] [1.0 - e^{-n_1 (t - T_F)}] Ve^{-p't}dt \tag{13-16}$$

$$C_{S2} = \int_{T_S}^{\infty} [S_s - S_{I0} - S_{I1}] [1.0 - e^{-n_2 (t - T_S)}] Ve^{-p't}dt \tag{13-17}$$

The following constraints apply to this model:

$$n_0 = a_1$$
$$n_1 = a_2 + b_1$$
$$n_2 = d_0$$

The constraints reflect the fact that the rate of capture of the slow followers' market share is equal to the rate at which the market share of the old market disappears.

Our model shows that in an industry in which much of the innovating is carried out not by one firm but by a group of firms, and if firms in this group are fast seconds to one another's innovations, this group's share of industry revenues will increase over time at the expense of the slow followers. So, the more that the largest firm in the industry innovates, the more rapid the industry's increase in concentration will be as the slow followers lose their overall market share to innovation competition. This model shows that concentration can develop without relying on economies of scale, advertising, or stochastic process. Also, the more quickly these new technological opportunities and new products based on these technologies appear over time, the more rapidly the industry will become concentrated.

MARKET STRUCTURE CONSIDERATIONS
IN THE SECURITIES INDUSTRY

Individuals do not usually switch brokers very often, and there are some moderate switching costs (mainly inconvenience) associated with a change. For institutions, the switching costs are virtually nil. Therefore, an innovator can penetrate its competitor's customer base with a new product, but much more slowly for the individual side of the market.

In this industry, scrapping costs are generally insignificant, as securities firms often have to change only their computer software. Also in this industry, firms have not attempted to patent all their new products (although this may be changing). Nor are the products difficult to copy. Imitators spend 50 percent to 75 percent less to imitate than innovators do. Without patent protection, mid-size firms would be unlikely to make large investments in product development. Larger firms could easily act as fast seconds and imitate their product, effectively preventing mid-size firms from capturing any quasi-rents.

These structural characteristics suggest that there would be incentives for the largest firms in this industry to act as innovators and fast seconds. They can pay the research and development costs and penetrate the market share of the slow followers. Mid-size and smaller firms might find research and development costs burdensome and would find that larger firms would likely be fast seconds to their innovations. A strategy of increasing market share by innovating would thus seem appropriate to the industry's largest firms.

EMPIRICAL RESEARCH ON INNOVATION
IN THE SECURITIES INDUSTRY

Tufano (1989) examined innovation rivalry in investment banking, with data consisting of fifty-eight financial innovations in corporate and mortgage-backed securities that produced publicly underwritten offerings in the United States from 1974 to 1986. These fifty-eight instruments raised over $278 billion in capital between 1974 and 1987, or 10.7 percent of the dollar volume of all U.S. public offerings in that period.

Innovators are defined as the sole managers of the first U.S. public offering of that security, or the lead manager of the syndicate if there are multiple managers. Imitators are banks that are the lead or sole managers of syndicates offering securities with similar terms to the products offered by the innovators. Innovators and most fast seconds are drawn almost exclusively from among the largest investment bankers, which developed and underwrote almost all financial innovations (Table 13-1).

Six investment banks account for 76.3 percent of all innovative (or pioneering) deals and 71.8 percent of all subsequent offerings using these fifty-eight instruments. The fifty-eight innovations generated revenues of $3.75 billion for the investment banks, which represented 15.9 percent of the total underwriting revenue reported by the ten national full-line firms and the ten large investment banks from 1976 to 1987. The full sample of fifty-eight products includes thirty-five products that were rapidly imitated by rivals (within one year of the innovative deal) and twenty-three that were imitated only after a long delay.

Consistent with our model, Tufano found that innovators capture long-lived quantity advantages, that for the thirty-five imitated products, innovators captured market shares almost two and a half times as large as those of the imitators in those markets. Innovators continued to capture larger shares in subsequent years; in year 1 of the life of the thirty-five imitated products, the innovator's average share of the market was 31.3 percent; the second entrant captured 14.7 percent; and the third entrant captured 13.4 percent of the underwriting market.

Table 13-1. Innovation and Rapid Imitation by Leading Industry Firms

Investment Bank	Markets in Which the Bank Was the Innovator		Markets in Which the Bank Offered an Imitative Product	
	No. of Products	Average Share as Innovator (%)	No. of Products	Average Share as Imitator (%)
Salomon Brothers	7	47.8	16	18.7
First Boston	6	54.5	12	16.8
Morgan Stanley	5	45.3	12	18.3
Goldman Sachs	4	35.5	10	12.4
Shearson Lehman[a]	4	47.3	15	15.8
Merrill Lynch	3	37.4	12	23.0
Smith Barney Harris	2	54.7	2	1.4
Blyth Eastman Dillon	2	61.6	1	49.9
Drexel Burnham	1	69.2	7	15.1
Bear Sterns	1	11.7	3	4.5
Shearson Loeb Rhodes	1	62.2	1	0.6
Mean	36[b]	47.9	91	15.4

[a]Includes Lehman Brothers and Shearson Lehman.

[b]The number of banks here is thirty-six because two banks pioneered competing identical products on one day.

Source: Tufano (1989), p. 233.

Tufano also used the innovator–imitator experience of Salomon Brothers to determine whether a bank captures a larger underwriting share as an innovator or an imitator. Salomon Brothers was the innovator of seven of the thirty-five products that were imitated and, on average, was the lead underwriter for 47.8 percent of the deals during the first year of these products' lives. Salomon also offered imitative products in sixteen markets and in these markets underwrote an average of 18.7 percent of the offerings in the first year of these products' lives.

This evidence supports the fundamental prediction of the model, that banks gain and keep market share by innovating. According to Tufano (1989), the data suggest that innovation and market share are linked. The largest banks innovate and, in turn, become larger. It appears that innovators even underprice their services (perhaps following a limit pricing strategy), which may contribute to their ability to gain and hold market share. That banks undertake costly actions with the apparent result of increasing or holding market share suggests that banks believe that bigger is better.

Tufano added that bankers report that innovators use their knowledge of the buyers of the innovative product to set up secondary trades and to become dominant market makers of new instruments. Active market making gives a bank valuable information about the identities and preferences of investors and reduces the search costs for subsequent underwriting and market making. By innovating, banks may signal their abilities and attract the attention of, or open the door to, corporate treasurers and potential investors. This may lower the innovators' overall marketing costs.

With these advantages, an innovator may be able to dominate the market for the product in the short run. However, if the innovator has no real cost advantage that persists in the long run, the innovator's market power will melt away over time. This is what we have seen in the market for mortgage-backed, asset-backed, and high-yield (junk) bonds, which are institutional markets with low switching costs. The innovators no longer dominate the market, and pricing is at "commodity" levels.

On the other hand, switching costs are higher for individual customers. Therefore, once a customer shifts to another securities firm to purchase the new product, he or she is not likely to switch to another firm for some time. An example of a retail product that attracted customers was Merrill Lynch's Cash Management Account.

CONCLUSION

Although the innovation process is complex and subject to many influences, our model describes the market structure forces at work in innovation. The securities industry does not have substantial economies of scale but has increasing concentration. The predictions of the model for this industry are that the largest firms would be the leading innovators, and this is what we have seen. The model also suggests that the largest firms in the industry can maintain their leadership positions by following a strategy of innovation leadership. Merrill Lynch, especially, has been able to maintain its position as the largest firm in the industry from almost the entire period from 1940 to 1992, by acting as an innovation leader on both the retail and the institutional sides of the business.[3]

Part of the development costs for new products are legal and regulatory costs, and so regulators should make every effort to minimize them. If these costs are substantial, they may be partly responsible for the reluctance of some mid-size firms to innovate. But more innovation by firms outside the oligopoly groups would help reduce increases in concentration that are due to the existing innovation pattern.

NOTES

1. The stimulus for innovation in many cases is exogeneous to the industry. Finnerty (1988) identified eleven different factors that were responsible for financial innovations.

2. Finnerty (1988) identified fifty-two new products or services introduced over the past twenty years.

3. Merrill Lynch ran a full-page ad in the *Wall Street Journal* (May 10, 1988) in which the firm identified itself as the leader in innovations and cited its six "landmark" innovations "as just one part—though an absolutely vital part—of being the leader in financial services."

14

Diversification by Securities Firms

The securities firms that have survived and grown over the past twenty years have altered and adapted their organizational forms to respond to changing economic conditions, by diversifying into new lines of business. Because there have been various motives for these diversifications, various economic models are helpful in exploring these motives. Teece (1980, 1982) shows the advantages of using firm know-how across several lines of business; Williamson (1975) argues that diversification is a method of employing excess capital; Chandler (1969) discusses the ability of a technical staff to find and develop diversification opportunities; Amit and Livnat (1988) consider the risk-reduction benefits of diversification; and Levy and Haber (1986) believe that diversification provides benefits in organizational flexibility and bankruptcy protection.

We also will discuss the efficacy of the various entry modes (Hill, Hwang, and Kim 1990) that have been used by securities firms to enter a new line of business. Then we will examine the conditions that have led to or facilitated diversifications. An important argument of this book is that successful diversification is necessary for securities firms to maintain or improve their relative position in their industry. Those firms that successfully entered the important new lines of business in the 1980s were those that either grew or at least maintained their position relative to that of their competitors. Those firms that failed to diversify, or on balance made the wrong diversification decisions, declined in size relative to that of their competitors. Finally, we will consider the organizational issues associated with the failure of Lehman Brothers, E. F. Hutton, and Drexel Burnham Lambert.

MOTIVES FOR DIVERSIFICATION

Various authors have contributed to the development of a theory of multiproduct organization that explains why firms diversify into related and unrelated product lines. Teece (1982) argues that to construct this theory, it is necessary to modify the neoclassical theory of the firm to emphasize the distinctive properties of *organizational knowledge* and the *transaction cost properties of market exchange*. He argued that the earlier literature failed to explain the multiproduct firm; that is, those theories that explain the multiproduct firm as a result of managerial discretion or taxes and regulation, or based on "synergy" motives, are incomplete.

Teece focused on the incentives most likely to be operative in an economy that is dynamically competitive in the Schumpeterian sense and in which firms are profit maximizing. Here the competitive process is dynamic, involving uncertainty, struggle, and disequilibrium. Two fundamental characteristics of such a dynamic competitive system are the following:

1. Firms accumulate knowledge or "know-how" through research and development (R&D) and learning, some of it incidental to the production process.
2. The market conditions facing the firm are constantly changing, creating profit opportunities in different markets at different times.

If at some point, competitive returns can no longer be obtained by reinvesting in traditional lines of business, because of secular decline due to life-cycle or other considerations, a profit-maximizing firm will be faced with three choices:

1. Selling the services of its unused assets to other firms.
2. Diversifying into other markets, through either acquisition or de novo entry.
3. If the unused resource is cash, returning it to shareholders through higher dividends or stock repurchase.

A theory of diversification emerges when the conditions are such that the second option appears to be the most profitable. Multiproduct diversification will be selected over the market alternative (Option 1) when transaction cost problems are likely to confound efficient transfer.

Various types of excess firm resources are likely to be used in diversification. For securities firms, the relevant resources include (1) human capital or know-how[1] as a common input to two or more products and (2) excess financial capital.

Know-how

Proprietary individual and organizational knowledge plays an important role in Teece's notion of the nature of the multiproduct firm. To the extent that human capital or know-how has fungible attributes, it can represent a common input into a variety of products. Know-how may also display some of the characteristics of a public good, in that it may be used in many noncompeting applications without its value in any one application being substantially impaired.

Markets do not, however, work well as an institutional mode for trading know-how. Much organizational knowledge is tacit,[2] but the transfer of such tacit knowledge from one enterprise to another is likely to be difficult and costly. The intrafirm transfer of know-how reduces these transaction costs, and it also avoids the need for repeated negotiations and lessens the hazards of opportunism. Better disclosure, easier agreement, better governance, and therefore more effective execution of know-how transfer are likely to result in a multiproduct organization.

Excess Capital

Financial capital can be a financial firm's excess capacity. Williamson (1975, p. 162) postulates that multidivisional firms can establish internal capital markets with resource allocation properties superior to those obtained by (external) capital markets. Inferior access to the inside information and the weak control instruments exercised by the stock market and financial intermediaries provide the basis for Williamson's assertion that the "miniature capital market" in a firm may provide the most efficient means of diversifying a firm's excess capital.

Stockholders can benefit from this internal capital market. If managers have access to more information than stockholders do and if it is difficult and costly to transmit this information to stockholders, then managers may be able to increase the shareholders' wealth by making investment decisions on their behalf. Thus, if a specialized firm possesses financial resources beyond reinvestment opportunities in its traditional business, there will be circumstances in which both stockholders and allocative efficiency can benefit if managers allocate funds to new products. And it is generally with respect to related businesses that an information advantage seems likely. It is the investment opportunities in which the firm has a decided information advantage that managers are likely to take advantage of the information by diversifying (Teece 1982, p. 56).

Technical Staff

Chandler (1969) identified another motive for firm diversification based on his historical analysis of organizational change. He observed that the pioneers in the strategy of diversification were the firms that had the technological and research skills to develop new products and the administrative experience to produce and distribute them. So the modern diversified corporation is the rational response of technically trained professional managers to the needs and opportunities of changing markets and technologies.

Flexibility

Levy and Haber (1986) argue that in the face of an unanticipated event, a multiproduct firm provides certain advantages (beyond excess capacity arguments) not available to the single-product firm. The multiproduct firm may reallocate its firm-specific inputs among production lines, thereby mitigating the potential disruption of an unanticipated shock. For example, a decline in demand for the output of a single-product firm would lead to a decline in the marginal revenue product of firm-specific inputs employed by the firm. A single-product firm would have to continue using the input in its present use or go out of business. The multiproduct firm has the additional option of transferring the input to a higher-valued use in another product line. Similarly, when the demand for an output unexpectedly increases, a multiproduct firm can obtain the required firm-specific inputs by transferring them from other product lines. This enables the multiproduct firm to avoid the high cost of rapidly accumulating firm-specific inputs.

In discussing know-how, Levy and Haber contend that although knowledge is often considered a joint input that may be used without congestion, the information may be embodied in particular individuals who must be transferred in order to use this information. They note that in the face of unanticipated changes in demand or technology, firms often react by transferring employees to different product lines.

Transaction Costs

By considering transaction costs, Levy and Haber's results qualify some of the earlier literature on multiproduct firms. For example, Panzar and Willig (1981) propose that multiproduct firms originate where there are cost economies of joint production—that is, economies of scope. This happens when firms possess certain public inputs that, once procured for the production of one output, would be available (wholly or in part) to aid in the production of other outputs.

Teece (1980, 1982) believes that contractual mechanisms can be derived to share the inputs that are yielding the scope economies, so that scope alone does not explain multiproduct firms. It is the transaction costs inherent in market contracting that actually determine a firm's organization. Levy and Haber's analysis goes on to imply that inputs need not be joint in order to provide advantages to the multiproduct firm; they need only be shareable.

Bankruptcy

Diversification may also provide benefits by reducing the likelihood of bankruptcy. Bankruptcy will occur when a firm cannot generate sufficient revenues to meet expenses, including fixed payments to debtholders. When bankruptcy is declared, the firm incurs not only legal costs but also the possibility of losing the value of firm-specific capital in the future if the firm is not successfully reorganized. A multiproduct firm has more flexibility in avoiding bankruptcy, as it has the option of employing firm-specific capital in alternative uses that may generate enough revenue to enable it to avoid bankruptcy.

Risk Reduction

To reduce risk, a firm adds lines of business that have a revenue pattern different from the firm's original one. The firm's objective is to create a more stable flow of revenue to the firm and to lessen the risk of relying too much on a particular business. Amit and Livnat (1988) discussed this management literature, and Scherer (1980) looked at the industrial organization literature on risk reduction through diversification.

THE SECURITIES INDUSTRY ENVIRONMENT

The securities business in the 1980s provided an environment conducive to diversification. Each of the motives that we just discussed was at work. It was also clear that substantial profits were being earned by the firms that introduced a new line of business and held a large market share in that business.

Changes in the Regulatory and Tax Framework

Changing conditions made diversification by securities firms unavoidable. The traditional mainstay of the securities industry—the brokerage business—had dramatically declined in importance for securities firms. In addition, with competitive commissions, the business became less profitable. Shelf registration reduced the profitability of what had been a very lucrative line of business; indeed, underwriting had been referred to in the 1970s as the "last gold mine" for the industry. Then the Tax Reform Act of 1986 drastically reduced the top income tax rates and made municipal bonds less attractive as a tax shelter. Accordingly, a number of securities firms, including Salomon Brothers, responded to this change by getting out of the munibond business.

Know-how

Securities firms, with multiple lines of business, can rapidly reallocate professional personnel from lines with declining profitability to those with increasing profit opportunities. Many securities professionals start their careers in one line of business and move to another, as their knowledge can be quickly transferred and so can be considered a public input. Those types of know-how that can be transferred include the ability to develop new products, a knowledge of the risk–return characteristics of various instruments, information about sources of capital, the ability to place securities, a knowledge of the structure of institutional portfolios and the investment objectives of the institutions, and experience in using new financial instruments to construct sophisticated trading strategies.

Professional and Technical Staff

Securities firms have highly trained administrative staffs with strategic planning responsibilities, and they also employ product development groups. Large securities firms use financial theorists, many with doctorates in finance or related areas, who help develop sophisticated securities products. These "quants" or "rocket scientists" can contribute to the development of products in their own areas and also provide useful input for product development in other areas. A society of "financial engineers" has been established. Salomon Brothers, for example, had forty-one Ph.D. holders at the firm in 1986 (*Institutional Investor,* March 1986, p. 75).

Hayes and Hubbard (1990) report that annual planning meetings utilizing proposed position papers became common at firms like Morgan Stanley and Goldman Sachs as a means of setting firm strategy and direction and keeping executives abreast of developments and opportunities in those areas of the business with which they were not directly associated.

Flexibility

Highly skilled professionals are a firm's most valuable asset. A multiproduct firm offers its employers an opportunity to move from a declining area to a new "hot" area, which means that a slowdown in one line of business will not necessarily result in the defection of some of the firm's best personnel. A multiproduct firm can also more readily adapt to a change in the legal, tax, or regulatory framework or an unanticipated shift in demand that has an important effect on a line of business. Eccles and Crane (1988) describe securities firms as organizations that tend to be decentralized, relatively loose, and compartmentalized, with ad hoc task-directed teams calling on the assistance of specialized departments only as required.

An article in *Business Week* (June 10, 1991) discussing the growing importance of trading for broker-dealers illustrates the importance of adapting the organization to changing conditions:

If you think the trading boom is just a one-quarter blip, look at what's happening at some big houses. Once-omnipotent investment bankers have been forced to give ground to traders. At Merrill, the latest reorganization promoted trading chiefs to head two of the firm's six divisions, while the merchant banking function was downgraded. Shearson has promoted hotshot trader Richard S. Fuld, Jr. to share the helm with investment banker J. Tomilson Hill. But Hill has eliminated Lehman's M&A department and reassigned bankers to other areas. Fuld, on the other hand, is building the firm's trading operation.

At CS First Boston Inc., Allen D. Wheat, the CEO of its new product-trading unit, is the firm's reigning rainmaker—a role once held by investment banker Bruce Wasserstein, who left to start his own firm. "In the past year, it has looked like the M&A guys are the bygone era," says Wheat.

Firms that do not possess this adaptability will not be able to take advantage of fleeting high-profit opportunities.

Excess Capital

With the declining importance of securities brokerage and increased competition from discount brokers, many firms were forced to look for new areas in which to employ their excess capital. In addition, a number of firms went public in the early 1980s or were acquired by larger financial entities. In both cases, large amounts of capital were added to the firm, in hopes that it would expand its activities in the new, highly profitable lines of business.

Eccles and Crane (1988) describe the broker-dealers' allocation of capital, which is typically closely controlled at the top. They observe that senior management has the ability to redeploy capital to take advantage of emerging opportunities in a constantly shifting market environment.

Bankruptcy

The multiproduct securities firms are less subject to potential bankruptcy than is the single-product firm or the firm that is too specialized in one line of business. The bankruptcy of Drexel Burnham Lambert, the junk bond king, was attributed to a lack of diversification. One Wall Street executive noted that Drexel was a one-product company centered on junk bonds and that one-product companies have not had long-run success on the street (*Wall Street Journal,* February 13, 1990, p. C-23).

Risk Reduction

Firms follow two types of strategies to reduce risk: (1) expanding into those businesses that provide some countermovement to the bull-and-bear cycles of the securities markets (e.g., real estate, insurance) and (2) developing hedging strategies to help manage the day-to-day risks of operating in highly volatile securities markets. The effect of adding real estate and insurance to the portfolios of securities firms' businesses was to smooth out the volatile boom-or-bust pattern in the industry. Greater stability in the performance of the industry was perceived by both management and investors as less risky, all other things remaining equal.

The new financial instruments developed on the options and futures exchanges allow securities firms to hedge larger securities positions and manage the increasing risks associated with larger day-to-day swings in securities prices. These instruments also provide the basis for complex new trading strategies such as program trading and the development of derivatives that have become profitable new lines of business.

MODES OF ENTRY

After a firm has decided to enter a new line of business, it must choose a mode of entry. Three possible entry modes are (1) starting from scratch with the firm's own staff (as an innovator or imitator), (2) hiring from competitors professionals experienced in the new product line, and (3) acquiring another firm's complete product group.

Starting from Scratch

A firm may choose to enter a new line of business using its own personnel. For example, a regional firm can join a junk bond syndicate and thereby enter this business. However, to be a junk bond originator, it is probably better to hire away someone with originating experience at a larger firm.

Hiring Experienced Professionals

Hiring experienced professionals is a strategy that a number of securities firms have pursued in order to enter a new line. Often a firm pays a premium in the form of a bonus or a large salary to hire away an experienced professional to start a new business. Firms in this industry have always had a tradition of hiring some of the best professionals from other companies.

Acquiring Another Firm's Product Group

Acquiring another firm's product group is a route used by many firms to enter a new line of business. The resource costs in this approach can be relatively low if the product group acquired is part of a firm that is leaving the business. Often, a large firm that is in trouble has one group in the firm that is regarded as a strong performer, and such groups are often acquired intact. But even this approach is subject to potential defections to another firm by individuals in the group.[3]

FACILITATING CONDITIONS

Other factors are relevant when considering the potential for success of a new line of business: (1) the completeness of markets, (2) the customer base for the new line of business, and (3) the switching costs that will be incurred by customers buying the new product.

Incomplete Markets

Van Horne (1985) states that an important factor in producing financial innovations is the movement toward market completeness. A complete market exists when every contingency in the world corresponds to a distinct marketable security. In contrast, incomplete markets exist when the number and types of securities available do not span these contingencies. That is, there is an unfilled desire for a particular type of security on the part of an investor. An example is the pension funds' desire for zero coupon bonds before 1981. If the market is incomplete, it will pay a broker-dealer to exploit the opportunity by tailoring a financial product to investors' unfilled desires, whether those desires pertain to maturity, coupon rate, protection, call features, cash-flow characteristics, or whatever.

The Customer Base and Switching Costs

The three primary customer bases for broker-dealers are individual investors, institutional investors, and issuers of securities. Individuals traditionally have transacted through one broker-dealer, and so they would incur some switching costs if they moved their account to a different firm in order to purchase that firm's product. These costs include the inconvenience of closing out the old account and ending what may have been a satisfactory relationship with a registered representative. Nonetheless, some products are attractive enough to cause individuals to switch firms. Merrill Lynch's Cash Management Account was such a product.

Institutions generally do business with many broker-dealers. In 1989, the average number of brokers that institutions considered necessary for execution services was 9.8, and the average number considered important to research was 10.6 (Greenwich Associates 1990, p. 5). The cost of switching from one broker-dealer's product to another's for institutions is minimal.

Issuers historically have had long-term alliances with selected investment-banking houses—"their principal bankers" (Hayes, Spence, and Marks 1983, p. 12). Although neither party was legally bound to maintain the alliance during future flotations of securities, there were strong bonds that tended to last for years. However, in the era of shelf registration, though these relationships did not disappear, they did change. *Institutional Investor* (December 1986) reports that issuers were dealing with two to four investment-banking houses that knew the company well. Issuers were also more open to other investment bankers' suggestions for new products.

THE DECISION FRAMEWORK

Figure 14-1 shows how motives, entry mode, and facilitating conditions form a framework for the entry decision. Hayes and Hubbard (1990, p. 330) note that generally a consensus is reached only on the broad outlines of the diversification strategy and that the implementation of specific decisions is left to the senior management of the particular area. Management in the new product area thus decides whether the new business requires recruitment of outside personnel or transfers of existing staff from one area to another; the implementation of such changes requires time and negotiation. The assembling of the new product line team calls for team balance and harmonious working arrangements. The managers of the new group are then asked for a postaudit of the new initiative at a subsequent planning meeting.

DIVERSIFICATION AND RELATIVE POSITION
IN THE INDUSTRY

One hypothesis suggested by the preceding discussion is that those firms that improved or maintained their relative industry position in the 1980s were successful at diversification, whereas those firms that slipped in the rankings did not succeed

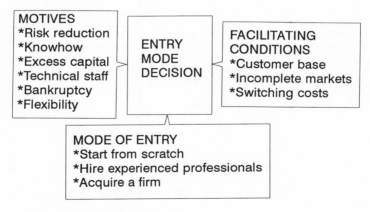

Figure 14.1. The decision framework.

in their diversification. To test this hypothesis, the total capital position of a set of large firms in 1981 was compared with the firms' total capital position in 1988. The firms were divided into three groups: (1) those that improved their relative position, (2) those that maintained their position, and (3) those that lost their position. The year 1981 was used as a starting point for the analysis because most of the major diversifications in the industry took place after 1981. New product areas included mortgage-backed securities (1983) and asset-backed securities (1984). Other important areas that represented diversification choices were the junk bond business and the mergers and acquisitions business. Activity in these areas accelerated after 1981.

Table 14-1 shows the firms' relative positions in each of these areas in 1988. Those firms that moved ahead or maintained their positions in the total capital rankings had strong positions in these expanding areas, and those that fell did not have strong positions in these areas.

Chapter 15 details the approaches used by Merrill Lynch, Salomon Brothers, and Morgan Stanley in adapting their organization to changing economic and industry conditions. These firms did not maintain their leadership positions by standing still

Table 14-1. Change in Position from 1981 to 1988 and Position in New Areas

			1988 Position in Rankings				
Firms that Improved Position	1981	1988	Worldwide Issues	Junk Debt	Mortgage Backed	Asset Backed	M&A
Shearson Lehman Hutton	4	1	6	12	5	10	4
Goldman Sachs	5	4	3	7	1	4	1
Drexel Burham Lambert	12	5	7	1	9	6	5
First Boston	9	6	1	2	3	1	2
Paine Webber	8	7	20	11	11	N1	19
Bear Stearns	15	8	13	13	7	N1	12
Smith Barney, Harris Upham	20	12	24	9	14	N1	21
Kidder Peabody	17	14	16	10	10	12	10
Firms that Maintained Position	1981	1988					
Salomon Brothers	2	2	4	5	2	2	8
Morgan Stanley	10	10	5	3	6	9	3
Donaldson Lufkin	13	13	29	8	13	N1	15
Firms that Declined in Position	1981	1988					
Merrill Lynch	1	3	2	4	4	7	9
Dean Witter Reynolds	7	9	39	N	17	8	N2
Prudential-Bache	6	11	10	6	8	N1	20
Stephens	11	17	N	N	N	N1	N2
A.G. Edwards	18	21	N	N	N	N1	N2

N = Not ranked in top 15.
N1 = Not ranked in top 12.
N2 = Not ranked in top 25.

Sources: Investment Dealers' Digest, various issues; *Institutional Investor,* various issues.

and relying on their existing strengths, but by adding new lines of business to take advantage of new opportunities.

DIVERSIFICATION CHOICES AT PROBLEM FIRMS

Three of the largest and most important firms at the start of the 1980s were not around when the industry entered 1991. In 1980, E. F. Hutton was the third-largest firm in the industry in the capital rankings; Lehman Brothers Kuhn Loeb was eleventh; and Drexel Burnham Lambert was thirteenth. In the 1980s, each firm faced difficult decisions regarding its organizational structure. Although each of these firms had significant problems in other areas, the their inability to resolve organizational problems played an important role in their demise.

Lehman Brothers

Ken Auletta detailed the fall of Lehman Brothers in two articles in the *New York Times Magazine* (1985a, 1985b) and in a subsequent book. Although he discussed the clash of personalities and the struggle for power and compensation among the traders and the investment bankers, he also made it clear that an important element in the conflict was a difference of opinion among the partners regarding the ultimate shape of the firm. Chairman Peter G. Peterson had committed the firm to becoming a full-service investment banker, a financial supermarket. Auletta described Peterson's view of the firm:

Retail, institutional, corporate and government customers could come to Lehman if they were shopping to merge, to divest, to undertake a leveraged buyout, to swap debt for equity, to have bonds underwritten, to trade stocks, to purchase zero coupon bonds or Treasury notes or municipal bonds, to invest in a money fund real estate. (Auletta 1985b, p. 42)

Some of the other partners, however, were concerned about the firm's ability to raise the capital necessary to achieve the goal of a full-service investment bank. Some of the partners thought that a better approach would be to shrink the firm, believing that Lehman should concentrate on the usual investment-banking services, in which the firm had a distinguished history, and on those products—perhaps commercial paper, money management, or retail sales—in which the firm was already strong.

Drexel Burnham Lambert

Drexel Burnham Lambert was the most profitable firm in the industry in 1986 when it was reported to have earned $545.5 million (*Wall Street Journal,* May 8, 1987, p. 2). But then it was severely weakened when it was required to pay $650 million in fines and restitution to settle charges stemming from the government's insider-trading investigation of the firm. Payment of part of this fine plus a weak junk bond market put the firm under financial stress in late 1989. When the firm needed cash in late 1989 and early 1990, its inventory of private placements, junk bonds, and bridge loans, carried on the books for $2 billion, could not be sold for anywhere near that price (*Fortune,* March 12, 1990, p. 88). In addition, many of the bridge loans were related to junk-financed mergers and acquisitions. Unable to raise funds to meet its short-term obligations, the firm filed for bankruptcy in early 1990. This inventory of private placements, junk bonds, and bridge loans resulted from the rapid growth of its junk bond business. Indeed, Drexel's success was clearly related to its dominant position in the junk market, but it could not rely on strength in other lines of business to pull it through a difficult period.

E. F. Hutton

Although E. F. Hutton was one of the most profitable public securities firms in the 1970s, it did not adapt well to the competitive environment of the 1980s.

Institutional Investor (April 1985, pp. 59–64) described the difficulties that E. F. Hutton had in attempting to broaden its lines of business. Hutton's great strength was its highly successful retail sales force—the "envy of the industry." It also had done well in the municipal bond area, and in 1977 it owned a profitable insurance company. But it was not successful in two key areas that would be important in the 1980s: institutional brokerage and corporate finance. This remained true despite its strong efforts, especially in corporate finance. Even though Hutton had difficulty in becoming a major investment banker, it did have success as an underwriter in the initial public offering (IPO) market. However, even this success was constrained by the reluctance of key executives to do some types of IPOs (e.g., fast foods) that were viewed as not suitable for E. F. Hutton. Another hindrance in investment banking was Hutton's practice of allowing corporate debt and equity underwritings to be priced by its corporate finance department, whereas at most firms it is done by bond traders and equity syndicators.

Hutton had always been known as an equities house, true to its retail orientation. It had been unwilling to devote much of its resources to such cyclical businesses as private placements, Euromarket syndications, energy deals, and real-estate partnerships that were replacing equities in institutional portfolios in the 1970s. The firm also shied away from the capital commitment and risks associated with fixed-income trading, another important element in an institutional strategy. Hutton also did not aggressively pursue large block trades on the equity side, and it made little headway in the areas of mergers and acquisitions, junk bonds, and securities-backed issues.[4] So Hutton entered the 1980s without having developed the type of flexible organization it needed to adapt to changing market conditions.

DIVERSIFICATION INTO THE SECURITIES INDUSTRY BY LARGE FINANCIAL INSTITUTIONS

The diversifications into the securities industry by American Express and Prudential did not meet with the success they anticipated. Press reports suggest that organizational issues regarding these acquisitions were part of the problem.

Prudential-Bache

Prudential Insurance Co. bought Bache Halsey Stuart Shields in June 1981 for $385 million. The purchase was billed as a natural marriage linking the vast financial resources of Prudential with the upscale market potential and securities savvy of Bache. The expected ''synergy'' was expected to transform Bache, known as a retail house, into a more broad-based financial services company. In 1982, Prudential brought in George Ball, formerly president of the E. F. Hutton Group, to become the president and chief executive officer of Bache. Early on, Ball ordered a recruiting campaign that brought in more than 1,100 experienced brokers through the lure of large, up-front bonuses (*Institutional Investor,* July 1984, pp. 77–79).

In 1985, Prudential contributed $600 million of equity capital to Prudential-Bache in order to help it gain corporate and municipal investment-banking clients. A firm spokesman stated that these clients usually look at the capital rankings of firms that are competing for their business. George Ball noted that the equity capital infusion also could give the firm greater freedom to make acquisitions and to diversify (*Wall Street Journal,* November 18, 1985, p. 2). But by the fall of 1989, Bache had not achieved the hoped-for success in investment banking. Prudential executives also did not appear to support the idea, which originated at Bache, that a global investment-banking strategy was right for the firm. At that time, an outside management consulting firm recommended that Bache contract, rather than expand, the services that the firm would offer. The recommendation for contraction won the day and resulted in the firm's discharging fifty or more of its professionals, nearly one-quarter of the core investment-banking force.

American Express–Shearson Lehman

American Express's acquisition of Shearson was motivated by the notion that AmEx could provide one-source delivery of various financial services and cross selling to various AmEx customers. AmEx's plans for an integrated financial services network, however, never materialized on a grand scale.

In 1981, American Express bought Shearson Loeb Rhoads, and then Shearson took over Lehman Brothers Kuhn Loeb in 1984 and E. F. Hutton four years later. But the cyclical nature of the securities industry turned out to be too disruptive to AmEx's bottom line. By 1987, AmEx had sold about 40 percent of Shearson to the public, partly because the expected synergies had not materialized (*Wall Street Journal,* March 6, 1990, p. A-6). For example, although Shearson's brokers were eager to have access to lists of AmEx cardholders, AmEx never turned over complete lists, fearing that the cardholders might blame AmEx if the investment ideas turned sour.

Shearson also ran into trouble in the late 1980s when the bull market died out. The *Wall Street Journal* (March 6, 1990, p. A-1) reported that one Wall Street executive who had seen Shearson's books said the firm faced as much as $500 million to $1 billion in writedowns from bad loans and other underperforming investments. AmEx responded by reorganizing Shearson through layoffs, closings, and the consolidation of some branch offices and the decision to quit some business lines. The firm also changed the basic structure by creating a Lehman Brothers division for institutional investing and capital markets and a Shearson Lehman Brothers division for retail and asset management.

THE POTENTIAL FOR CREATING STRATEGIC BARRIERS TO ENTERING NEW LINES OF BUSINESS

Jacquemin (1987) argues that the strategic creation of barriers to entry rests on two requirements. First, a firm that embarks on such a strategy must confirm its credibility in the eyes of its rivals in a way that effectively constrains their behavior. Second, the firm must be certain of its profitability, in that the expenditure caused by creating barriers is more than offset by the additional revenue resulting from it. To modify the expectations of rivals in a credible way, what is required is an irrevocable engagement with would-be entrants if information is complete or, if information is incomplete, an engagement that is perceived as irrevocable.

In this industry, an innovator cannot prevent competitors from employing know-how, capital, and personnel to introduce an imitative product. Although it appears that limit pricing is used, perhaps as a strategy to slow imitation, innovators do not make the kind of long-term strategic commitments that Jacquemin cited as necessary to block entry by competitors.

Strategies that rely on building large capacity that may deter a competitor's entry in manufacturing industries do not work in this industry. Securities firms generally do not make a large fixed cost investment in a product line. Although they do incur sunk costs in developing a product (e.g., R&D, regulatory approval, computer-program development, training of personnel), such investments are usually a fraction of a percentage of the firm's revenues. The industry thus has not been subject to the kinds of "economic warfare" observed in other industries. Instead, most new product areas are characterized by substantial entry over time. Hayes and Hubbard (1990) observe that in certain cases successful new products have been copied so effectively that they have evolved into what is referred to as *commodity-type* businesses with many sellers, reduced commissions, and sharply declining profitability.

This is not to say that the strategic groups described in Chapter 13 are not relevant to new products. Indeed, the six firms in Groups I and II were the leading product innovators and fast seconds on the investment-banking side of the business, as shown in Table 13-1. After a product does become a commodity-type product, the usual pecking order emerges, with the oligopoly group as the managing underwriters at the top of the rankings. The regional and smaller firms then generally fill out the roster of firms handling the product.

Table 14-2 compares the business activities of a selected group of publicly held broker-dealers listed in the Securities Industry Association (SIA) *Fact Book*. The table clearly shows that the regional firms have followed the national full-line firms and investment bankers into new lines of business. For example, firms such as Legg Mason, Morgan Keegan, Piper Jaffray, McDonald & Co., First of Michigan, Scott

Table 14-2. Lines of Business of Selected Publicly Held Broker-Dealers

Firm	January 1, 1992 Capital (000s)	Brokerage				Underwriting							
		Retail	Institutional	International	Wrap Accounts	Equities	Corporate Fixed Income	Municipals	High-Yield Fixed Income	Mortgage-Backed	Asset-Backed	International Issues	Real-Estate Partnerships
Merrill Lynch & Co., Inc.	$11,782,512	x	x	x	x	x	x	x	x	x	x	x	x
Morgan Stanley Group, Inc.	5,421,515	x	x	x		x	x	x	x	x	x	x	x
Salomon Brothers, Inc.	4,122,417	x	x	x		x	x	x	x	x	x	x	x
Paine Webber Group, Inc.	1,866,206	x	x	x	x	x	x	x	x	x	x	x	x
The Bear Stearns Companies, Inc.	1,835,820	x	x	x	x	x	x	x	x	x	x	x	x
A. G. Edwards, Inc.	417,412	x	x	x	x	x	x	x	x	x	x		x
Charles Schwab & Co., Inc.	285,595	x	x	x	x	x	x	x					
Alex. Brown & Sons, Inc.	248,350	x	x	x	x	x	x	x	x	x		x	x
Legg Mason, Inc.	176,928	x	x	x	x	x	x	x	x	x			x
Raymond James Financial, Inc.	144,037	x	x	x	x	x	x	x	x	x			
Inter-Regional Financial Group	130,796	x	x	x	x	x	x	x	x	x	x		
Jefferies & Company, Inc.	113,159		x	x		x	x	x	x		x		
Advest Group, Inc.	97,881	x	x		x	x	x	x	x	x			x
Piper Jaffray, Inc.	83,398	x	x	x	x	x	x	x	x	x			
Interstate/Johnson Lane Corp.	75,350	x	x	x	x	x	x	x	x				
McDonald & Company Securities, Inc.	68,488	x	x	x	x	x	x	x		x	x	x	x
Morgan Keegan, Inc.	59,875	x	x	x	x	x	x	x		x	x	x	x
The Ziegler Companies, Inc.	49,122	x	x			x	x	x		x	x		
Fahnestock & Co., Inc.	40,006	x	x	x		x	x	x					
Rodman & Renshaw, Inc.	32,514	x	x	x	x	x	x	x	x	x	x	x	x
First of Michigan Corp.	31,259	x	x		x	x	x	x					x
Stifel, Nicolaus & Company, Inc.	27,715	x	x		x	x	x	x		x	x		x
Southwest Securities, Inc.	24,169	x	x			x	x	x		x			x
First Albany Corp.	23,932	x	x	x	x	x	x	x					
Scott and Stringfellow Investment Corp.	19,722	x	x		x	x	x	x					x
Waterhouse Securities, Inc.	11,416	x	x	x		x	x	x					
John G. Kinnard & Co., Inc.	7,915	x	x	x	x	x	x	x	x	x	x		

Market-Making and Trading

Firm	Equities	Corporate Fixed Income	Municipals	High-Yield Fixed Income	Mortgage- or Asset-Backed	Derivatives	Swaps	Currencies	U.S. Government	Arbitrage	Commodities	Proprietary Trading
Merrill Lynch & Co., Inc.	x	x	x	x	x	x	x	x	x	x	x	x
Morgan Stanley Group, Inc.	x	x	x	x	x	x	x	x	x	x	x	x
Salomon Brothers, Inc.	x	x		x	x	x	x	x	x	x	x	x
Paine Webber Group, Inc.	x	x	x	x	x	x	x	x	x		x	x
The Bear Stearns Companies, Inc.	x	x	x	x	x	x	x	x	x	x	x	x
A. G. Edwards, Inc.	x	x	x	x	x	x			x			
Charles Schwab & Co., Inc.	x	x	x	x	x	x	x		x			
Alex. Brown & Sons, Inc.	x	x	x	x	x				x			
Legg Mason, Inc.	x	x	x		x				x		x	x
Raymond James Financial, Inc.	x	x	x	x	x	x	x		x			
Inter-Regional Financial Group	x	x	x	x	x	x	x		x	x	x	x
Jefferies & Company, Inc.	x	x		x	x	x				x		x
Advest Group, Inc.	x	x	x	x	x			x	x		x	
Piper Jaffray, Inc.	x	x	x	x	x				x			
Interstate/Johnson Lane Corp.	x	x	x	x	x	x			x	x	x	
McDonald & Company Securities, Inc.	x	x	x	x	x			x	x	x	x	
Morgan Keegan, Inc.	x	x	x		x	x			x		x	
The Ziegler Companies, Inc.		x	x		x	x						x
Fahnestock & Co., Inc.	x	x	x	x	x							x
Rodman & Renshaw, Inc.	x	x	x	x	x	x	x	x	x	x	x	x
First of Michigan Corp.	x	x	x						x			x
Stifel, Nicolaus & Company, Inc.	x	x	x						x		x	
Southwest Securities, Inc.	x	x	x						x		x	
First Albany Corp.	x	x	x	x	x				x			x
Scott and Stringfellow Investment Corp.	x	x	x						x			
Waterhouse Securities, Inc.	x	x	x						x		x	
John G. Kinnard & Co., Inc.	x	x	x						x		x	

Table — Non-Securities-Related Business and Other Securities-Related Business by Firm

Firm	Mergers and Acquisitions	Restructuring	Valuation	Merchant Banking	Bridge Loans	Private Placements	Mutual Fund Origin	Asset Management	Specialist Unit	Venture Capital	Leasing	Mortgage Banking	Other Real Estate	Insurance
Merrill Lynch & Co., Inc.	X	X	X	X	X	X	X	X	X	X	X	X	X	X
Morgan Stanley Group, Inc.	X	X	X	X	X	X	X	X	X	X	X	X	X	X
Salomon Brothers, Inc.	X	X	X	X	X	X	X	X		X		X	X	X
Paine Webber Group, Inc.	X	X	X	X	X	X	X	X	X	X			X	X
The Bear Stearns Companies, Inc.	X	X	X	X		X	X	X	X	X		X		
A. G. Edwards, Inc.	X	X	X			X	X	X				X	X	X
Charles Schwab & Co., Inc.							X	X						
Alex. Brown & Sons, Inc.	X	X	X	X		X	X	X		X			X	X
Legg Mason, Inc.	X	X	X	X		X	X	X		X		X	X	X
Raymond James Financial, Inc.	X	X	X		X	X	X	X		X	X	X	X	X
Inter-Regional Financial Group, Inc.	X	X	X	X	X	X	X	X	X	X	X	X	X	X
Jefferies & Company, Inc.	X	X	X		X	X			X					
Advest Group, Inc.	X	X	X		X	X	X	X						X
Piper Jaffray, Inc.	X	X	X			X	X	X		X			X	X
Interstate/Johnson Lane Corp.	X	X	X			X	X	X					X	X
McDonald & Company Securities, Inc.	X	X	X			X	X	X		X			X	X
Morgan Keegan, Inc.	X		X	X		X	X	X		X		X	X	X
The Ziegler Companies, Inc.	X				X	X	X	X			X	X		X
Fahnestock & Co., Inc.	X	X	X			X	X	X		X				X
Rodman & Renshaw, Inc.	X	X	X			X	X	X	X	X				X
First of Michigan Corp.	X	X	X			X	X	X		X	X		X	X
Stifel, Nicolaus & Company, Inc.	X	X	X			X	X	X	X					X
Southwest Securities, Inc.	X					X	X	X						X
First Albany Corp.	X		X			X	X	X					X	X
Scott and Stringfellow Investment Corp.	X	X	X			X	X	X		X				X
Waterhouse Securities, Inc.							X	X						X
John G. Kinnard & Co., Inc.	X				X	X	X	X		X			X	X

Note: The last five columns (Venture Capital, Leasing, Mortgage Banking, Other Real Estate, Insurance) fall under "Non-Securities-Related Business"; the nine columns from Specialist Unit through Mergers and Acquisitions fall under "Other Securities-Related Business."

Source: Annual Reports and 10-Ks

and Stringfellow, the Jeffries Group, Rodman and Renshaw, and most of the other firms are in the mergers and acquisitions line; Legg Mason, Jefferies, Piper Jaffray, Advest, and several others are in junk bonds.

This table suggests that firms outside the oligopoly group also diversified in order to meet the changing industry environment and needs of their customers, that firms in the oligopoly group have not been able to erect permanent barriers to these businesses, and that mid-sized and regional firms played their traditional roles as followers and participants in the newly opened lines of business.

NOTES

1. For a complete discussion of know-how, see Teece (1980).

2. Tacit knowledge is known and understood by employees but cannot be easily documented or transferred to another production setting. Teece (1982, pp. 51–53) identified the transaction cost problems associated with the transfer of tacit knowledge.

3. For a discussion of Drexel Burnham Lambert's groups that were attractive to other firms, see *Wall Street Journal,* February 15, 1990, p. C-1.

4. For an explanation of the other problems that contributed to E. F. Hutton's failure, see *Business Week,* December 21, 1987, pp. 98–102.

V

Performance and
Public Policy

15

Merrill Lynch, Morgan Stanley, and Salomon Brothers Adapt

In order to illustrate how successful firms have adapted their structures to changing economic conditions, we will look at Merrill Lynch, Morgan Stanley, and Salomon Brothers. Each of these firms has been a leading firm in the industry for fifty years or more and has a unique identity in the industry. Merrill Lynch has been a leading innovator and a dynamic force in the industry since the 1940s in both retail and investment banking. Its size alone dominated the industry from the 1940s through the early 1980s. Yet it has been one of Wall Street's great mysteries. No other firm can boast such strength and diversity in revenues while having so much trouble in consistently bringing them to the bottom line (*Business Week,* July 17, 1989, p. 122).

In many respects, Morgan Stanley has been the premier investment banker in the industry since the 1930s. Among its longtime clients are many of this country's largest firms, including General Motors, Standard Oil of New Jersey, IBM, Mobil Oil, Texaco, U.S. Steel, DuPont, Shell Oil, and Standard Oil of Indiana (Hayes, Spence, and Marks 1983, pp. 102–3). The firm is an offshoot of the banking house of J. P. Morgan and is sometimes described as patrician. It has managed to remain highly profitable while making the organizational changes that turned the "classic" investment banker into a firm providing a broad range of corporate and investor services.

Salomon Brothers is the premier trading house on Wall Street. In the mid-1980s, the firm was an overwhelming force in the industry: In 1985, it was the most profitable publicly held securities firm in the world, with pretax profits of $760 million. It was the top underwriter of corporate equity in the United States, with 30 percent of the market share. It was also the largest underwriter of all securities and the largest dealer in U.S. government securities; its total fixed-income trading transactions were estimated to be more than those of its two nearest competitors. From its offices in New York, London, Tokyo, Zurich, and Frankfurt, the firm helped raise more than $150 billion for governments and corporations around the world (*Institutional Investor,* March 1986, p. 68). Salomon's dominance has declined a little since those halcyon days, but it continues to be one of the most important firms in the business. Salomon has had a reputation for creating a rough-and-tumble atmosphere that comes with a high-pressure trading environment. As one employee pointed out, "No one holds your hand and tells you what to do. You have to live by your wits. And don't look for a sympathetic shoulder to cry on if you drop the ball'' (*Institutional Investor,* March 1986, p. 75).[1]

Each of these firms survived and prospered in the turbulent markets of the 1970s and 1980s. This chapter will examine how each adapted its organizational structure from its early days. We will demonstrate that there are no easy rules or guidelines to decide what businesses to enter and how to enter them. Indeed, each firm made significant mistakes relating to new business. Nevertheless, the history of each shows that these firms understood the importance of diversification as a competitive strategy and were able to implement a strategy that works.

MERRILL LYNCH

Merrill Lynch has been one of the most dynamic forces in the securities industry since the 1940s. The firm has been very deliberate in choosing innovation and diversification as a strategy to maintain leadership. In the words of the former chairman of the firm, Donald T. Regan: "If we don't come up with new ideas to suit modern times, we could be overtaken by our competitors. We can't afford to atrophy" (*Business Week,* August 8, 1977, p. 50).

The firm was created in 1940 when Merrill Lynch, an investment-banking firm, merged with E. A. Pierce & Co., the largest member of the New York Stock Exchange (NYSE). The firm became the first to use the techniques of mass merchandising to sell securities. In the 1940s, Merrill Lynch was the first firm to build a nationwide network of sales offices. Bache, E. F. Hutton, Paine Webber, and others followed suit (*Financial World,* June 1, 1977, pp. 62–70). Until Merrill Lynch's move, the securities business had been a regional or local business. Throughout the 1950s and 1960s, the firm maintained its leadership position by opening new offices and expanding its client base. In the 1960s, the firm substantially increased its underwriting position on the strength of its retail distribution capabilities and became a major managing underwriter (Hayes 1979).

In 1963, the firm entered the government securities business by acquiring a number of the employees of the large government securities firm C. J. Devine, whose chief executive had just died. In 1970, Merrill took over Goodbody & Co. at the request of the NYSE, following the back-office crunch described in Chapter 6. At the time, Goodbody was the fifth largest retail brokerage house and had a strong position in municipal bonds (Harvard Business School, case 1-380-140 [1980], pp. 7–10).

In 1969, Merrill expanded into money management and advisory services by acquiring Lionel D. Edie & Co., economic consultants and investment advisers to large pension funds. Later, Merrill sold the firm back to its employees to avoid conflicts of interest that may have arisen under the Employees Retirement Income Security Act of 1975. To replace these businesses, in 1976 Merrill established Merrill Lynch Economics, an economic consulting firm, and Merrill Lynch Asset Management, which offers investment counseling to individuals and institutions.

In 1972, Merrill entered into physical commodity trading through a partnership with a metals-trading company. By 1979, Merrill owned a 50 percent interest in

Merrill Montagu, Inc., a precious metals–trading firm. It also owned Merrill Lynch Wood Markets, Inc., a wholly owned subsidiary formed in 1975 to deal in plywood, lumber, and other wood products on a wholesale basis. In 1978, Merrill Lynch acquired financially troubled White Weld, a premier investment banker with 450 of the most productive retail reps in the industry. As often happens with such acquisitions, other firms were able to pirate away a number of White Weld employees. Over 195 reps left to join other firms, and 15 out of the 78 employees left the Corporate Finance group. Nonetheless, this acquisition made Merrill a much stronger competitor in investment banking.

Merrill's major foreign involvement began in 1969 with the acquisition of a Canadian investment-banking and brokerage firm. In 1972, the firm entered the European markets through a joint venture with a London merchant bank. Merrill gradually bought out its partners and organized a bank in Panama in 1977 to oversee the operations of the London unit. Within a short time, the banking subsidies in London and Panama were actively engaged in international banking, including accepting deposits and making loans.

In 1976 the firm established Personal Capital Planning Group, Inc., to assist individuals, on a fee basis, with investment planning. In 1977, Merrill acquired Ticor Relocation Management, a firm that provided employee relocation services, including home-sale and home-finding services for major corporations.

Before the elimination of fixed commissions, Merrill Lynch began to diversify out of traditional securities lines of business. The decision to diversify out of traditional businesses was taken in 1968 when a severe market downturn added up to paper losses of $300 billion for investors. When investors left the market in large numbers, Merrill Lynch decided to follow them by providing a wider variety of financial services. The eventual demise of the fixed-commission-rate system was realized early at Merrill Lynch. In 1970, Donald Regan was one of the first Wall Street executives to call for competitive rates (*Wall Street Journal,* September 1980, p. 18). The diversifications were also intended to provide a more stable source of revenue, or a countercyclical source, to offset a large swing in the traditional securities business.

In 1974, it entered the insurance-underwriting business when it acquired Family Life Insurance Company. Merrill Lynch Realty Associates, a residential-real-estate entity, was formed in 1978 and was involved in real-estate brokerage and real-estate management. Merrill Lynch argued when it entered the real-estate business that real estate was similar to the securities business in the 1940s, and the firm expected to use its know-how at building a nationwide network of offices just as it had done in the securities industry. After a long effort to try to find synergy between the securities business and the real-estate business, Merrill Lynch unloaded its real-estate business in the late 1980s. Real estate was too much of a local business and did not benefit from the nationwide network of offices. In retrospect, Merrill concluded that it was unrelated to its main securities business (*Business Week,* July 17, 1989, pp. 122–25).

When Merrill's Cash Management Account was introduced in 1977, it was called the most important financial innovation in years by *Fortune.* (October 20, 1980, p. 135). The firm invested over 150 labor years to develop the product. The first firm to follow with a similar account was Dean Witter, in March 1982, but by the end of 1982, six other firms were offering their own versions of the account.

In the 1980s, Merrill was credited with pioneering the "bridge loan," which enables a client to complete a takeover without first lining up permanent financing. The firm also moved into junk bonds and merchant banking in this decade.

Critics argue that in the past Merrill did not do all those things that well-managed companies are expected to do, such as scrutinize expense accounts and fire mediocre people. As one employee observed, "It's a wonderful place to work. There is an enormous culture of looking out for each other. It is virtually impossible to get fired. Who wants to work where it's easy to get fired?" (*Institutional Investor,* November 1990, p. 75). Recently Merrill tightened management controls and has been successful at instituting tough cost-cutting measures. An important element in this restructuring is a change in focus from attempting to be number one in its businesses to being the most profitable.

MORGAN STANLEY

Morgan Stanley was created in the aftermath of the Banking Act of 1933. In 1934, J. P. Morgan & Co., with its Philadelphia office, Drexel & Co., was one of the nation's most important private banking and investment houses. Forced to choose, by the enactment of Glass–Stegall, between the commercial-banking business and the securities business, it chose commercial banking. One year later, three Morgan partners and two from Drexel resigned and organized the investment-banking corporation of Morgan Stanley & Co., Inc. Morgan Stanley continued the investment-banking business of the old J. P. Morgan & Co. and retained many of this country's largest corporations as clients (Harvard Business School, case 1-380-140 [1980]). The firm was able to maintain these relationships from the 1930s through to the 1980s. Hayes and Hubbard (1990) describe Morgan as the bluest of the "blue blood" houses, relying on performance and "old school ties" to maintain these relationships.

In 1942, Morgan joined the NYSE and began to offer brokerage services to institutional customers and corporations. Morgan remained a pure investment-banking house until the late 1960s, when with no trading capability, the firm began to lose the ability to place new issues. Without a strong trading presence, it became difficult to price offerings in increasingly volatile markets. In addition, many of the regional houses that had joined Morgan's syndicates had disappeared in the industry turmoil of the late 1960s or had become competitors.

This changing environment led to conflicts among Morgan's partners as to what organizational form the firm should take. Some argued that the firm should remain a pure investment banker. Another group, led by Robert Baldwin, believed that the firm should expand the range of services offered to institutional investors. Initially, the partnership resisted the expansionary approach, and in 1968—some say out of frustration—Baldwin actually quit the firm to become chief executive officer of Hartford Fire Insurance Company. But his departure was thwarted when ITT chairman Harold Geneen announced, a few days before Baldwin was to assume the job, that ITT would tender for Hartford (*Fortune*, February 27, 1978, p. 85). Soon afterward, Baldwin's expansionist view won out, and he led the firm throughout the 1970s. Starting from scratch in 1971, the firm began building up its bond sales trading. Shortly thereafter, it entered equity sales and trading and added a research capability. By 1974, Morgan had "bootstrapped" itself into being one of the top bond-trading houses on Wall Street (*Institutional Investor*, June 1974, p. 62). In July 1977, Morgan acquired the San Francisco retail firm of Shuman, Agnew in order to develop its "big ticket" retail business.

Traditionally, Morgan underwrote and distributed bonds for foreign corporations and governments in the United States, and in 1967, it established its first physical presence abroad. In collaboration with an affiliate of Morgan Guaranty Trust Co., Morgan Stanley established a new company in Paris to manage and participate in the underwriting and distribution of securities. In 1975, Morgan acquired complete ownership of the entity, which then became Morgan Stanley International. The firm also opened a representative office in Tokyo in 1971, an investment bank in Montreal in 1972, and a London office in 1977.

Morgan Stanley entered real estate in 1969 by entering mortgage banking through a partnership with one of that business's largest firms. Subsequently, Morgan established a wholly owned real-estate-development subsidiary.

After the diversifications of the early 1970s, the firm did not keep pace with the diversifications of other firms, and by 1981, large gaps in Morgan Stanley's production lines had become evident. In addition to being weak or not a presence in such trading areas as commercial paper, foreign exchange, and mortgage-backed securities, the firm came late to leveraged buyouts and the fast-expanding municipal bond area (*Institutional Investor*, June 1984, pp. 86–94). Between 1982 and 1984, the firm engaged in another burst of diversifications intended to enable it to regain its stature. It added commercial paper, gold, and futures trading, foreign exchange, municipal finance, mortgage-backed securities, and leveraged buyouts.

Morgan has followed a strategy of enticing established leaders from other firms to open up an unfamiliar line of business. These new arrivals, some brought in as partners, have been given virtual autonomy to implement detailed business plans approved by management. A firm executive conceded that "we seem to have taken longer to make decisions (on diversifications) than we should have." On the other hand, he pointed out: "When we do move, we have a deep commitment. That carries a lot of weight when you're trying to get people to join you in very senior roles" (*Institutional Investor*, June 1984, p. 94).

In the 1980s Morgan was one of the most profitable firms in the industry. It was the first firm to establish a full-time mergers and acquisitions group (in 1972) and has been a strong player in this profitable area. It has been one of the most active program traders, and its relatively new merchant-banking group has been highly profitable; indeed, the merchant-banking group may have contributed as much as half of the firm's $442 million profit in 1989 (*Forbes*, February 19, 1990, pp. 94–98).

Morgan has been successful at maintaining a certain uniqueness or mystique even among investment bankers. One difference that contributed to this mystique was the firm's approach to its relationships with its clients. It insisted on being the sole manager of any of the deals it underwrote, even into the 1980s. The *Wall Street Journal* reported that in 1979, when IBM demanded that Morgan share managership of a $1 billion issue of notes and debentures with Salomon Brothers, Morgan walked out of the deal, even though it meant losing IBM as a client (*Wall Street Journal,* July 17, 1980, p. 19). Morgan was very effective as sole manager in the 1960s: On the basis of proportional credit to the managing underwriter, Morgan Stanley was the leading underwriter of the 1960s. From 1960 to 1969, Morgan Stanley was the manager or comanager on 183 issues for $12.3 billion, compared with $11.7 billion on 484 issues for its nearest rival, First Boston (*Investment Dealers Digest,* 1970, p. 308). Following First Boston was Lehman Brothers, with 495 issues for $7.9 billion. The numbers show that Morgan Stanley did many fewer underwritings than its closest competitors, but that on most of those offerings it did not share managership with any other underwriter. Of course, the firm no longer maintains this policy, but it continues to exhibit a certain uniqueness.

SALOMON BROTHERS

Salomon Brothers was founded in 1910 by three brothers with $5,000 in capital. By the late 1920s, the firm had become prominent as a bond-trading house, even though it did not do much underwriting (Harvard Business School, case 1-380-140 [1980]). During the 1930s, the bond market underwent a major change, with bond ownership shifting from individuals to institutions, and so much of the bond trading went to the "upstairs" bond-trading rooms of firms like Salomon's that were equipped to block position.

In the 1960s, Salomon instituted curbs on capital withdrawal by partners, thereby becoming one of the best capitalized firms on Wall Street. The firm also built up its bond research capabilities with the addition of well-known research analysts, including economist Henry Kaufman. In response to the institutionalization of the equities markets, Salomon began the block trading of equities in the mid-1960s, and by 1969, it had become a strong player, willing to risk capital and position blocks that were difficult to sell. Salomon became the leader in the largest blocks, whereas on smaller blocks, institutions preferred to deal with brokers who provided research. Salomon there upon responded by establishing a research department for equities.

While a bond-trading powerhouse, Salomon had difficulty breaking into the ranks of the leading managing underwriters. Morgan Stanley's partners could rely on strong relationships with top executives at many Fortune 500 companies based on old school ties, but Salomon did not have these connections. Rather, it was a firm of traders who relied on a very sophisticated understanding of the market and good gambling instincts. In fact, thirteen of Salomon's twenty-eight general partners in 1970 lacked college degrees. Despite efforts to bring aboard personnel who would help the firm break into the top tier of underwriting, in 1977, Salomon Brothers was investment banker to fewer than 10 of the top 500 industrials. Only in the 1980s, with a breakdown in "relationship" banking, did Salomon move into the ranks of the leading underwriters.

The firm set up a small operation in London in 1968 handling U.S. stock business. Then in 1973, it began a trading operation in London—its first outside the United

States—trading Eurodollar certificates of deposit and then Yankee bonds. In 1975, it entered the expanding Eurobond market and, based on its willingness to handle huge blocks at low spreads, became one of the top six Eurobond-trading firms. Some of foreign governments that were Salomon's customers in the United States began to use the firm to underwrite their Eurobond issues. In 1976, Salomon established its second foreign branch, in Hong Kong.

The firm increased its equipment-leasing business and began trading financial futures for its own account in 1977, and later on for its customers as well. Salomon was at this point a significant player in the mergers and acquisitions business. Ira Harris, hired by Salomon from Blair in 1969, was credited with building this business. By the 1970s, Salomon also was in the oil and gas business.

In 1981, Salomon was acquired by Philbro, a large worldwide commodities-trading firm. At the time of the acquisition, Philbro was much larger than Salomon. But as the 1980s progressed, the securities side of the business grew in dramatic leaps while the commodities business tumbled following the collapse of demand for commodities from 1982 to 1984. Eventually, Salomon executives took control of the firm from the Philbro executives and sold a number of commodities businesses. Salomon remained, however, in the oil commodities business, earning high profits with the outbreak of the Persian Gulf War in 1991.

The markets of the 1980s were perfect for Salomon Brothers. Enormous growth in the government bond market, interest rate volatility, stock market volatility, and the development of new financial theories all played to its strengths. Salomon Brothers became perhaps the leading financial innovator on Wall Street, with mortgage-backed bonds, interest rate swaps, zero coupon bonds, and other novel instruments (*Institutional Investor,* March 1986, p. 70).

It is interesting that many of the firm's most important strategic decisions were made without exhaustive study and planning. For example, the managing partner of the firm during the 1960s and 1970s, William R. Salomon, stated that the decision to move into large block stock trading in 1967, to move overseas in 1969, and to form a corporate finance department in the late 1960s all were "made by a few executive partners." He also said that the firm did not have massive deliberations on these issues, that things were done informally (*Business Week*, April 3, 1978, p. 79). Another executive was quoted in 1986 as implying the firm does not rely on a detailed, long-term strategy. As an example, he pointed to the firm's decision, made with virtually no debate, to establish a foreign-exchange group and let it expand at its own pace. In three years the group had grown from two to thirty people.

Mortgage-backed securities illustrate the benefit that can result from good decisions. From an uncertain start and several difficult years, the department finally took off. By 1986, the mortgage and real-estate finance department had more than 300 professionals and was reported to account for as much as 30 percent of Salomon's pretax income in 1984.

The strategy that Salomon followed in developing new products was described by the *Institutional Investor:*

[The firm] is well aware that although volume is the key to significant revenues in fixed income trading, there isn't a great deal to be earned on the basis of volume alone, as margins are slim and under constant pressure. So the best way to make money is to create new volume. The strategy allows Salomon to enjoy wide margins in the early stages of a product's life cycle (in structuring financing and in underwriting), than to create a secondary market and finally to bring in huge trading programs for institutional clients. (March 1986, p. 70)

Mobility of resources is also an element in Salomon's diversification approach. "Here, people, capital and technology are highly mobile. We don't need five years to decide to move in a new direction," said Robert Salomon, Jr., managing director (*Institutional Investor*, March 1986, p. 71).

Toward the end of the 1980s, Salomon was faulted for not playing a significant role in mergers and acquisitions, merchant banking, and junk bonds. *Business Week* (February 27, 1989, pp. 98–103) discussed the infighting that kept Salomon behind in junk bonds. One reason cited was that the firm did not want to jeopardize its reputation as a high-grade underwriter by moving into the riskier world of junk bonds and corporate raiders. Another reason was infighting among the firm's traders and bankers over the structure and management of the unit. In retrospect, Salomon chairman John H. Gutfreund admitted that he should have demanded a better organizational plan for the management of the junk bond unit (*Business Week*, February 27, 1989, p. 103).

Salomon's culture is quite different from that of Merrill Lynch or Morgan Stanley. It was a trading culture that was perfect for the volatile markets of the 1980s. Salomon emphasized its distribution power as a way to attract investment-banking clients, and it worked. And Salomon had a reputation for playing hardball both inside and outside the firm. Yet these days this is not the image that the firm wants to convey to the outside world. Senior Salomon officials talk about consensus seeking, collegiality, and meritocracy. The firm rightfully prides itself on the successes of some of its employees who did not come to the firm with typical investment-banking credentials. A notable example is Lewis Ranieri, who joined Salomon in 1966 at age nineteen as a $70-a-week night clerk in the mailroom while attending St. John's University part-time. Within a short time, he was a bond trader and eventually was credited with being a key developer of the mortgage-backed securities market (*Business Week*, August 17, 1987, p. 90). Ranieri was made a vice president at twenty-six, a general partner three years later, and in 1984 the youngest member of the executive committee. He did, however, resign from the firm in 1987, in the course of a firm reorganization.

Salomon's Treasury-Bidding Scandal

In April 1991, three members of senior management at Salomon Brothers—John Gutfreund, Thomas Strauss, and John Meriwether—were informed that Paul Mozer, the head of the firm's government trading desk, had submitted a false bid of $3.15 billion in an auction of U.S. Treasury securities on February 21, 1991.[2] John Meriwether (vice chairman of Salomon) was Mozer's superior. Thomas Strauss (president of Salomon) was Meriwether's superior. John Gutfreund (chairman and chief executive officer) was Strauss' superior. The executives were also informed by Donald Feuerstein, the firm's chief legal officer, that the submission of the false bid appeared to be a criminal act and, although not legally required, should be reported to the government. Gutfreund and Strauss agreed to report the matter to the Federal Reserve

Bank of New York. Mozer, a managing director, was told that his actions might threaten his future with the firm and would be reported to the government. For months, however, none of the executives took action to investigate the matter or to discipline or impose limitations on Mozer. The violation was also not reported to the government for a number of months. During that period, Mozer committed additional violations of the federal securities laws in connection with two subsequent auctions of Treasury securities.

Gutfreund, Strauss, and Meriwether were not charged by the Securities and Exchange Commission with any participation in the underlying violations. However, the SEC believed that their supervision was deficient and that this failure was compounded by the delay in reporting the matter to the government.

The SEC emphasized the responsibility of broker-dealers to properly supervise their employees and pointed out that it is imperative, especially in larger organizations, for those in authority to quickly act on any indications of irregularity. Further, there must be an adequate follow-up and review, and, if more than one supervisor is involved, there must be a clear definition of the efforts to be taken and a clear assignment of those responsibilities to specific individuals within the firm. Supervisors are also required to increase supervision of involved employees and to place appropriate limitations on their activities. The fact that these steps were delayed or nonexistent led the SEC to conclude that Meriwether, Strauss, and Gutfreund should be held accountable for their individual supervisory errors.

The Economics and the Ethics of the Case

Smith (1992) used Salomon's bond-trading scandal to illustrate the relationship between ethics and economics in a free market. During the week the scandal became public, Salomon's stock dropped by one-third, representing a loss of $1.5 billion in market value. The loss suggested that the market expected Salomon to bear costs far in excess of the fines and other costs arising from expected legal and regulatory sanctions.

Whenever it is difficult to determine the quality of a product or service prior to purchase, buyers will reduce their demand prices to reflect their uncertainty. The damage to Salomon's reputation as a result of the bidding scandal reduced the expected value of its underwriting business as potential customers found it difficult to determine the quality of Salomon's service. The firm's ability to ''certify'' a new issue was impaired and concerns were raised concerning its future viability.

While Salomon's bond underwriting was satisfactory, its stock underwriting, far more sensitive to the quality of the underwriter, was significantly affected by the incidents. Salomon experienced reduced demand volume and had to accept reduced demand prices from clients in order to get the stock-underwriting business. Also, in a class-action suit stemming from the buyout of Revco Drug Stores, Inc., Salomon agreed to pay $30 million to the security holders. The scandal may have contributed to a less favorable settlement because this additional suit would likely consume much managerial time and the firm's bargaining position was impaired as a result of its loss of credibility.

These loses are only part of those that are relevant to the firm. Of the losses that cannot be directly measured in terms of dollar value is the loss of valuable employees because of the firm's uncertain future. Because coordinated teams of employees throughout the organization take years to develop, personnel losses could affect the firm's productivity and competitiveness.

Smith observes that markets impose significant costs on individuals and firms that engage in unethical behavior. Ethical behavior is profitable. A more widespread understanding of the costs of unethical behavior, combined with corporate reward systems that give employees incentives to act ethically, would surely result in fewer ethical-conduct violations.

Effects of the Scandal on Salomon's Long-Term Health

Salomon was able to survive this problem. With $139 billion in assets—and with most of that in high-quality government and other securities—the firm was in a much stronger financial position than was Drexel before its downfall. (Drexel's assets consisted mainly of illiquid junk bonds.) And it is the quality of Salomon's assets that gives the firm its real liquidity. As Donald S. Howard, Salomon's chief financial officer, stated, the firm had the most liquid balance sheet of all U.S. financial institutions (*Business Week,* September 9, 1991, pp. 78–80).

Fortunately, Salomon had developed a financial crisis–management plan for the firm two years before the scandal. Although the plan's architects never thought it would be used to save Salomon from its own transgressions, it is seen as a critical element in the firm's strategy to stem the damages from the scandal. The plan took advantage of the liquidity of the firm's assets, by replacing its entire $6.9 billion in outstanding commercial paper with repurchase agreements. The firm also developed lines of credit, committed loans that could be borrowed from banks, and reduced inventory positions and other assets in order to raise cash.

CONCLUSION

It is clear from the history of these three firms that securities firms make diversification choices in an environment of uncertainty and risk—that is, an environment of bounded rationality. Sometimes firms must respond quickly to opportunities that present themselves as the result of other firms' misfortunes. Sometimes diversifications are part of a well-thought-out plan. The firms must be flexible enough to respond to the changing environment, but also must be able to adjust when their efforts are not completely successful.

It does not appear that most of the diversifications discussed in this chapter include a well-thought-out strategy to erect barriers to entry to a line of business. Nor does it appear that once one of these firms makes a commitment to enter a new line, it faces any strategic barriers.

Although there are risks inherent in diversification, it is clear that none of these three firms would be as effective a competitor in the world's securities markets if it could not provide a relatively wide range of financial services. The analysis of this book and this chapter therefore concludes that if U.S. firms are to remain competitive both domestically and internationally, they must be allowed the freedom to adapt their organizations to changing economic conditions despite the risks and occasional setbacks along the way. Regulatory concerns about the riskiness of new products and new lines of business must be balanced by an understanding of the adverse consequences of restricting innovation and diversification.

NOTES

1. For a humorous look at working at Salomon Brothers, see Lewis (1989).

2. U.S. Securities and Exchange Commission Release No. 34-31554 (December 3, 1992). This release contains a discussion of the SEC's findings in this case.

16

Competition in the
International Securities Markets

Competition among securities firms is now worldwide, with many U.S. firms staffing large offices in London, Tokyo, and other foreign financial capitals. Foreign firms also have made inroads into U.S. securities markets. The top four Japanese securities firms, larger in size than the largest U.S. firms, are attempting to increase their presence in many U.S. securities lines. At the same time, U.S. firms have had significant success in Japanese securities markets.

DEVELOPMENTS IN WORLD SECURITIES MARKETS

During the 1980s, stock markets around the world experienced bull markets, with world stock market capitalization increasing from $2.7 trillion in 1980 to $11.4 trillion in 1991. The U.S. market's share, however, fell during this period, and by 1987, Japan had surpassed the United States as the world's largest equity market in terms of market capitalization. Then a decline in the Japanese stock market in 1990 and 1991 put the United States back on top. But even though the equities markets of the industrialized countries grew rapidly in the 1980s, the stock markets of some less-developed countries grew at an even faster pace.[1]

In the 1980s, regulatory barriers came down around the world. The "big bang" in London and the regulatory restructuring associated with the passage of the United Kingdom Financial Services Act in 1986 is probably the most noteworthy. Not only were stock brokerage commission rates deregulated on the London Stock Exchange (LSE), but the United Kingdom's domestic securities markets were opened up by permitting foreign financial-service firms to become members of the LSE. The Financial Services Act also provided for investor protection safeguards not unlike those found in U.S. securities markets.

Canada and France also took steps to restructure their domestic securities markets and to open their markets to greater foreign participation. Canada now permits foreign ownership of Canadian securities firms and greater diversification by formerly specialized financial institutions.[2] France's stock market was opened to greater foreign participation ("le petit bang"). French financial institutions were also permitted a wider range of securities activities, including membership on the stock exchange, which was previously limited to brokers who had a monopoly on stock trading. The French government is even attempting to promote broader stock ownership among individuals (*Wall Street Journal,* November 5, 1986, p. 1).

In Spain, a major reform of the Spanish stock market began in 1987. One of its most significant aspects was the establishment of a national securities market commission similar to the U.S. Securities and Exchange Commission (SEC). In 1988, the Netherlands' Central Bank announced the formation of a new organization to strengthen that country's position in the international market for financial services.

As Europe progresses toward a unified capital market, it is believed that the members of the European Economic Community (EEC) will harmonize their investor protection regulations in banking and securities or operate on the principle of mutual recognition of one another's regulations.

STOCK MARKET CAPITALIZATION

The explosive growth in the world's stock market capitalization over the past decade was fueled by the bull market of the 1980s. From 1980 to 1991, U.S. stock market capitalization (all stock exchanges and the over-the-counter NASDAQ market) increased by 189 percent, and the equity markets outside the United States increased by 470 percent (Table 16-1). The U.S. share of global equity market capitalization dropped from 53.3 percent in 1980 to 36.7 percent in 1991.

The decline in the U.S. share of the world's equity markets can be attributed in part to the decline of the dollar, which began in early 1985. But several other factors were also important. Although U.S. stock prices appreciated rapidly by historical

Table 16-1. Global Equity Markets' Capitalization, 1980–1991 (Market Value in $ Billion)

Country	1980	1986	1987	1988	1989	1990	1991
United States	1,448	2,637	2,589	2,794	3,506	3,090	4,186
Japan	380	1,843	2,803	3,907	4,393	2,918	3,131
United Kingdom	205	440	681	771	827	868	1,003
Germany	72	258	213	252	365	379	393
France	55	150	172	245	365	342	374
Canada	118	166	219	242	291	242	267
Switzerland	38	132	129	141	104	166	180
Netherlands	29	84	86	114	158	149	169
Italy	3	140	120	135	169	149	154
Spain	17	49	71	175	123	111	148
Australia	60	94	172	183	137	107	145
South Africa	100	103	129	126	131	138	124
Hong Kong	NA	54	54	74	77	83	122
Sweden	13	63	71	100	119	92	97
Other developed markets	93	157	184	230	331	244	266
All emerging markets	86	145	201	368	611	472	643
World	2,715	6,514	7,893	9,857	11,706	9,548	11,403

Source: Securities Industry Association, *Fact Book,* various issues.

standards, many foreign stock markets displayed larger price increases than did those in the United States. Whereas the supply of stock generally expanded overseas, the supply of stock publicly traded in the United States contracted during the 1980s. In the United States, a significant increase in tender offers, leveraged buyouts, and corporate repurchase programs during this period substantially reduced market capitalization.

Even though $171 billion in common stock (gross) was registered with the SEC from 1980 to mid-year 1988, the Federal Reserve Board estimated that the amount of equity capital removed from the market exceeded the supply of new issues by nearly $350 billion. In contrast, *net* bond financing by U.S. corporations increased by $475 billion over this period.

The expansion of foreign stock markets, conversely, benefited from the rapid stock appreciation accompanied by the increased public float associated with the privatization of many state-owned enterprises. Privatizations raised equity market capitalization not only in Europe and Japan but also in a number of less-developed capital markets.

The Japanese market was the world's fastest growing equity market through the 1980s, and in 1987, Japan surpassed the United States as the world's largest equity market in terms of market capitalization. Nevertheless, because of the large amount of intercompany holding of Japanese shares, the amount of stock available to trade on any particular day was not as large as that available in the U.S. stock market. The 1990s, however, have so far not been as rewarding for the Japanese market: The Nikkei index of 225 Japanese stock dropped 49 percent from its peak in December 1989 to March 1992 (*Wall Street Journal,* March 19, 1992, p. C-1).

Although the equity markets of the leading industrialized countries have grown rapidly in recent years, the stock markets of some of the newly industrialized countries, known as emerging markets, have grown even more quickly.[3] The stock markets of the Group of Seven industrialized countries (the G-7 nations), excluding Japan, grew at annual rate of 14 percent from 1982 to 1988 (measured in U.S. dollars), and the emerging stock markets grew at an annual rate of 26 percent.[4]

The securities markets of less-developed countries (LDCs) have also become more integrated into global securities markets. Foreign portfolio investment in these countries has increased substantially as more emerging markets have opened to foreign investment. In 1989, there were nine closed-end country funds listed on U.S. stock exchanges that invest exclusively in the emerging securities markets. As recently as 1984, the Mexico Fund and the Korea Fund were the only closed-end country funds listed on a U.S. stock exchange that pooled securities from LDC markets. Closed-end country funds investing in Taiwan, Thailand, Brazil, India, and Malaysia also have been listed on U.S. stock exchanges. In addition, funds investing in less-developed capital markets are traded in London and in other major financial centers around the world.

Investment abroad by Americans expanded dramatically in the 1980s as foreign markets exceeded U.S. performance. In 1988, gross transactions by U.S. investors in foreign corporate stocks totaled over $151 billion, down from the record total of over $189 billion in 1987, but still representing almost nine times the total of such transactions in 1980. Gross U.S. transactions in foreign debt securities amounted to $445 billion in 1988, more than a twelvefold increase since 1980. American investors' net investment in foreign stocks in 1988 came to $1.7 billion, with their net investment in foreign debt securities totaling $10 billion.[5]

UNITED STATES FIRMS IN LONDON

In anticipation of the "big bang" in London in 1986, American banks and securities firms quickly enlarged their London presence. Total staffing at Credit Suisse/First Boston, Drexel Burnham Lambert, Goldman Sachs, Merrill Lynch, Salomon Brothers, and Shearson Lehman increased from 2,311 in 1984 to 5,519 in 1986 (*New York Times,* September 28, 1986, p. F-8).

The major firms were attempting to build a "critical mass" in sales, trading, and investment banking. Japanese securities firms also built up a large London presence, and the result was to add capacity to markets with existing overcapacity.[6] The buildup was also in response to a surge in Euromarket activity from 1983 to 1986, as the volume of new Eurobond and Euroequity issues increased nearly fourfold, to $191.7 billion (*New York Times,* September 20, 1987, p. F-29). This surge was fueled by a worldwide trend toward easing government restrictions on capital flows and the rush by countries, corporations, and supranational institutions to securitize their debt and reduce bank loans with tradable securities.

Growth in the market slowed in 1987 as Eurobond issues dropped by 25 percent and many U.S. firms cut back their London staffs. The overall London-based Euromarket industry experienced a shakeout that eliminated about 10,000 jobs in 10 months (*Wall Street Journal,* March 29, 1988, p. 24). During this period, there was also a shift away from dollar-denominated issues as the dollar fell relative to other currencies. Some argue that the Euromarket's difficulties began with the 1984 repeal of the U.S. withholding tax on interest paid to foreign bondholders, which made domestic bonds, particularly U.S. Treasuries, more attractive to international borrowers. Another factor was the U.S. mergers and acquisitions boom. Top-rated Eurobonds issued by U.S. corporations turned overnight into noninvestment-grade junk bonds.

Courtadon (1985) examined the competitive structure of the Eurobond underwriting industry. The purpose of her study was twofold: (1) to identify the shifts since 1979 in market share, borrower loyalty, the economic rents available to underwriters, and the conditions giving rise to these changes; and (2) to use this information to assess the major factors shaping future competitive conditions in the Eurobond-underwriting industry. Based on data from 1979 to 1984, she found that the market share in the largest sectors of the Eurobond market was increasingly concentrated in very few of the uppermost lead managers. Despite this, competition did increase in the industry owing to the greater rivalry between the top-tier lead managers and the greater number of lead managers overall.[7]

COMPETITION WITH THE
JAPANESE SECURITIES INDUSTRY

Japanese Securities Firms

A fixed-commission-rate system is still in place in Japan. The artificially high commission rates, combined with the booming Japanese securities markets and the appreciation of the yen relative to the dollar resulted in Japanese securities firms that dwarf U.S. and other competitors. Table 16-2 shows the market capitalization of the "Big Four" Japanese securities firms—Nomura Securities, Daiwa Securities, Nikko Securities, and Yamaichi Securities—compared with the three largest U.S. firms at the end of 1986 and in 1990. Nomura, the largest securities firm in the world, had almost seven times the capitalization of Salomon Brothers, the largest U.S. firm in 1986. In 1990, Nomura had 3.6 times the capital of the largest U.S. firm (Merrill Lynch).

Even though the Tokyo Stock Exchange is gradually bringing down its commission rate to be more in line with those of New York and London, Japanese securities firms benefit enormously from the artificially high rates (*Wall Street Journal*, November 2, 1987, p. 27). Commissions accounted for 53.4 percent of revenues for Nomura, 22.9 percent for Merrill Lynch, and only 3.2 percent for Salomon in 1986 (data from *Annual Reports*).

Both Japanese securities firms and Japanese banks also benefit from the high savings rate of the Japanese people, which is higher than that of any other nation and can be traced to several factors. One is the society's ethic of thriftiness, another is intense savings by parents to finance their children's education; and a third is the lack of adequate pension schemes for wage earners, which forces Japanese workers to put away a significant portion of their earnings for their retirement. Finally, government-imposed savings incentives were used after World War II to supply the funds necessary to rebuild the Japanese economy. The main measure was to free

Table 16-2. Market Capitalization of Four Largest Japanese and U.S. Securities Firms, 1986 and 1990 ($ Billion)

	Market Capitalization	
Firm	1986	1990
Japan		
Nomura Securities Co.	$33.6	$14.7
Daiwa Securities Co.	—	7.9
Nikko Securities Co.	—	6.1
Yamaichi Securities Co.	11.0	6.1
United States		
Salomon Brothers, Inc.	$ 5.9	$ 2.8
Shearson Lehman Brothers, Inc.	—	2.0
Merrill Lynch, Pierce, Fenner & Smith, Inc.	4.0	3.2

Source: 1986: Securities Industry Association, *Yearbook,* 1987/1988; 1990: *New York Times,* March 10, 1991, sec. 7, p. 6.

certain types of savings accounts from taxes. The most important kind of tax-free savings account today is with the postal savings system. Deposits accumulated through its 23,000 postal outlets equal over $600 billion, making it the largest body of savings in the world, greater than the four largest commercial banks in Japan combined. The lucrative postal savings system's money is tightly controlled and managed by an inner core of Japanese securities firms (Wright and Pauli 1987, p. 48).

The Termite Strategy

Wright and Pauli (1987) see the Japanese as having as a goal the domination of the world market for financial services. They suggest that Japanese securities firms will employ the strategy that was used to enable Japanese firms to take over other industries, like the automobile and the semiconductor chip. Wright and Pauli call this the *termite strategy* because it involves no master plan and no single leader to orchestrate the steps. Yet each Japanese securities firm is driven toward the same target, each seeking to maximize its strengths and minimize its weaknesses, seeking out the areas of greatest demand and the path of least resistance from competitors. With this strategy, there is no big thrust for the target, no single front line, just a thousand small steps.

In following this strategy, Japanese firms identify segments of an industry and enter a suitable one. Then they join with domestic competitors in other segments in which the know-how or technology is superior to that of the Japanese. After establishing themselves in foreign markets through high quality and low prices, they are accused of dumping. Then at the request of the foreign government, they raise their prices. The increased prices means high profits for Japan. The Japanese then transfer the high value-added operations to Japan. Profits and expertise flow back to Japan while the lower value-added jobs are reinstated abroad under the umbrella of Japanese investment. Finally, the Japanese take over failing companies and finance research and scholarships at leading Western universities to secure access to the most recent research and best-trained graduates.

Thurow (1992, p. 185) offered another version of this story: American firms set high return-on-investment (ROI) goals. Japanese firms force the ROIs below these hurdle rates with aggressive pricing in some market segments. In time, the U.S. firms retreat from that segment, since they are not making the necessary ROI. Once that market segment is conquered, the Japanese firms move on to price aggressively in some other market segment.

The way that this strategy is unfolding in the United States, it could be argued, is that the Japanese have entered the financial services market through the government-lending segment, to which margins are crucial and the government's appetite seems insatiable. The Japanese have already entered into a number of joint ventures with successful U.S. securities firms in order to acquire unique American know-how. Nomura acquired 20 percent of Wasserstein, Perrilla and Co., mergers and acquisitions specialists, and Nikko has a 20 percent interest in the Blackstone Group, another New York merger firm (*New York Times,* June 11, 1989, p. F-1). Other Japanese financial organizations have acquired an interest in U.S. firms: Sumitomo

Bank acquired a 12.5 percent stake in Goldman Sachs, and Nippon Life Insurance Co. acquired a 13 percent interest in Shearson Lehman (*New York Times,* April 12, 1987, p. E-14). And Nomura Securities endowed both a $1.6 million chair at the Massachusetts Institute of Technology and a $1.5 million chair at New York University (Wright and Pauli 1987, p. 74).

Strategic Response

Wright and Pauli contend that unless the U.S. government, industry, and consumers understand this strategy, we will design the wrong policies, ask for protection that will not help, and seek cooperative arrangements that will result in draining our expertise to our major competitors. They suggest strategic responses by both the private sector and the government. Strategies for the government that appear beneficial to our securities industry include developing a comprehensive and finely tuned statistical framework and identifying potential areas of competitive advantage for the U.S. securities industry relative to its foreign competitors; creating a truly integrated policy for all traditional financial services sectors; relaxing antitrust legislation; and monitoring those financial strategies and policies of competitive nations that affect our securities industry.

Japanese governmental agencies perform an important role in helping the private sector identify areas of potential comparative advantage. Japan's Ministry of International Trade and Industry (MITI) and other government-sponsored think tanks perform a valuable service to their private sector by undertaking macroeconomic studies and providing strategic guidance to their private sector. Japanese securities organizations even go as far as translating into Japanese many of the research reports written by the SEC's Directorate of Economic and Policy Analysis. Japanese securities officials have been frequent visitors to the SEC, asking questions about various aspects of its regulatory programs, and they have also been interested in the availability from the SEC of structure–conduct–performance data on the U.S. securities industry.

Recent Performance of Japanese Securities Firms in New York

After more than five years of heavy spending on staff, office space, and computers and the commitment of hundreds of millions of dollars of capital, the Big Four Japanese firms—Nomura, Yamaichi, Nikko, and Daiwa—have had mixed results on Wall Street. In 1989, they were scaling back their presence (*Wall Street Journal,* June 11, 1989, p. C-1), cutting back sharply in the mainstream businesses in which they had been trying to build a presence—underwriting and trading equities and corporate bonds.

The Big Four firms have failed to establish strong bonds of trust with major corporate and institutional clients, which can take years to build. The result is that they have had to cut their staffs. Nomura cut its staff in the United States to about 500 from 650; Daiwa cut its staff from more than 400 to 360; Nikko cut back from 370 to 260; and Yamaichi also made a small cut.

These firms have had more success in the low margin, so-called commodities businesses, such as buying and selling Treasury securities for customers. And this has resulted less from acumen or the development of strong relationships with U.S. customers than from contracts with Japanese institutional investors. Japanese institutions are buying large amounts of American securities and having a powerful effect on U.S. markets. Because U.S. institutional investors would like to follow the Japanese institutions, American institutions have given Japanese securities firms some of their business. Nomura has had success in one high-tech area: In the spring of 1992, it was the leading program trader in New York.

Another problem has been that Japanese investors' taste for U.S. equities has been, at best, mercurial. In 1988, the Japanese bought only $3 billion of foreign stocks, most, but not all, of which were U.S. stocks, which is much less than the $16.87 billion they added in 1987 (*Wall Street Journal,* June 5, 1989, p. C-1).

Japanese firms have not turned to acquisitions of broker-dealers for growth. Rather, their reluctance to follow that route, despite the large capitalization of Japanese firms relative to that of U.S. firms, is based on the fear that a Japanese firm could pay a bundle for a company, only to see the good employees leave (*Wall Street Journal,* April 1, 1989, p. C-1).

United States Firms in Japan

In the 1980s, U.S. and European securities firms built up a strong presence in Japan. With New York and London, Tokyo has become the third leg of the international capital market. In addition to the enormous capital available in the Japanese market, Tokyo provides a different time zone from those of New York and London as stock trading moves to a twenty-four-hour trading day. American firms were initially attracted by the opportunity to sell U.S. Treasury securities to Japanese investors. American and European firms also sought to serve European, American, Middle Eastern, and Asian investors who were buying Japanese securities. Now, however, U.S. and foreign brokers want to be more than purveyors of foreign stock; they want to handle block trades for Japanese insurance companies and pension funds and function as full-service companies in Japan's domestic capital markets.

In 1986, responding to prolonged pressure from foreign governments, the Tokyo Stock Exchange (TSE) granted memberships (seats) to Merrill Lynch, Goldman Sachs, Morgan Stanley, and two British securities firms. Each firm paid around $5 million for its seat. In 1987, the TSE opened up sixteen new memberships to foreign securities firms. The U.S. firms admitted were Prudential-Bache, Smith Barney, Salomon Brothers, Kidder Peabody, First Boston, and Shearson. Other foreign firms admitted included four from Britain, two from France, two from Germany, and two from Switzerland. The new members paid around $8.6 million each for the seats (*New York Times,* December 17, 1987, p. D-2).

As of 1987, Salomon Brothers had 286 persons in its Tokyo office. Merrill Lynch, which has been in Japan for nearly three decades, employed 400 people there in 1987 and had several offices outside Tokyo. Morgan Stanley had a Tokyo staff of 430, and First Boston's was up to 185 (*Business Week,* September 7, 1987, p. 90).

Characteristics of Japanese Securities Markets

Japan's stock markets have several characteristics that differ from those of U.S. markets. One is that individuals have been the dominant traders on the TSE despite an increase in institutional and block trading in recent years. One factor responsible for this difference is Japan's tax law. Dividends are taxed, whereas capital gains (up to fifty trades, totaling no more than 200,000 shares a year) are tax free. Individuals accounted for about 55 percent of trades in 1983, and almost half of those trades were for margin accounts (*Forbes,* June 4, 1984, p. 54). This arrangement provides speculative interest to investing and adds depth and liquidity to a market that tends to be thin and volatile. Rapid price changes are the rule on the TSE, because in many issues there is comparatively little stock. This scarcity is a direct result of the fact that major industrial groups like Sumitomo, Mitsui, and Mitsubishi all own pieces of many of their publicly traded subsidiaries. Beyond these links lies a network of other inside holdings between manufacturer and supplier, bank and client, which are expressions of goodwill. All of these so-called policy investments are locked in and unlikely to move unless the unthinkable happens to break up this time-honored relationship. It is also common practice for a bank, a brokerage firm, or another intermediary to step in and help make sure that a block of loose stock does not wind up in the wrong hands.

Another factor that stabilizes ownership in Japan is "pure investment." For example, Yamaichi Securities might never sell its 2.2 percent interest in Mitsubishi Metal because it is one of the companies that it underwrites. Thus stock ownership helps cement business ties.

The Success of Japanese Firms in the Eurobond Market

Despite their limited success in New York, Japanese securities firms have had significant success in the Euromarket. In underwriting international bonds, Japanese firms have raised their relative position from that of 1980. In 1980, Nomura was ranked eighth, Daiwa thirteenth, and Yamaichi fifteenth. (Nikko was not ranked among the top twenty-five.) Then in 1989, Nomura was first, Daiwa second, Yamaichi third, and Nikko fourth. In 1990, Nomura was first, Daiwa fifth, Nikko ninth, and Yamaichi tenth, and in 1991, Nomura was first, Daiwa second, Yamaichi eleventh, and Nikko twelfth (*Institutional Investor,* various issues). But the Japanese firms' success was not just a reflection of the rise of yen-denominated issues; the Big Four also had similar success in new dollar–Eurobond issues.

The Success of U.S. Firms in Tokyo

American firms have had success in Tokyo using their skills at trading futures, options and other innovative "derivative" instruments, and program trading to win major corporate finance clients away from Tokyo's Big Four securities houses. *Business Week* (February 4, 1991, pp. 74–75) reported that many U.S. securities executives believe that the Big Four are leaning hard on long-time clients to discourage them from giving underwriting business to U.S. firms. At the same time, the Big

Four are building their futures- and options-trading capabilities in New York. In the long run, they will be able to bring these capabilities to the Tokyo market and compete more effectively with U.S. firms in this crucial aspect of the business.

Also in response to the inroads by U.S. firms, Japanese regulators are dragging their feet on their commitments to more open markets. For example, after permitting the introduction of stock index options and futures in 1988, the Ministry of Finance imposed trading limits early in 1990, despite protests by Salomon Brothers and Morgan Stanley. The Japanese are also slowing the introduction of new products. In 1990, the Tokyo Stock Exchange pressured the American Stock Exchange to stop listing its popular put and call warrants on the Nikkei average. These warrants, used by Salomon and others, allow investors to hedge Japanese stockholdings by placing long-term bets on whether the Nikkei will rise or fall. They were among the most heavily traded instruments on the Amex in 1990. With Japanese approval, the Amex has since introduced a new line of options based on the Tokyo market, but their appeal is limited because their three-month duration curbs their use in hedging.

CONCLUSION

American firms are strong competitors in international capital markets. Diversification into foreign securities markets is viewed as important to the long-run success of major U.S. securities firms. As markets become more global and trading becomes a twenty-four-hour-a-day activity, a strong presence in both the London and the Tokyo markets is viewed by many American firms as essential. Large U.S. firms aim to be a member of the worldwide oligopoly of securities firms that is expected to remain when the globalization of financial markets is complete.

It is clear that the Japanese have mounted a serious challenge to U.S. securities firms, both in the United States and in world markets. Given the success of Japanese competitors in other industries and the enormous capital resources of Japanese securities firms, the SEC should do all that it can to help U.S. firms face this challenge. As Wright and Pauli suggested, the SEC should actively work with U.S. securities firms, exchanges, and organizations to provide whatever support they might need. And it should more closely monitor the activities of Japan's MOF and MITI related to the securities industry. This would entail translating some of their documents into English.

NOTES

1. This section is based on Chuppe, Haworth, and Watkins (1989).

2. In Canada, commercial banks, securities broker-dealers, trust companies, and insurance companies are now permitted to offer the same financial products. In effect, Canada now permits investment-banking and commercial-banking services to be offered by the same financial institution. As a result, the United States and Japan, the two largest equity markets in the world, are the only major capital markets to maintain a separation between investment banking and commercial banking.

3. The International Finance Corporation classified twenty equity markets based in less-developed countries as emerging markets. These are the stock markets of Argentina, Brazil, Chile, Colombia,

Greece, India, Indonesia, Jordan, Malaysia, Mexico, Nigeria, Pakistan, Philippines, Portugal, South Korea, Taiwan, Thailand, Turkey, Venezuela, and Zimbabwe (*Emerging Markets Data Base* [Washington, D.C.: IFC, May 1988]).

4. The G-7 countries are the United States, Japan, Great Britain, Germany, Canada, France, and Italy.

5. Testimony of SEC chairman David S. Ruder before U.S. Senate Subcommittee on Securities, U.S. Senate Committee on Banking, Housing, and Urban Affairs, *Concerning the Globalization of the Securities Markets,* June 15, 1989.

6. The Euromarket is centered in London, and its largest segment is the Eurobond market. The term *Eurobond* is loosely applied to bonds that are offered outside the country of the borrower and usually outside the country in whose currency the securities are denominated.

7. For a discussion of investment banking in Europe, see also Walter and Smith (1990).

17

Performance of the Securities Industry

This chapter examines the performance of the securities industry and relates it to the analysis of structure and conduct in the previous chapters. Overall, the securities industry has performed well as a conduit to the financial markets for both borrowers and lenders. It has managed the large financial risks it takes in its business and has done so with very few firm failures and minimal losses to its customers.

Industrial organization studies attempt to identify the main forms of competition in an industry. The conclusion of this book is that innovation and diversification strategies are what drive this industry. That is, they are consciously chosen strategies that are intended to accomplish several different objectives. As an innovator, a firm has an opportunity to take customers away from rivals, perhaps permanently. Also, by following fast-second strategies, the larger firms not only prevent their other large competitors from taking away their customers, but also send a message to the mid-size and smaller firms that if they innovate, the large firms will act as fast seconds and prevent them from earning substantial profits from their innovation. Furthermore, successful firms realize that if they do not adapt their structure to changing market conditions, they will be unable to provide the range of services that their customers expect.

This chapter examines measures of performance to judge how well the industry has fulfilled its economic function. These performance measures include profitability, managerial effectiveness, risk management, technological progressiveness, and the stability of securities firms. Our performance analysis will provide the basis for the policy recommendations that follow in Chapter 18.

WHAT WE HAVE LEARNED FROM STRUCTURE AND CONDUCT ANALYSIS

The securities industry has relatively easy entry and exit: The number of National Association of Securities Dealers (NASD) member firms increased from 2,933 in 1980 to 6,722 in 1987 and fell to 5,576 in 1991 (Securities Industry Association, *Trends,* August 16, 1991, p. 3). The size distribution of firms is at loose oligopoly levels. The largest firms in the industry, the national full-line firms and investment-banking houses, dominate the industry in terms of pricing and innovation and diversification policies. The moderate concentration levels and the dominant position of these large firms permit the possibility of profit levels somewhat higher than competitive levels. That is, there may be some type of tacit cooperation among the largest firms.

Barometric pricing for individual brokerage suggests that price changes are related to cost changes. Brokerage on the institutional side is complicated by soft dollars. However, more recent pricing data indicate that despite some inefficiencies in the institutional brokerage market, institutional commissions are more flexible than they were in the past, reflecting more responsiveness to the declining costs associated with larger institutional orders.

Underwriting profits declined on some offerings with the introduction of shelf registration and are currently closer to competitive levels than in the past. A strong underwriting market does, however, produce healthy profits in investment banking. Shelf registration has also led to more bought deals; that is, investment bankers are taking down whole new issues and taking on the risk of distributing these larger portions. But even with shelf registration, the managing underwriters have been able to maintain at least partially the long-standing barriers to entry to this group.

There still is a substantial profit potential in traditional businesses. As 1991 revealed, the rise in stock prices and underwriting volume combined with increased activity by small investors and declining interest rates, all converged to return very high industrywide profits. In addition, innovative broker-dealers are able to enjoy transient supernormal profit opportunities with the introduction of some, but not all, of their new products. Computer-driven trading strategies relying on new financial instruments allow firms to take advantage of any momentary arbitrage profit opportunities in the securities markets. The new instruments give firms more hedging opportunities in increasingly volatile markets and a greater ability to manage risk.

The high-profit opportunities are related less to tacit cooperation among the firms than to a strategy of competition through innovation and diversification. Here innovators and fast seconds are able to capture these transient profits until the innovation or service is diffused throughout the industry. Although the innovators tend to limit entry into a new line by following a limit-pricing approach, eventually a broad range of firms will offer the new product, and profit margins will drop toward competitive levels.

LACK OF EVIDENCE OF WIDESPREAD COLLUSION IN THE INDUSTRY

Because of the interactive nature of the securities business, with firms trading with one another and cooperating on deals and underwriting, there is a potential for collusion. But despite the incidents discussed earlier, our analysis does *not* show any clear evidence of patterns of conduct suggesting that there currently are collusive arrangements among firms in this industry. Without specific cost data, we cannot determine with certainty that prices are close to competitive levels. However, considering the vigor of the competition among firms and the lack of any strong evidence of systematic, ongoing collusion, our structure and conduct analysis does indicate that competition in the industry is workable.

OVERALL PROFITABILITY IN THE SECURITIES INDUSTRY

Table 17-1 compares the profitability of securities firms, banks, and manufacturing firms. The average pretax return on equity for New York Stock Exchange (NYSE) firms doing a public business between 1972 and 1990 was 20.7 percent, compared with 14.2 percent for banks and 20 percent for all manufacturing firms.[1] The standard deviations of the returns for NYSE firms is 14.3 percent, compared with 3.1 for banks and 3.5 for all manufacturing firms.

Hay and Morris (1979, p. 217) show that the higher the risk level of an industry is, the higher its equilibrium profits will be. They also state that the variance of profits may be an acceptable proxy for risk. Table 17-1 shows that manufacturing corporations earned an average of 40.1 percent more profit than banks did, with only a 13 percent increase in the profit risk (standard deviation of profits). NYSE member firms earned only 3.5 percent more profit than did manufacturing firms but experienced 300 percent more profit risk than manufacturing firms did. In view of the high risk of the securities industry, it is clear that at least part of the return is a risk premium for the industry's investors.

Table 17-1. Pretax Return on Equity for NYSE Member Firms Doing a Public Business, All Insured Commercial Banks, and All Manufacturing Corporations

	NYSE Member Firms	Commercial Banks	All Manufacturing Corporations
1972	23.8%	15.0%	18.4%
1973	(2.5)	16.2	21.8
1974	1.5	15.7	23.4
1975	30.3	14.0	18.9
1976	32.0	13.7	22.7
1977	13.0	14.6	23.2
1978	20.3	17.3	24.5
1979	28.8	18.4	25.8
1980	46.8	18.1	21.9
1981	35.5	15.6	21.5
1982	37.0	13.8	14.1
1983	36.8	13.4	16.3
1984	13.3	13.0	19.2
1985	28.8	13.9	15.8
1986	28.3	12.4	14.8
1987	4.5	4.9	19.2
1988	9.5	17.3	22.6
1989	7.0	12.2	20.0
1990	(0.5)	10.7	15.3

Sources: NYSE member firms: *SEC Monthly Statistical Bulletin,* various issues; commercial banks: *FDIC Annual Report,* various issues; all manufacturing firms: U.S. Department of Commerce, *Quarterly Financial Reports for Manufacturing, Mining and Trade Corporations,* various issues.

Table 17-2. Pretax Return on Equity (In Percent)

Firm Category	1980	1981	1982	1983	1984	1985	1986	1987	1988	1989	1990	1991	Average 1981–1991
National full line	45.0	24.6	29.7	28.1	(2.6)	17.9	20.3	(2.1)	(0.7)	(0.3)	(8.3)	19.9	11.5
Large investment banks	55.7	56.7	54.8	43.8	31.1	38.5	34.2	9.2	18.2	9.2	5.4	25.2	29.7
Regionals	N.A.	37.2	36.0	40.5	6.8	29.0	32.7	14.0	5.4	10.4	1.0	34.9	22.5
New York City–based	N.A.	42.1	43.3	50.7	19.9	31.2	38.3	5.2	15.0	11.4	3.1	16.3	25.1
NYSE discounters	N.A.	52.2	53.9	46.8	0.8	25.6	49.5	19.7	5.0	14.5	15.4	35.5	29.0
All NYSE Firms	49.2	35.9	40.5	36.6	13.3	29.4	28.6	4.7	9.6	6.9	(0.7)	23.7	20.8

Source: Securities Industry Association, *Fact Book*, various issues.

Table 17-2 traces profitability by type of firm between 1981 and 1991. The most diversified firms, the national full-line firms, were the least profitable. Since they are the most diversified, their low profitability may mean that the overall synergy or economies of scope across business lines was not that strong. This result is consistent with the findings in Chapter 10, indicating diseconomies of scope for larger firms in the production of brokerage, market-making, and underwriting services.

Large investment banks were the most profitable group, with an average pretax return equity of 29.7 percent. They were the dominant underwriters, developed many of the industry's new products, and did much of the highly lucrative mergers and acquisitions (M&A) business. In explaining the returns in this industry, shown in Table 17-1, it should be kept in mind that a large part of these profits were earned by the investment bankers.

Regional firms doing a full-line business earned 22.5 percent on pretax equity, slightly more than all manufacturing firms did. These firms did not open new markets but did follow the lead of the more innovative firms into such areas as mortgage-backed and asset-backed securities and the M&A business.

New York City–based firms are like large investment banks in that they earn revenues from merchant banking, trading activities, and investment positions. Their profit trends were similar to those of investment banks.

Discounters had the highest average return on equity. Of course, these firms operate with very low levels of equity because they act primarily as agents.

DUPONT ANALYSIS OF PROFITS OF PUBLICLY HELD FIRMS

We will use the DuPont method to examine the profitability of publicly held firms, as this method brings together various financial ratios and shows how these ratios interact to determine the profitability of assets.[2] Table 17-3 shows the average return on equity between 1985 and 1989 of those broker-dealers whose financial information was available on Compustat.[3] The return on equity was divided into three fundamental factors of turnover, margin, and leverage:

Return on equity = Profit margin $\times$ Asset turnover $\times$ Financial leverage   (17-1)

These three fundamental factors are also expressed in terms of ratios:

$$\frac{\text{Net income}}{\text{Equity}} = \frac{\text{Net income}}{\text{Sales}} \times \frac{\text{Sales}}{\text{Total assets}} \times \frac{\text{Total assets}}{\text{Equity}} \qquad (17\text{-}2)$$

Firms were divided into the following categories: national full-line firms, large investment banks, discounters, regional firms, and other miscellaneous firms. Comparing national full-line firms, we see that A. G. Edwards is the most profitable firm as measured by return on equity. A. G. Edwards has been unique among national full-line firms in that it has been able to make the retail brokerage business highly profitable. This firm earned approximately 60 percent of its revenues over the these five years from the retail brokerage business, compared with 22 percent for Merrill

Table 17-3. DuPont Analysis of Firms' Profitability Average Between 1985 and 1989

	Return on Equity	Profit Margin	Revenues/Assets	Assets/Equity
National full-line firms				
A. G. Edwards	.165	.089	.502	3.746
Shearson Lehman	.116	.019	.143	51.568
Paine Webber	.095	.023	.152	28.810
Merrill Lynch	.087	.028	.174	18.866
Large investment banks				
Bear Stearns	.278	.085	.070	45.517
Morgan Stanley	.276	.077	.103	35.823
Salomon Brothers	.132	.014	.321	30.335
Discounters				
Quick & Reilly Groups	.209	.156	.266	5.085
Charles Schwab Corp.	.109	.036	.181	16.572
Regionals				
McDonald & Co., Investments	.144	.076	.458	4.127
Raymond James Financial Corp.	.143	.052	.338	9.388
Piper Jaffray, Inc.	.137	.049	.470	5.935
Robert C. Brown & Co., Inc.	.135	.143	.622	1.817
Alex Brown, Inc.	.132	.059	.336	6.248
Scott & Stringfellow Financial	.124	.052	.607	3.800
Legg Mason, Inc.	.115	.060	.470	4.219
First of Michigan Capital	.114	.047	.644	3.721
Advest Group, Inc.	.107	.041	.245	10.247
First Albany Companies	.106	.030	.207	17.431
Ryan Beck & Co.	.105	.115	.417	1.866
Morgan Keegan, Inc.	.099	.057	.370	5.060
Ziegler Co., Inc.	.097	.129	.336	2.288
Miscellaneous				
DCNY Corp.	.123	.048	.069	34.077
Jefferies Group, Inc.	.115	.064	.400	4.851

Source: Matthews and Dellva (1991), p. 14a.

Lynch, 15 percent for Shearson, and 26 percent for Paine Webber. A. G. Edward's performance contradicts a widely held industry view that brokerage is not a profitable line of business.

Among large investment bankers, Bear Stearns has always had a reputation as an efficient firm that pays close attention to costs. Morgan Stanley, of course, continues to rely on its strength as a prestige underwriter and has successfully expanded into other high-profit lines of business. Salomon Brothers is the largest bond-trading house and has historically made money by trading with very low profit margins and high turnover.

Leverage is much lower for the regionals than for the national full-line and investment-banking firms, at least in part related to the fact that regionals are not primary government dealers. However, there is no strong relationship between leverage or turnover and profitability among the regionals.

The analysis also suggests that the large investment bankers remain in a position to earn top industry profits. Unencumbered by costly retail networks, they have been able to take advantage of emerging profit opportunities.

An examination of the regionals suggests that no one configuration of a firm ensures high profits. Rather, alternative configurations can earn high profits, because the key to strong profits is the ability to select a configuration for a firm that is suitable for its business. Furthermore, a firm must be able to adapt its organizational structure to the changing mix of industry products and services. Those regionals that have remained profitable have generally been successful at introducing the new product lines pioneered by the national full-line firms and the large investment bankers.

Other than A. G. Edwards, the national full-line firms rank below the investment bankers and many of the regional firms in return on equity. In this industry, larger size alone does not bring higher profits. Investment bankers must be nimble in order to earn consistently high profits, yet they operate under higher risk conditions than do other securities firms. The recent rapid demise of Drexel Burnham Lambert and the poor returns for investment banks in 1987, 1989, and 1990 show how risky investment banking can be.

The lower profit rates for the national full-line firms compared with those of large investment bankers provides some support for the finding of little, if any, economics of scope between the retail brokerage business and investment banking. Although a large retail network does not represent the kind of traditional large fixed-cost base usually associated with manufacturing firms, it is a cumbersome part of the business to downsize following a market downturn.

EMPLOYMENT BY FIRM CATEGORY IN THE 1980s

Regionals and national full-line firms have similar business mixes, but regionals have been more profitable than national full lines. Hiring practices might, in part, explain the differences in profitability. Table 17-4 shows hiring by all categories of firms and the percentage increase in number of employees between 1981 and 1991. Total industry employment increased by 55.7 percent from 1981 to 1987 at the peak of the bull market. From its peak of 262,000 jobs in October 1987, employment declined by 20 percent to 209,900 in 1991.

The national full lines as a group have been the dominant employers in the industry. In 1981, they employed 58 percent of industry personnel; in 1991, 54.6 percent. But from 1981 to 1987, the national full lines increased their employees by 50.9 percent, compared with an increase of 30.4 percent by the regionals. The national full lines significantly cut their staffs following the October 1987 crash. This may

Table 17-4. Securities Industry* Employment by Firm Category, 1981–1991 (In Thousands, End of Period)

Firm Category	Employment						Percentage Change 1981–1991
	1981	1983	1985	1987	1989	1991	
National full-line firms	97.0	121.0	133.8	146.4	128.0	116.8	20.4
Large investment banks	19.0	25.7	29.1	38.1	32.1	29.5	55.3
Regionals	32.6	36.4	36.1	42.5	36.0	39.3	20.6
New York City–based	10.9	12.4	12.1	15.2	15.2	15.8	45.0
Discounters	0.8	0.9	2.8	5.0	4.8	5.7	612.5
Total firms*	167.2	205.6	224.5	260.4	227.6	213.8	27.9

*NYSE member firms doing a public business.
Source: Securities Industry Association, *Fact Book,* various issues.

mean that hiring practices at the national full lines, which employ more than half the industry's total employees, may contribute to instability in the industry.

The experience of Merrill Lynch, the industry's largest employer, is instructive. Merrill Lynch laid off 5,000 employees between the October 1987 stock market crash and the end of 1989. Then in early 1990, with 40,500 employees worldwide, the firm eliminated about 3,000 more jobs. Analysts argue that such large-scale cuts were necessary for the firm to earn a respectable return on equity. A senior Merrill Lynch official commented that the mind-set at Merrill is to adjust to the new business levels, and the firm tends to get carried away on the upside (*Wall Street Journal,* January 15, 1990, p. C-1).

Paine Webber and Shearson also report low returns on equity relative to that of other firms. This information provides some evidence that hiring patterns of rapid increases in staff in booms followed by a lagged adjustment to declining markets may contribute to the variability of profits for the overall industry.

RISK IN THE INDUSTRY

Earlier in this book, we proposed that the industry's revenues were being based more and more on riskier lines of business. The industry's leverage also increased dramatically from 1972 to 1991. In addition, securities markets became more volatile in the 1980s. These factors may indicate that the industry became more risky in the 1980s.

An important part of the growth in assets over this period is the growth in customer cash and securities left with the firm. These accounts are insured by the Securities Investor Protection Corporation, and therefore, increases in risk levels in the industry would be of concern to securities industry personnel, potential bank entrants, and regulators.

On the other hand, securities firms and exchanges have developed new approaches to hedging and risk management. This development suggests that the industry has been able to prevent risk from increasing. We will use a *market model* approach to measure the risk levels that are reflected in the security prices of publicly traded securities firms.

Model

Following a method used by Kane and Unal (1988) to examine the riskiness of U.S. banks and savings and loans, we will use the familiar market model of asset returns expanded with an interest rate index. This model's focal return-generating process is the two-index model developed by Stone (1974). With it, we can estimate the stock market and interest rate sensitivity and unsystematic risk of a portfolio of publicly held securities firms. The U.S. Securities and Exchange Commission (SEC) argued in 1985 that broker-dealers, because of the changing nature of their business, are *less* affected by fluctuations in stock market prices and are *more* affected by volume and price changes in the debt market (U.S. Securities and Exchange Commission 1985, p. 19). The two-variable Stone model will allow us to separate the stock and bond market effects on securities firms' returns. We will also test for a structural shift in risk between 1972 and 1988, by using a dummy variable. We chose 1982 as the year of the structural shift because the bull market of the 1980s started then. Also, by 1982, many of the new financial instruments and trading strategies were in place to enable broker-dealers to manage risk. The dummy variable will enable us to determine whether the securities firms were operating in a riskier environment in the 1980s than they were in the 1970s.

The model is

$$R_p = B_0 + B_m R_m + B_i R_i + e_p \tag{17-3}$$

where B_m and B_i are measures of the asset's systematic market and interest rate risk; R_m and R_i represent stock market returns and bond market returns; R_p is the return on the asset; and e_p is the error term. The model was estimated first as a one-factor model with stock market returns only. Then it was estimated as a two-factor model with both stock and bond returns. Then both models were estimated separately for both the bear (until June 1982) and the bull markets.

Firms included in the sample were all those publicly held securities firms included on the monthly CRSP tapes from 1972 to 1988. In the portfolio of securities firms, each firm was equally weighted.

Regression Results

One-Factor Model

The regression results are shown in Table 17-5. Regression 1 shows that the beta $(B_1)$for the securities firm portfolio is 1.63. That is, the securities firm portfolio is riskier than the overall market portfolio (which has a beta of 1.0). The intercept term, B_0, is negative and statistically significant. This suggests that after the effects of the overall markets are explained, other factors yield a significantly negative return for securities firms.

The addition of the dummy variable (Regression 2) to the original market model had little effect on the model. The coefficient of the dummy was insignificant. Alternatively, the addition of an interactive term (the dummy times R_m in Regression 3) also results in an insignificant variable.

Two-Factor Model

Regressions 6, 7, 8, and 9 were estimated based on the two-factor model. Regression 6 included both the stock index and the interest rate index. Both indexes were statistically significant, indicating that both the stock and the bond markets are important to determining securities firms' returns. However, the addition of the interest rate factor does little to improve the performance of the equation. The adjusted R^2 increased only from 0.736 to 0.741 owing to the addition of the interest rate factor. This suggests that the stock market is probably more important than the bond market in explaining the returns of this portfolio.

Regressions 7, 8, and 9 show the effect of the dummy variable in the two-factor model. Regression 7 reveals that the intercept dummy variable is now significant and negative. Regression 8 shows the interaction between the dummy and the stock index. The coefficient is negative and statistically significant, suggesting that the overall stock market risk of this portfolio of securities firms was lowered from 1.65 to 1.63, a minor reduction. On the other hand, the interactive term of the dummy and the interest rate index in Regression 9 has a stronger effect. The dummy was significant and reduced the interest rate riskiness from 0.58 to 0.38, a substantial reduction. The interpretation of these results are that (1) the riskiness of securities firms relative to the stock market changed very little from the bear market to the bull market and (2) the riskiness relative to the bond market declined in the 1980s.

Bear and Bull Market Results

The single-factor and two-factor models were also estimated separately for the bear and bull markets. Regressions 4 and 5 show the estimates of the single-factor model. The stock market beta fell from 1.66 in the 1970s to 1.58 in the 1980s, so there was moderate decline in stock market risk. Regressions 10 and 11 show the estimates for the two-factor model. In this model, the stock market beta showed a slight decline from 1.66 to 1.59, and the bond market variable fell from statistically significant to insignificant. This means that the overall riskiness of the securities firms relative to the stock and bond markets declined in the 1980s. That is, the industry is better at managing the risks of its business now than it was in the 1970s. This result suggests

Table 17-5. Market and Interest Rate Factor Models: Sensitivity of Broker-Dealer Portfolio Returns to Changes in Stock Indexes and Market Interest Rates

No.	Period	N	Constant	CRSPEQ	LTGBY	D1	D2	D3	AdjR2	Standard Error
1	1/72–12/88	204	−.6327 (−9.097)	1.6313 (23.795)	—	—	—	—	.736	.058
2	1/72–12/88	204	−.6329 (−9.140)	1.6367 (23.950)	—	−.0137 (−1.658)	—	—	.738	.057
3	1/72–12/88	204	−.6372 (−9.197)	1.6410 (23.960)	—	—	−0.137 (1.684)	—	.738	.057
4	1/72–5/82	125	−.6567 (−7.613)	1.6601 (19.489)	—	—	—	—	.753	.059
5	6/82–12/88	79	−.5940 (−5.030)	1.5849 (13.658)	—	—	—	—	.704	.054
6	1/72–12/88	204	−.6748 (−9.429)	1.6359 (24.072)	.3943 (2.180)	—	—	—	.741	.057
7	1/72–12/88	204	−.6896 (−9.720)	1.6458 (24.473)	.5304 (2.836)	−.0208 (−2.452)	—	—	.747	.056
8	1/72–12/88	204	−.6963 (−9.780)	1.6524 (24.504)	.5316 (2.843)	—	−.0207 (−2.479)	—	.747	.056
9	1/72–12/88	204	−.6942 (−9.759)	1.6455 (24.470)	.5840 (2.999)	—	—	−.2053 (−2.449)	.747	.056
10	1/72–5/82	125	−.7164 (−8.151)	1.6697 (19.984)	.5604 (2.474)	—	—	—	.763	.058
11	6/82–12/88	79	−.6484 (−5.205)	1.5928 (13.773)	.4513 (1.318)	—	—	—	.707	.054

CRSPEQ = Center for Research in Security Prices equally weighted stock index.

LTGBY = Long-Term Government Bond Index.

$D1$ = Dummy variable = 0 from 1972-1 to 1982 and 1 from 1982-9 to 1988-12.

$D2$ = $D1 \times$ CRSPEQ.

$D3$ = $D1 \times$ LTGBY.

$R_P = B_0 + B_1\text{CRSPEQ} + B_2\text{LTGBY} + B_3D1 + B_4D2 + B_5D3 + e$

Source: Matthews and Dellva (1991), p. 20a.

the possibility that the new financial instruments have been helpful in allowing broker-dealers to manage risk in more volatile markets.

LIQUIDATION RISK

Table 5-3 shows the number of securities firms liquidated by the Securities Investor Protection Corporation (SIPC) from 1971 to 1991. The combined effect of more stringent regulatory capital requirements put in place in the early 1970s and better management of firms brought on by a more competitive environment following the deregulation of commission rates in 1975 resulted in fewer failures following the end of the bull market of the 1980s than following the end of the bull market of the 1960s.

COMPENSATION IN THE SECURITIES INDUSTRY

The securities industry has always had a number of highly paid individuals. Indeed, the *Wall Street Journal* (April 18, 1990, pp. R-19–R-20) reported that six of the fourteen highest paid executives among all the publicly held financial services firms in 1989 (including banking and insurance) were from the securities industry, and *Institutional Investor* (March 1983, p. 70) reported that one retail broker grossed $3.6 million in 1982. A bond trader earned $20 million at Salomon Brothers in 1990, and an oil trader earned $23 million at the same firm that year. Michael Milken is said to have amassed a fortune of $1 billion (or more) as the primary architect of the junk bond market (*New York Times,* January 26, 1988, p. D-7). Individuals with experience in a new market area also earn substantial premiums by taking that experience to another firm. In fact, bonuses are so important in this industry that Eccles and Crane (1988, chap. 8) devote an entire chapter of their book to the process of determining bonuses and they provide figures for investment banking.[4] The years of Eccles and Crane's study were very good for investment bankers. In 1986, entry-level associates were paid $70,000 or more, with guaranteed bonuses of $20,000 to $50,000. Fourth- and fifth-year associates could earn bonuses of several hundred thousand dollars, and vice presidents could earn middle six-figure bonuses. A number of managing directors (the next level above vice president), who in most firms had salaries between $100,000 and $150,000 a year, were receiving over $1 million in bonuses.

Eccles and Crane observe that the potentially large size of the bonuses provides a strong incentive for people to identify new business opportunities, which reinforces the tendency to formulate strategies at lower levels of the organization. Investment bankers who are willing to take the personal career and financial risks of pursuing a new business will be generously rewarded if they are successful. These innovators share substantially in the quasi-rent earned in the new business before competition drives margins down.

High profits for some securities firms and high incomes for some professionals persist despite considerable competition in all facets of the industry. There are no artificial (legal) barriers to entry that could hinder competition (with the exception of Glass–Steagall). There are some natural barriers, in that some activities require large amounts of start-up capital (e.g., merchant banking and Rule 415 underwriting), but several potential competitors have access to the capital necessary to enter these businesses (Mead and O'Neil 1986, p. 362).

Although the brokers, traders, and investment bankers earn high incomes during a bull market, their incomes fall sharply with a market downturn. In addition, they face job insecurity. From the third quarter of 1987 to the first quarter of 1991, industry employment dropped from 262,000 to 209,000, a decline of 20 percent (Securities Industry Association, *Trends,* August 16, 1991, p. 3). This decline was similar to the cutbacks following the end of the bull market of the 1960s when the industry's work force dropped by 25 percent.

Part of the high incomes earned by employees and the high profits earned by firms is the economic rents awarded to special skills and special market placement (e.g., mergers and acquisitions departments). If banks were permitted to enter all securities lines of business, these economic rents would probably decline with more competition.[5] These rents will continue to be earned by securities firms as long as they are better able to exploit market inefficiencies than other firms are.

THE TECHNOLOGY OF TRADING AND FRAGMENTED MARKETS

The analysis by Minnerop and Stoll (1985) shows that securities firms' back-office operations are technically efficient. Firms rapidly improve their back office to take advantage of new technology that can give them a competitive advantage; that is, the push of new technology is changing securities markets.

Stoll (1992) argues that changes in automation and improvements in communication technology have dramatically reduced the cost of providing standardized trading, which has resulted in market fragmentation. NYSE stocks can now be traded in a variety of markets—on a regional exchange, in the NASDAQ market, in a foreign market, or on proprietary trading systems such as Instinet. Some NASDAQ firms claim to offer low-cost, automated execution of orders at prices equal to or better than NYSE quotes. Standardized, automated trading services are also being offered to institutional investors by systems such as Instinet and Posit.

In addition, there has been a trend toward tailoring trading services aimed primarily at institutions. Investment bankers' research, sales, and trading operations have become more integrated as trading strategies are devised to implement institutions' portfolio objectives.

For brokers and their customers, the new world of fragmented markets has expanded the range of available trading services, and it has also increased the cost to brokers of ensuring that their customers receive the best price. In this environment, Stoll asks how regulators intend to regulate the new trading systems that do not fall easily into the current regulatory cutbacks of "broker-dealer" or "exchanges." Many of the new trading systems fall into neither category and are currently operating under "no action" letters from the SEC. Some of the new trading systems are not exchanges, since they may simply be computer facilities and have no members. Some systems are operated by registered broker-dealers, but the system itself need not be a broker-dealer.

Stoll also asks which rules of best execution regulators should promulgate. Should the SEC specify what constitutes best execution, or should a broker's execution be evaluated by the customer? The evaluation of ''best execution'' is complicated by the fact that the customer's *net* price depends not only on the spread but also on commissions, other costs incurred in the trade, and the services provided by the broker—for example, research that the investor would otherwise be required to pay for. Stoll believes that accepted standards of best execution should apply to brokers, as they decide on the markets in which to trade, but detailed best-execution rules put an overtight straitjacket on the markets, invariably favor established markets, and are almost impossible to oversee. In a free market, the evaluation of best execution must be left to the customer, and competition for customers will push markets toward high-speed, low-cost trading arrangements.

COMPARING THE COST OF CAPITAL FOR U.S. AND JAPANESE SECURITIES FIRMS

McCauley and Zimmer (1991) estimated the cost of capital for U.S. and Japanese securities firms in the 1980s. They found that the Japanese firms in their sample faced an average cost of equity of 5.1 percent between 1982 and 1991 compared with 7.8 percent for their sample of U.S. securities firms.[6] McCauley and Zimmer offered two sets of explanations for the Japanese advantage. Macroeconomic explanations focus on the relatively low equity costs that characterized the whole Japanese corporate sector in the latter 1980s. Even though international capital became more mobile in the 1980s, capital costs were not equalized across countries, and national factors still played a predominant role. In Japan, higher household savings resulted in lower equity costs. In addition, smoother growth in Japan, resulting from successful macroeconomic policies, meant less risk in profits, and lower profit risks meant lower cost of equity.

Additionally, investors in Japanese securities firms have more reason to suppose that their downsize risk is substantially lessened by the possibility of government intervention in favor of a securities firm in trouble, as they witnessed the government's efforts on behalf of Yamaichi Securities in the 1960s. Yamaichi's difficulties were related to losses on stock market holdings that had impaired the firm's capital. Customers began to withdraw liquidity. Then the Bank of Japan worked with the Ministry of Finance to devise a rescue plan involving largely unsecured advances by the Bank of Japan; eventually Yamaichi recovered and repaid the loans over four years.

Contrast this effort with the case of Drexel Burnham Lambert. In this case, the SEC worked with the Federal Reserve Bank of New York to achieve an orderly reduction of Drexel's balance sheet, and the firm sought protection from creditors under Chapter 11 of the Bankruptcy Code. Although these cases are different, market participants may view the equity of major U.S. securities firms as subject to more risk than that of major Japanese securities firms.

The cost of capital of U.S. security firms is substantially lower than that of U.S. banks or manufacturing firms. One reason the authors cite for the advantages enjoyed by securities firms is that they issued new equity in the mid-1980s when the U.S. cost of equity was most favorable.

SOURCES OF EXTRAORDINARY PROFIT
FOR BROKER-DEALERS

Broker-dealers have years of very high profits. From 1980 through 1984, their pretax return on equity exceeded 30 percent. Such extraordinary profits come from a number of different sources. The NYSE composite index rose from a high of 63.69 in 1979 to a high of 81.02 in 1980, a gain of 27.2 percent. Average monthly new stock issues went from a monthly average of $949 million in 1979 to $1.7 billion in 1980, an increase of 80 percent, and average new monthly bond issues climbed from $3.3 billion in 1979 to $4.4 billion in 1980, an increase of 32.3 percent. Reported volume on the NYSE increased from 8.2 billion shares in 1979 to 11.4 billion shares in 1980, an increase of 39.2 percent. Activity levels remained high in 1981, and in 1982 the stock market began the prolonged bull run of the 1980s. In the early 1980s, mortgage-backed securities also generated enormous profits for some firms, followed by asset-backed securities in 1985. The junk bond and mergers and acquisitions business generated large profits for a handful of firms in the mid- and late 1980s.

Very high profits arise from the rapid rise in stock- and bond-price levels, increased volume, and increased underwriting activity. In a bull market, many firms rush to enter the business. But then, as the market turns down, many firms leave the business, as illustrated in Figure 17-1.

The potential for extraordinary profits is balanced by the potential for extraordinary losses. In April 1987, Merrill Lynch reportedly lost $275 million on a particularly risky form of mortgage security in which the firm had held a position of about $1.7 billion (*Wall Street Journal,* May 20, 1987, p. 3). The loss stemmed from pricing and trading mistakes on a complex new instrument called "stripped" mortgage-backed securities (*Business Week,* May 18, 1987, pp. 112–13). That same April, Salomon Brothers was reported to have lost about $100 million owing to violent swings of bond prices, mainly in municipal bond trading. Other firms were reported to have lost millions in the same period on complex Treasury bond options (*New York Times,* June 18, 1987, p. D-1).

FOCUSING ON REVENUES RATHER THAN PROFITS

Eccles and Crane (1988) report that many investment bankers describe their business as "revenue driven." During the early and mid-1980s, generating revenue was of more concern than controlling costs. In fact, the problem for some firms was increasing costs fast enough by hiring the necessary personnel to handle the available business. In addition, bonuses—which are a large share of compensation and, in turn, one of the largest components of total cost—are variable and linked to revenues.

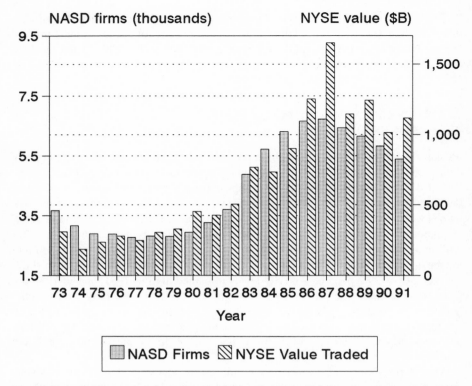

Figure 17-1. Firm entry and market performance. (Securities Industry Association, *Securities Industry Yearbook;* New York Stock Exchange, *Fact Book*)

On the investment-banking side, it is difficult to measure the profitability of deals. The loose relationship between value contributed and revenues earned is one problem. As discussed in Chapter 9, it is difficult to measure the accuracy of the production expenses of the many people who spend time working on a deal, and the difficulty of allocating administrative and operating costs further constrains measures of deal profitability.

Eccles and Crane observed that because of the difficulty of measuring profitability, broker-dealers put great emphasis on measuring market share. The greater a firm's market share is in any line of business, the more extensive its contracts with issuers and investors will be, and the more information it will have about the market. The more active a firm is, the better able it will be to price deals and thereby to lower the risk of loss. So, since market share and profitability are believed to be highly correlated for a number of products, market share is used as a proxy for profitability.

OVERALL PERFORMANCE OF THE SECURITIES INDUSTRY

Competition is vigorous among securities firms. It occurs in all lines of business. The large firms compete to bring out new products and capture quasi-rents. Investment bankers compete to be at the top of the syndication charts. Block traders compete for the largest share of the business. Discounters provide competition for individual brokerage services. In securities brokerage, municipal bonds, private placements, and mergers and acquisitions, commercial banks are either effective or potential competitors. Despite rigorous competition in almost all lines of business, however, the industry can earn high profits, during a strong bull market. Areas that provide extranormal profit opportunities, largely through innovations, will continue to be available to securities firms.

Almost 20 percent of the population of the United States use the services of securities firms directly as customers of securities firms. Through pension funds and other institutions, many more Americans use securities firms' services. Generally these customers are treated fairly and honestly in the securities markets, and the fees they pay are reasonably related to costs. But there is room for improvement. The next chapter discusses specific policy recommendations for the SEC.

NOTES

1. The SEC has published profitability measures for NYSE member firms doing a public business, based on pretax income. Pretax income is used for a number of reasons: Most broker-dealers are organized as partnerships, closely held corporations, or sole proprietorships, although some are publicly held corporations. The SEC uses pretax income, since it is the closest approximation of profits that places these firms on a comparable accounting basis (i.e., before adjustments for distributions to shareholders or partners). These comparisons are also limited because it is difficult to distinguish between owners' employment compensation and their return on investment.

2. For a discussion of the DuPont method, see Weston and Copeland (1989), pp. 228–31.

3. Compustat is a computer-based data system available from the University of Chicago.

4. They also discuss the framework for the compensation of sales, trading, and research personnel but do not provide specific figures.

5. Banks earned only 5 percent of M&A fees in 1989 (Securities Industry Association, *Trends,* (May 31, 1990, p. 14).

6. The Japanese firms included in their sample were Daiwa, Nikko, Nomura, and Yamaichi. The U.S. firms were Merrill Lynch, Morgan Stanley, Salomon Brothers, Bear Stearns, and Paine Webber.

18

Policy Implications
and Recommendations

This chapter discusses policy recommendations for the broker-dealer industry based on the analysis of this book and my own experience as a financial economist at the U.S. Securities and Exchange Commission (SEC) from 1977 to 1984. The basic recommendation of the study is that regulators provide a framework that facilitates organizational change so that U.S. securities firms can maintain their position as world leaders in this dynamic industry. This should be added to the traditional objectives of preventing fraud and abuses of investors in financial markets and ensuring the safety and soundness of broker-dealers.

Many of the SEC's policies date from legislation passed many years ago, before global competition was much of an issue. Now, however, if our securities industry does not remain sound, innovative, and flexible, we could lose our industry to larger, better capitalized competitors.

INTERNATIONAL COMPETITION

The internationalization of securities markets presents U.S. securities firms with both opportunities and challenges. American broker-dealers are the most competitive and innovative firms in the world today, a model of how firms can seek out the profit opportunities available in incomplete markets.

An example from 1982 illustrates a decision by the SEC that hurt the competitive position of U.S. exchanges relative to other country's exchanges. In 1982, the SEC voted to prohibit foreign securities firms from offering their securities in the United States unless they met U.S. accounting and disclosure standards. The SEC's Division of Corporate Finance argued that this rule would pressure foreign issuers to adopt U.S. disclosure standards in order to raise capital in U.S. markets. This meant that foreign issuers would have to meet U.S. accounting standards, at considerable expense, no matter how successful or well regulated the companies were in their home country.

Economists from the SEC's Directorate of Economic and Policy Analysis argued that it was unrealistic to expect that foreign firms would prepare their disclosure documents according to accounting standards mandated by the Financial Accounting

Standards Board of the United States and the SEC.[1] Each country's accounting standards have evolved within its own financial and industrial history and tax laws, and other countries' accounting systems often are substantially different from those of the United States. The SEC economists also contended at the time that U.S. investors will buy foreign securities anyhow, so why not give them lower costs by allowing U.S. trading. But the SEC nevertheless approved the rule change.

In a speech in March 1991, William Donaldson, chairman of the New York Stock Exchange (NYSE), argued that we need to adjust regulatory policies that are tying the hands of the U.S. securities industry in global competition. He identified the U.S. accounting requirement for foreign issuers as just such a policy, pointing out that twenty years ago, the United States accounted for about two-thirds of all the capitalization of publicly traded companies in the world. Today, we have less than one-third. The NYSE estimated that there are more than 2,000 companies outside the United States that could meet the NYSE's financial criteria for listing, and at least 350 of them are world class.

If this nation is to be *the* international marketplace for securities, we must recognize the obvious—that not all the quality companies in the world are U.S. companies, nor are all U.S. accounting standards and practices necessarily the only way of approaching disclosure.

We have a strong advantage. Overseas companies want access to the most active investors in the world. And our investors should have the benefit of the broadest possible choice of quality investments.

Not only *should* they have that benefit, they *will*, whether we act or not. It's just a question of whether the benefit accrues to *our* market or to somebody else's. (Donaldson 1991, p. 4)

Greg Jarrell explained the SEC's position in the context of the political support theory. If lower-disclosing foreign firms trade without problems side by side with higher-disclosing U.S. firms, then the basis for strict U.S. disclosure standards will come under scrutiny. Even though the NYSE might gain with this regulatory change, other SEC constituents could be losers, including accountants, securities lawyers, and the SEC staff (*Wall Street Journal,* June 19, 1992, p. A-10).

THE VALUE OF U.S. SECURITIES FIRMS AS INTERNATIONAL COMPETITORS: THE CASE OF SALOMON BROTHERS

Commenting on the chances of Salomon Brothers surviving the scandal in the bond-trading market revealed in the summer of 1991, David Vise, coauthor of *Eagle on the Street,* commented, ''The answer to your question of whether Salomon Brothers will survive is in the federal government's hands. It depends on the severity of the sanctions against Salomon. Right now the Justice Department, the Securities and Exchange Commission, the Treasury, and the Fed are all investigating Salomon'' (interview on ''Crossfire,'' CNN, September 20, 1991).

If Salomon Brothers had failed, the United States would have lost one of its most effective competitors in international competition. As this book has shown, securities firms are complex organizations that must be able to adapt their organizational forms to changing economic conditions. Salomon has been highly successful at adaptation, but if it had failed, there might have been adverse economic consequences for the U.S. securities industry as a whole, especially in the competition between U.S. and Japanese securities firms.

Salomon and other firms in the oligopoly group are currently leaders in providing sophisticated, high-tech trading services in the United States and in the Tokyo and London markets. As we have seen, if a firm fails, other firms will acquire its best units. For example, Salomon acquired much of Drexel's junk bond capabilities following the demise of that firm. However, given the size of Salomon, perhaps only a firm as large as one of the top four Japanese firms could acquire a large Salomon unit. A Japanese firm could combine Salomon's technical strengths in various lines of business with its existing capital and become a powerful competitor in U.S. markets and enhance its position in Japanese markets.

PROPERTY RIGHTS FOR NEW PRODUCTS AND SERVICES

Innovation is primarily the province of the largest firms in the industry. Small and mid-sized firms are reluctant to innovate because of the rapid imitation of successful products by firms in the oligopoly group. Recent court decisions, however, recognized that protection can be accorded to some innovations in finance (Petruzzi, DelValle, and Judlowe 1990, pp. 624–25). Broad interpretation of copyright and patent laws, along with the fact that many of the recent innovations in finance require the use of a computer for practical implementation, have provided a framework that has led to patent awards. The seminal case of patenting computer programs was the patent awarded to Merrill Lynch's Cash Management Account (CMA). Most innovations are combinations of other inventions or known technologies in nonobvious ways. The CMA was a combination of this type. Each part of this account (e.g., money market funds, VISA accounts) existed before the patent, but had never before been combined in this way.

Even though some patents have been acquired, the current ambiguity in patent law makes it unclear which other recent financial innovations might have been eligible for a patent. Until 1992, many innovators did not anticipate that a patent could be won for their innovation. For those new products that do not qualify for a patent, there remains the unresolved issue of a property right that should belong to the developer of a new idea. This is part of the larger question of whether and how to allocate property rights in intangible things. Macey (1991, pp. 2–3) noted that we have not yet developed a sensible, efficient, and coherent system for allocating such property rights. Despite these issues, Trzyna (1992) argues that industry attitudes toward patents are changing. He contends that many more firms are applying for patents now than in the past, and firms will be forced to give more consideration to patent issues.

At a practical level, Joseph S. Rizzello, president of the Philadelphia Board of Trade, proposed that innovators who develop new financial products should be given a grace period of perhaps eighteen months, during which the innovator would have patentlike protection for its product.[2] With this grace period, it is more likely that smaller and mid-sized securities firms would accept the risks and expenses of developing new products.

SEC–CFTC JURISDICTIONAL DISPUTES

The SEC has the authority to regulate trading of options on securities, and the U.S. Commodities Futures Trading Commission (CFTC) regulates the trading of futures contracts (including futures on stock indexes) and options on futures contracts. The two agencies have frequently struggled with jurisdictional confusion. Some disputes were resolved by negotiation, but others were resolved only when the courts sorted out jurisdictional disputes. The related industries have also used the threat of litigation to thwart competition through innovation and perhaps to thwart regulation as well (U.S. Office of Technology Assessment 1990, pp. 169–72). A major source of difficulty is the "exclusive jurisdiction" phrase in the Commodity Futures Trading Commission Act: "The Commission (CFTC) shall have exclusive jurisdiction with respect to . . . transactions involving . . . contracts of sale (and options on such contracts) for future delivery of a group or index of securities (or any interest therein or based on the value thereof)" (7 U.S.C. 2a [ii]). Most new contracts—if they are not standard corporate stock or bonds—have some aspects of "future delivery," and the likelihood that they will be found by the courts to fall under the CFTC's jurisdiction may effectively discourage stock markets from product innovation.

Serious disagreements have erupted between exchanges seeking to innovate, and between the regulatory agencies, over products at the intersection of the agencies' jurisdictions (U.S. Office of Technology Assessment 1990, p. 170). In 1981, the chairs of the SEC and the CFTC entered into an agreement clarifying the two agencies' jurisdictional responsibilities, pending the enactment of clarifying amendments to the securities and commodities laws. This agreement gave the CFTC exclusive jurisdiction over futures contracts and options on futures contracts, and it recognized the SEC as the sole federal regulator of options on securities and on foreign currencies traded on national securities exchanges. The agreement specified certain criteria that the CFTC would use in approving futures contracts on a group or an index of municipal and nonexempt securities. As part of the Futures Trading Act of 1982, Congress enacted the CFTC–SEC agreement into law, adding a provision that the SEC had the right to object to a futures contract on a stock index (or an option on such a contract). After a hearing, SEC's objection would be taken into judicial review.

Because of this awkward structure, innovation in products is hampered or completely stymied because when products "fall between the stools," they are likely to involve the exchanges in protracted wrangling between agencies or in lengthy judicial proceedings to determine the proper jurisdiction (U.S. Office of Technology Assessment 1990, p. 177). This wrangling between agencies can have serious consequences for the relative competitive positions of U.S. exchanges and broker-dealers and foreign competitors. Nicholas Giordano, president and chief executive officer of the Philadelphia Stock Exchange claimed:

The lack of coordination between regulatory markets has . . . exacted a toll in the development of new products. As a nation, we have created a competitive disadvantage for ourselves because foreign markets take away market share while we battle over jurisdictional rights to these new instruments. Jurisdictional debates should not be a factor when introducing new products. . . . [R]egulators encounter confusion as new and complex market instruments are introduced to the marketplace. As a result, new products can be held hostage to courtroom antics. When the competition marches into the courtroom to challenge a competitor's new product, the cost of innovation increases. Therefore, we disadvantage ourselves vis-à-vis our foreign competitors who do not pay these costs or bear the additional burden. (Giordano 1991, p. 28)

Giordano illustrated his point using the Philadelphia Stock Exchange's experience with its new product called Cash Index Participations (CIPs). CIPs, which began trading in May 1989, reflected the overall value of Standard & Poor's 500-stock index. As with stock ownership, investors buying CIP shares would receive dividends and would see the price of their shares rise and fall in relation to the value of the 500 stocks that make up the index. This product would allow individual investors to take advantage of the movement of the entire stock market just as large institutions have been able to do. But after the introduction of CIPs, a court of appeals, in response to a suit brought by the commodities industry, ordered the Philadelphia Stock Exchange to stop trading them because of their "futureslike" characteristics. Meanwhile, the Philadelphia Stock Exchange's CIPs were copied in Canada and Europe, where these products are currently being traded. The Philadelphia Stock Exchange is no longer trading its own innovative product because of this jurisdictional dispute between government agencies.

Accountability to Encourage Efficient Resolution of SEC–CFTC Disputes

Milton Friedman (1985) argues that making the Federal Reserve more accountable to Congress and the public would improve its performance. This study book recommends more accountability by the SEC and the CFTC to the public, the industry, and Congress on the subject of jurisdictional disputes. To eliminate the protracted wrangling between agencies, a clock should start running when a jurisdictional dispute arises. Within a reasonably short time, if the dispute has not been resolved, both agencies would be required to publicly issue a report on the nature of the dispute, the reason it remains unresolved, and the consequences of not resolving it. If these consequences are that a foreign securities firm or exchange will be able to offer a product while a U.S. securities organization may not, the agencies should disclose that fact. Such an admission would provide a strong incentive for resolution.

BANKS' ENTRY INTO THE SECURITIES INDUSTRY

Litan (1987) contends that unless Congress prohibits them, banks and other financial institutions will inevitably find ways to offer a full range of financial services. In the absence of federal legislation, therefore, transforming the financial marketplaces will probably be inefficient and beset by legal uncertainties that will impede an orderly transition to a more competitive financial system.

A number of legislative proposals have been made that would allow greater bank participation in the securities industry. There have also been a number of studies that have analyzed the arguments for bank participation (Benston 1990; Kaufman and Mote 1988; Litan 1987).

Rather than discussing in detail the legislative proposals or the studies, our approach is to accept Litan's premise that banks will inevitably find ways to offer a full range of securities services and outline what this will mean for the banks, broker-dealers and regulators.

In the 1920s, the banks were able to use their networks of branch offices to make rapid inroads into the securities business, as we pointed out in Chapter 4. However, at that time, securities firms had not developed the extensive network of offices or the well-developed market for middle-class investors that they currently possess. Today, banks would have to persuade retail customers to move an account to a bank securities subsidiary from a broker-dealer, in order to penetrate the retail brokerage market. Banks have had some experience in this area through the discount brokerage services that many currently offer their customers. With an unrestricted ability to offer services, banks would be able to offer investment advice, but it is not clear that the availability of this advice would prompt customers to incur the switching costs to shift accounts.

In institutional brokerage, the banks' securities subsidiaries would be able to hold and trade from large securities positions. They also would be able to block positions to facilitate institutional sales. And in this line of business, they would be able to capture some of the order flow over time, although this does not appear to be a high-profit area for broker-dealers.

In underwriting, Litan (1987, pp. 66–67) argues that the high profits conceal the high salaries and profit-sharing draws that investment banks pay their personnel. Litan cites the higher personnel costs for the largest investment banks, which in 1985 averaged over $100,000 per employee, including partners, compared with approximately $50,000 for the two leading wholesale commercial banks, Bankers Trust and Morgan Guarantee, and $33,800 for all twelve money-center banks. Bank entry, he believes, would compress these differentials in personnel costs, since this would lower the profits that investment banks earn, as well as permit personnel that commercial-banking organizations employ to be involved in a broader range of investment-banking activities.

Concentration in the Eurobond market, in which banks are permitted to participate, has been substantially lower than in the American market for corporate securities offerings. Concentration levels have also been lower for underwriting general-obligation municipal bonds than for revenue bonds, which have been off limits to banks. Litan also notes that additional competition in investment banking would lower fees, citing research reviewed in Silber (1979) and Pugel and White (1985) on the municipal bond market.

With regard to the lucrative mergers and acquisitions business, banks have faced a severe disadvantage, since they cannot underwrite securities and may be unwilling to extend bridge loans necessary to complete the deals. If allowed to underwrite securities, banks would be able to provide a more complete range of services for mergers and acquisitions (M&A) customers (e.g., underwriting junk bonds). More competition should bring down M&A advisory fees.

The analysis of this book suggests that some of the supranormal profits and high compensation in this industry result from the quasi-rents earned by innovators and fast seconds from new products. Bank entry would tend to reduce these quasi-rents because the large banks that would compete head to head with the oligopoly group firms would provide a wider group of innovators and fast seconds for the industry. Bankers Trust has already shown an ability to be a leader in the field of derivatives. Although it will take some time, it is expected that banks will develop abilities in these areas.

Adapting the Organizational Structure

Walter Wriston argues that by blocking American banks—but not General Electric Capital, Ford Credit, or General Motors Acceptance Corporation (GMAC)—from diversifying their product lines, the regulatory framework forces banks not only to put all their eggs in one basket, but also to fill the basket with the same kinds of eggs. Banks lost mid-size corporate customers to the junk bond market and car-loan customers to GMAC and were forced to lend more into high-risk markets like real estate. (*Wall Street Journal,* December 19, 1990, p. A-16). Banks' income comes only from interest on loans and securities; it does not flow from diversified financial services products like life or casualty insurance premiums, underwriting fees, and commissions or other financial services. Wriston thinks that if banks restricted their revenue sources to mainly interest income as a result of management decisions, instead of by law, any alert regulator would severely and justifiably criticize the practice as unsafe and unsound.[3]

Our analysis contends that those broker-dealers that have survived, grown, and prospered over the past ten years have adapted their organizations to the changing market by diversifying into new lines of business. Those firms that have run into difficulty, such as Lehman Kuhn Loeb, E. F. Hutton, and Drexel Burnham Lambert, all had difficulty shaping their organizations to meet the changing environment. Our analysis also supports Wriston's argument. Keeping banks in their current regulatory straitjacket will make them become weaker and weaker as financial markets change. Therefore, banks should be allowed to have more freedom to adapt their organizations to changing opportunities.

Likelihood of Broker-Dealer Subsidiaries Failing

The framework that will be established to regulate the relationship between the bank holding company and the broker-dealer subsidiary should be flexible enough to allow for the failure of the broker-dealer subsidiaries. Because three of the largest broker-dealers have failed over the last ten years, a broker-dealer subsidiary of a large bank could also have a chance of failing. Regulators should make clear from the outset that the "too big to fail" philosophy that prevailed in bank regulation will not apply to the broker-dealer subsidiary. That is, proposed limits on the amount of bank capital that would be tied up in the broker-dealer must be such that a total failure would not bring down the bank.

This recognition should also be a part of the framework for regulating broker-dealer subsidiaries of mid-size and smaller banks. Small broker-dealers have a high rate of entry and exit from the securities industry in response to the profit opportunities associated with the bull and bear markets. As we stated in Chapter 14, if small broker-dealers have problems that the firms themselves cannot solve, the self-regulators should arrange mergers of the failing firm with a healthier firm. This would probably be more difficult if the problem broker-dealer were a subsidiary of a bank and would present a different type of problem for regulators. Regulators of the securities subsidiary should prepare a framework for this type of problem. More organizational flexibility would allow banks to devise more types of hedging and investment strategies to manage their risks and avoid failure.

BROKER-DEALERS' CAPITAL AND SIPC INSURANCE

A study by Deloitte and Touche (1990) of the Securities Investor Protection Corporation (SIPC) fund argues that SIPC liquidations are becoming larger and costlier and that industry trends toward concentration and riskier business activities pose new threats of larger firm failures. They believe that based on the failure of large firms in the past few years, the fund must prepare to fund larger liquidations in the future than it did in the past. The report also explores various scenarios for large firm failures.[4] The study concludes that the SIPC funding structure is adequate to cover maximum probable losses and intermediate cash flows associated with the failure of a very large firm but that the liquidation of such a firm could deplete the SIPC fund. Therefore, there is a significant policy question as to whether a fully depleted SIPC fund would provide the kind of public confidence in broker-dealers that the existence of the SIPC is intended to foster (Deloitte and Touche 1990, pt. 3, p. 28). This is a policy question for the SIPC board.

There are other recommendations related to the soundness of broker-dealers that I would make. If customers know more about the financial soundness of their broker-dealer, they are less likely to leave their cash and securities with unsafe firms. Currently, privately owned broker-dealers are required only to file an audited annual statement of financial condition, which is available for public inspection (National Association of Securities Dealers 1985, pp. 4073–74). If broker-dealers have economic problems that show up between annual reports, customers may be unaware of them, which, if known, might cause them to withdraw their funds and securities from the broker-dealer. Thus requiring broker-dealers to supply quarterly unaudited reports on their financial condition would bring the customer into the loop as an active participant in maintaining the soundness of the broker-dealer system. Although such a policy might impose short-term costs on some broker-dealers, the long-term benefit would be less reliance on government and industry regulators for maintaining a sound industry and relying more on the market. Such a change could also mean lower SIPC insurance premiums for broker-dealers. In addition, a change of this importance would be best implemented when the industry is healthy and profitable rather than when many firms are in economic difficulty.

MORE ECONOMIC INPUT INTO SEC POLICYMAKING

The *Wall Street Journal* pointed out that many high-ranking Washington officials are trained as lawyers, in part because they were asked to interpret the law. But when technical market issues arise that are related to economic or finance theory, the lawyers are often at a loss to understand just what is involved. As of August 1991, the SEC had no commisioners with an economics background, and, as has typically been the case, the heads of all major divisions were lawyers. Joseph A. Grundfest, a former SEC commissioner with a joint economics and legal background, pointed out how inappropriate it would be if the FDA had no chemists and biologists and was staffed totally with lawyers (*Wall Street Journal,* August 28, 1991, p. A-10).

The Brady Report also argued that the SEC should expand its scope of competence in the new, more complex market environment:

The SEC's experience and expertise is focused primarily on regulating intramarket activities, not on rationalizing the interactions among markets. To be effective as an intermarket regulator the SEC might have to fund the acquisition of expertise in a wide variety of financial markets, in the credit and banking system, and in international markets. (Brady 1988, p. 61)

The SEC's major rule proposals originate in the Division of Corporate Finance, the Division of Investment Management, or the Division of Market Regulation. The Division of Corporate Finance is responsible for the rules and regulations relating to corporate disclosure and tender offer disclosure; the Division of Investment Management is responsible for investment company regulation; and the Division of Market Regulation regulates the broker-dealers and the exchanges.

During my years at the SEC (1977–1984), the lawyers who headed these divisions had varying interests in economic analysis. Some were interested in using all the economic data and analysis available to provide a strong empirical and economically sound basis for rulemaking. Others were less interested in investigating and debating the economic consequences of proposed rule changes.

Today, each incoming SEC chairman determines the role that the staff economists will play at the SEC. But this is not true at the U.S. Commodities Futures Trading Commission. When Congress created the CFTC in 1974, it defined a specific role for economists: The three main divisions at the CFTC are Enforcement, Trading and Markets, and Economic Analysis. By establishing the Division of Economic Analysis (DEA), Congress recognized the importance of economic analysis in the regulation of the commodities and futures markets.

The DEA is responsible for market surveillance, analysis, and research. It monitors futures and options trading for potential manipulation and other disruptive market situations (U.S. Commodities Futures Trading Commission 1985, p. 47). The DEA reviews exchange contract proposals, advises the CFTC and other divisions about the economic aspects of regulatory policy issues, and conducts economic research.

The role that economists play at the CFTC has been enhanced by the fact that the two most recent chairwomen of the CFTC—Susan M. Phillips and Wendy L. Graham—are economists by training. I do not recommend that the role played by economists at the SEC be patterned after that played by the economists at the CFTC. Rather, my recommendation is that the current Office of Economic Analysis at the SEC be upgraded to a division and expanded to include more expertise in areas suggested by the Brady Report. I also think that this new division should be given authority to make rule proposals to the commission. With economists and financial economists on a more equal footing with the lawyers, their role can evolve toward giving the SEC a more extensive technical financial and economic competence, which is necessary in order for our regulatory structure to provide the adaptability necessary to ensure that the U.S. securities industry will be competitive in the world economy.

In addition to upgrading our economic capability, Congress should ensure that there will always be a strong voice for economic analysis at the commission level, by requiring that at least two of the five commission members have strong economic and/or finance training.

NOTES

1. The "harmonization" of accounting standards across countries is a different long-term task that has been undertaken by the Organization for Economic Cooperation and Development (OECD). A report on the progress of that effort as of 1990 can be found in Organization for Economic Cooperation and Development (1991).

2. This suggestion was made in an interview with me.

3. Litan (1987, chap. 3) examined empirically how significant the benefits of broader financial activity diversification would be. He found that taken as a whole, the earnings of a typical banking organization could have been made more stable if it had been permitted to engage in various nonbanking activities. He also reviewed other studies of the same issue.

4. These scenarios include bad news that would discourage firms from trading with a firm with a problem, major fraud, back-office problems, complex regulatory and legal problems, and limits on trading and credit imposed by outside forces. The report argued that these factors in some combination could result in the sudden failure of a large firm.

References

Alchian, A. A. 1950. "Uncertainty, Evolution and Economic Theory." *Journal of Political Economy,* June, pp. 211–21.

Alchian, A. A., and W. R. Allen. 1969. *Exchange and Production: Theory in Use.* Belmont, Calif.: Wadsworth.

Altman, E. I., and S. A. Nammacher. 1987. *Investing in Junk Bonds: Inside the High Yield Debt Market.* New York: Wiley.

Amihud, Y., T. S. Y. Ho, and R. A. Schwartz. 1985. *Market Making and the Changing Structure of the Securities Industry.* Lexington, Mass.: Lexington Books.

Amit, R., and J. Livnat. 1988. "Diversification Strategies, Business Cycles and Economic Performance." *Strategic Management Journal,* March–April, pp. 99–110.

Aoki, M. 1976. *Optimal Control and System Theory in Dynamic Economic Analysis.* New York: North Holland.

Auerbach, J., and S. L. Hayes, III. 1986. *Investment Banking and Due Diligence: What Price Deregulation?* Boston: Harvard Business School Press.

Auletta, K. 1985. "The Fall of Lehman Brothers, Part II." *New York Times Magazine,* February 24, p. 36.

Bain, J. S. 1956. *Barriers to New Competition.* Cambridge, Mass.: Harvard University Press.

———. 1959. *Industrial Organization.* New York: Wiley.

Baldwin, W. L., and G. L. Childs. 1969. "The Fast Second and Rivalry in Research and Development." *Southern Economic Journal,* July, pp. 18–24.

Baron, D. P. 1979. "The Incentive Problem and the Design of Investment Banking Contracts." *Journal of Banking and Finance* 3, no. 2:157–75.

———. 1982. "A Model of the Demand for Investment Banking Advising and Distribution Services for New Issues." *Journal of Finance* 37, no. 4:955–76.

Baron, D. P., and B. Holmstrom. 1980. "The Investment Banking Contract for New Issues Under Asymmetric Information: Delegation and the Incentive Problem." *Journal of Finance,* December, pp. 1115–38.

Baruch, H. 1971. *Wall Street: Securities Risk.* Washington, D.C.: Acropolis Books.

Baumol, W. J. 1977. "On the Proper Cost Test for Natural Monopoly in a Multiproduct Industry." *American Economic Review,* December, pp. 809–22.

———. 1982. "Contestable Markets: An Uprising in the Theory of Industry Structure." *American Economic Review,* March, pp. 1–15.

Baumol, W. J., and Y. M. Braunstein. 1977. "Empirical Study of Scale Economies and Production Complementarity: The Case of Journal Publication." *Journal of Political Economy,* September, pp. 1037–48.

Baumol, W. J., J. C. Panzar, and R. D. Willig. 1982. *Contestable Markets and the Theory of Industry Structure.* New York: Harcourt Brace Jovanovich.

Baxter, W. F. 1970. "NYSE Fixed Commission Rates: A Public Cartel Goes Public." *Stanford Law Review,* April, pp. 675–712.

Becketti, S., and G. H. Sellon, Jr. 1989. "Has Financial Market Volatility Increased?" *Economic Review of the Federal Reserve Bank of Kansas City,* June, pp. 3–16.

Benston, G. J. 1983. "Federal Regulation of Banking: Analysis and Policy Recommendations." *Journal of Bank Research,* Winter, pp. 216–44.

———. 1990. *The Separation of Commercial and Investment Banking: The Glass–Steagall Act Revisited and Reconsidered.* New York: Oxford University Press.

Berkowitz, S. A., and D. E. Logue. 1987. "The Portfolio Turnover Explosion Explored." *Journal of Portfolio Management* 13, no. 3:38–45.

Berkowitz, S. A., D. E. Logue, and E. A. Noser, Jr. 1988. "The Total Cost of Transaction on the NYSE." *Journal of Finance* 43, no. 1:97–112.

Berlin, M. 1988. "Banking Reform: An Overview of the Restructuring Debate." *Business Review—Federal Reserve Bank of Philadelphia,* July–August, pp. 3–14.

Bloomenthal, H. S., and D. Salcito. 1983. "Customer Protection from Brokerage Failures: The Securities Investor Protection Corporation and the SEC." *University of Colorado Law Review* 52, no. 2:161–202.

Blum, G. A., W. A. Kracaw, and W. G. Lewellen. 1986. "Determinants of the Execution Costs of Common Stock Trades by Individual Investors." *Journal of Financial Research,* Winter, pp. 291–301.

Blum, G. A., and W. G. Lewellen. 1983. "Negotiated Brokerage Commissions and the Individual Investor." *Journal of Financial and Quantitative Analysis,* September, pp. 331–43.

Brady, N. F. [Chairman] 1988. *The Presidential Task Force on Market Mechanisms,* January 8, Washington, D.C.: Government Printing Office.

Brooks, J. 1973. *The Go-Go Years.* New York: Weybright and Talley.

———. 1980. "Corporate Pension Fund Asset Management." In *Abuse on Wall Street: Conflicts of Interest in the Securities Markets,* ed. R. A. Schotland, pp. 224–266. Westport, Conn.: Quorum Books.

Bull, C. 1983. "Implicit Contracts in the Absence of Enforcement and Risk Aversion." *American Economic Review* 73, no. 4:658–71.

Carlton, D. W., and J. M. Perloff. 1990. *Modern Industrial Organization.* Glenview, Ill.: Scott, Foresman Little Brown.

Carosso, V. P. 1970. *Investment Banking in America: A History.* Cambridge, Mass.: Harvard University Press.

Chandler, A. 1969. "The Structure of American Industry in the Twentieth Century: A Historical Review." *Business History Review,* Autumn, pp. 274–75.

Chen, N. F., R. Roll, and S. A. Ross. 1986. "Economic Forces and the Stock Market." *Journal of Business* 59, no. 3:383–403.

Chiswick, B. R., and S. J. Chiswick. 1975. *Statistics and Economics: A Problem Solving Course.* University Park: Pennsylvania State University Press.

Chuppe, T. M., H. H. Haworth, and M. G. Watkins. 1989. "Global Finance: Causes, Consequences and Prospects for the Future." *Global Finance Journal,* Fall, pp. 1–20.

Clareman, L. S. 1990. "The New Rules of Suing a Broker." *1991 Investors' Guide, Fortune,* Fall, pp. 207–8.

Coase, R. 1960. "The Problem of Social Cost." *Journal of Law and Economics* 3:1–44.

Cohen, J. B., E. D. Finbarg, and A. Zeikel. 1987. *Investment Analysis and Portfolio Management.* 5th ed. Homewood, Ill.: Irwin.

Cohen, M. F., and G. J. Stigler. 1971. *Can Regulatory Agencies Protect Consumers?* Washington, D.C.: American Enterprise Institute.

Condon, K. A. 1981. "Measuring Equity Transactions Costs." *Financial Analysts Journal,* September–October, pp. 57–60.

Courtadon, C. L. 1985. *The Competitive Structure of the Eurobond Underwriting Industry.* Monograph 1985-1. New York: Salomon Brothers Center, New York University.

Dale, B. 1988. "The Grass May Not Be Greener: Commercial Banks and Investment Banking." *Economic Perspectives,* November–December, pp. 3–13.

Deloitte & Touche. 1990. *The Securities Investor Protection Corporation: Special Study of the SIPC Fund and Funding Requirements,* October 8. New York: Deloitte & Touche.

Doede, R. W. 1967. "The Monopoly Power of the New York Stock Exchange." Ph.D. diss. University of Chicago.

Donaldson, W. H. 1991. "Enhancing America's Position in an Age of Global Markets." Remarks to the National Press Club, March 4.

Dougall, H. E., and J. E. Gaumnity. 1986. *Capital Markets and Institutions.* 5th ed. Englewood Cliffs, N.J.: Prentice-Hall.

Duffee, G., P. Kupiec, and P. White. 1990. "A Primer on Program Trading and Stock Price Volatility: A Survey of the Issues and the Evidence." *Board of Governors of the Federal Reserve System,* January, pp. 1–33.

Eccles, R. G., and D. B. Crane. 1988. *Doing Deals: Investment Banks at Work.* Boston: Harvard Business School Press.

Eckl, S., J. N. Robinson, and D. C. Thomas. 1990. *Financial Engineering: A Handbook of Derivative Products.* Oxford: Basil Blackwell.

Edmister, R. 1978. "Commission Cost Structure, Shifts and Scale Economies." *Journal of Finance,* May, pp. 477–86.

Epps, T. W. 1976. "The Demand for Brokers' Services: The Relation Between Securities Trading Volume and Transaction Cost." *Bell Journal of Economics,* Spring, pp. 163–94.

Fabozzi, F. J., and R. R. West. 1981. "Negotiated Versus Competitive Underwritings of Public Utility Bonds: Just One More Time." *Journal of Financial and Quantiative Analysis,* September, pp. 323–39.

Fama, E. F. 1991. "Efficient Capital Markets: II." *Journal of Finance,* December, pp. 1575–1617.

Färe, R., S. Grosskopf, and C. A. Lovell. 1985. *The Measurement of Efficiency of Production.* Amsterdam: Kluwer Nijhoff.

Federal Reserve Board. *Federal Reserve Bulletin,* various issues.

Finnerty, J. D. 1988. "Financial Engineering in Corporate Finance: An Overview." *Financial Management,* Winter, pp. 14–33.

Fischel, D. R. 1986. "Regulatory Conflict and Entry Regulation of New Futures Contracts." *Journal of Business* 59, no. 2:S85–S102.

Flannery, M. J. 1985. "An Economic Evaluation of Bank Securities Activities Before 1933." In *Deregulating Wall Street: Commercial Bank Penetration of the Corporate Securities Market,* ed. I. Walter. New York: Wiley.

Fons, J. S. 1987. "Economic Commentary: A Critical Look at SIPC." *Federal Reserve Bank of Cleveland,* July, pp. 1–6.

Fortune, P. 1989. "An Assessment of Financial Market Volatility: Bills, Bonds and Stocks." *New England Economic Review,* November–December, pp. 13–28.

Freedman, S. 1982. "The Unsafe Harbor: Section 28(e) of the Securities Exchange Act of 1934." *Securities Regulation Law Journal,* Fall, pp. 195–234.

Friedman, M. 1985. "The Case for Overhauling the Federal Reserve." *Challenge,* July–August, pp. 4–12.

Friend, I. 1977. "The Increase in Institutional Holdings Does No Harm to the Stock Market." *Financier,* February, pp. 31–34.

Friend, I., and M. Blume. 1973. "Competitive Commission on the New York Stock Exchange." *Journal of Finance,* September, pp. 795–819.

Furbush, D. 1990. "Program Trading in Context: The Changing Structure of Equity Markets." Paper presented at the Shadow Securities and Exchange Commission Meeting, Washington, D.C., November 9.

Garbade, K. D. 1982. *Securities Markets.* New York: McGraw-Hill.

Gaskins, D. W. 1971. "Dynamic Limit Pricing: Optimal Pricing Under Threat of Entry." *Journal of Economic Theory* 3, no. 3:306–22.

Geroski, P. A. 1990. "Innovation, Technological Opportunity, and Market Structure." *Oxford Economic Papers* 42, no. 3:586–602.

Giddy, I. H. 1985. "Is Equity Underwriting Risky for Commercial Bank Affiliates?" In *Deregulating Wall Street: Commercial Bank Penetration of the Corporate Securities Market,* ed. I. Walter. New York: Wiley.

Giordano, N. A. 1991. "Jurisdictional Debate Between the Securities and Futures Industry." *Journal of Commerce and Finance,* Fall, pp. 27–30.

Godfrey, M., C. Granger, and O. Morgenstern. 1964. "The Random-Walk Hypothesis of Stock Market Behavior." *Kyklos* 17, no. 1:1–30.

Goldberg, L. G., G. A. Hanweck, M. Keenan, and A. Young. 1991. "Economies of Scale and Scope in the Securities Industry." *Journal of Banking and Finance* 15, no. 1:101–7.

Goldberg, L. G., M. Keenan, L. Schrier, and A. Young. 1989. "Relative Revenue Distribution in the Securities Industry." *Quarterly Review of Economics and Business,* Autumn, pp. 86–94.

Golec, J. H. 1990. "Empirical Tests of a Principal–Agent Model of the Investor–Investment Advisor Relationship." Working Paper, Clark University, pp. 1–23.

Greenwich Associates. 1988. *Don't Fight the Problem—Institutional Investors 1988.* Greenwich, Conn.: Greenwich Associates.

———. 1990. *Getting Down to Business—Institutional Investors 1990.* Greenwich, Conn.: Greenwich Associates.

Greer, D. F. 1980. *Industrial Organization and Public Policy.* New York: Macmillan.

Haberman, G. 1987. "Capital Requirements of Commercial and Investment Banks: Contrasts in Regulation." *Federal Reserve Bank of New York—Quarterly Review,* August, pp. 1–10.

Hay, D. A., and D. J. Morris. 1979. *Industrial Economics: Theory and Evidence.* Oxford: Oxford University Press.

Hayes, S. L. 1971. "Investment Banking: Power Structure in Flux." *Harvard Business Review,* March–April, pp. 136–152.

———. 1979. "The Transformation of Investment Banking." *Harvard Business Review,* January–February, pp. 153–71.

———, ed. 1987. *Wall Street and Regulation.* Boston: Harvard Business School Press.

Hayes, S. L., and P. M. Hubbard. 1990. *Investment Banking: A Tale of Three Cities.* Boston: Harvard Business School Press.

Hayes, S. L., A. M. Spence, and D. Van Prazz Marks. 1983. *Competition in the Investment Banking Industry.* Cambridge, Mass.: Harvard University Press.

Hazen, T. L. 1990. *The Law of Securities Regulation.* 2nd ed. St. Paul: West.

Heggestad, A. A. 1979. "Market Structure, Competition, and Performance in Financial Institutions: A Survey of Banking." In *Issues in Financial Regulation,* ed. F. R. Edwards, pp. 449–90. New York: McGraw-Hill.

Herman, E. S. 1980. "Commercial Bank Trust Departments." In *Abuse on Wall Street: Con-*

flicts of Interest in the Securities Markets, ed. R. A. Schotland, pp. 23–157. Westport, Conn.: Quorum Books.

Hill, C. W. L., P. Hwang, and W. C. Kim. 1990. "An Eclectic Theory of the Choice of International Entry Mode." *Strategic Management Journal* 11, no. 2:117–28.

Ho, T. S. Y., and R. G. Macris. 1984. "Dealer Bid-Ask Quotes and Transaction Prices: An Empirical Study of Some AMEX Options." *Journal of Finance,* March, pp. 23–45.

Holmstrom, B. 1979. "Moral Hazard and Observability." *Bell Journal of Economics,* Spring, pp. 74–91.

Hymer, S., and P. Pashigian. 1962. "Firm Size and Rate of Growth." *Journal of Political Economy* 70, no. 6:556–69.

Ibbotson, R. G., and G. P. Brinson. 1987. *Investment Markets: Gaining the Performance Advantage.* New York: McGraw-Hill.

Ibbotson, R. G., and R. Sinquefield. 1982. *Stocks, Bonds, Bills, and Inflation: The Past and the Future.* Charlottesville, Va.: Financial Analysts Research Foundation.

Investment Company Institute. *Mutual Fund Fact Book,* various issues.

Investment Dealers Digest. 1970. *Corporate Financings: 1960–1969.* New York: Investment Dealers Digest.

Jacquemin, A. 1987. *The New Industrial Organization: Market Forces and Strategic Behavior.* Cambridge, Mass.: MIT Press.

Jaffe, S. M. 1977. *Broker-Dealers and Securities Markets: A Guide to the Regulatory Process.* New York: McGraw-Hill.

Jarrell, G. A. 1984. "Change at the Exchange: The Causes and Effects of Deregulation." *Journal of Law and Economics,* October, pp. 273–312.

———. 1987. "Financial Innovation and Corporate Merger." In *The Merger Boom,* ed. L. E. Browne and E. S. Rosengren, pp. 52–73. Boston: Federal Reserve Bank of Boston.

Jensen, M. C. 1989. "Eclipse of the Public Corporation." *Harvard Business Review,* September–October, pp. 61–74.

Jensen, M. C., and W. H. Meckling. 1976. "Theory of the Firm: Managerial Behavior, Agency Costs and Ownership Structure." *Journal of Financial Economics* 3, no. 4:305–45.

Johnsen, D. B., and D. L. Williams. 1991. "Soft Dollars: The Currency of Unpriced Exchange?" Working Paper, University of California at Los Angeles, June.

Kandel, M., and P. Greer. 1968. "Inside the New York Stock Exchange." In *The Anatomy of Wall Street,* ed. C. Role and G. J. Nelson. Philadelphia: Lippincott.

Kane, E. J. 1983. "Policy Implications of Structural Changes in Financial Markets." *American Economic Review,* May, pp. 99–100.

Kane, E. J., and H. Unal. 1988. "Parameter Variability, Event Studies, and the Two-Index Model." In *Proceedings of a Conference on Bank Structure and Competition,* pp. 178–201. Chicago: Federal Reserve Bank of Chicago.

Karmel, R. S. 1982. *Regulation by Prosecution: The Securities and Exchange Commission vs. Corporate America.* New York: Simon and Schuster.

Kaufman, G. G., and L. R. Mote. 1988. "Securities Activities of Commercial Banks: The Current Economic and Legal Environment." Staff memorandum no. SM88-4, Federal Reserve Bank of Chicago.

Keenan, M. 1979. "The Scope of Deregulation in the Securities Industry." In *The Deregulation of the Banking and Securities Industries,* ed. L. Goldberg and L. White, pp. 115–32. Lexington, Mass.: Lexington Books.

Kelley, E. J. 1985. "Legislative History of the Glass–Steagall Act." In *Deregulating Wall Street: Commercial Bank Penetration of the Corporate Securities Market,* ed. I. Walter, pp. 41–65. New York: Wiley.

Kerekes, G. T. 1970. "Evolution and the Economics of the Securities Industry in the United

States.'' In *The Stock Market Handbook*, ed. F. G. Zarb and G. T. Kerekes. Homewood, Ill.: Dow Jones–Irwin.

Kirvin, J. H. 1970. "The Cashiering Function." In *The Stock Market Handbook*, ed. F. G. Zarb and G. T. Kerekes. Homewood, Ill.: Dow Jones–Irwin.

Klein, B., and K. Leffler. 1981. "The Role of Market Forces in Assuring Contractual Performance." *Journal of Political Economy* 89, no. 4:615–41.

Kohlmeier, L. M. 1980. "State and Local Pension Fund Asset Management." In *Abuse on Wall Street: Conflicts of Interest in the Securities Markets*, ed. R. A. Schotland, pp. 267–319. Westport, Conn.: Quorum Books.

Kohn, M. 1991. *Money, Banking, and Financial Markets*. New York: Dryden.

Kupiec, P. H. 1990. "A Survey of Exchange-traded Basket Instruments." *Journal of Financial Services Research* 4, no. 3:175–90.

Leffler, G. L., and L. C. Farwell. 1963. *The Stock Market*. 3rd ed. New York: Ronald Press.

Levy, D. T., and L. J. Haber. 1986. "An Advantage of the Multiproduct Firm: The Transferability of Firm-specific Capital." *Journal of Economic Behavior and Organization* 7:291–302.

Lewis, M. 1989. *Liar's Poker: Rising Through the Wreckage on Wall Street*. New York: Norton.

Lipton, M., and R. B. Manzur. 1975. "The Chinese Wall Solution to the Conflict Problems of Securities Firms. *New York University Law Review*, June, pp. 459–511.

Litan, R. E. 1987. *What Should Banks Do?* Washington, D.C.: Brookings Institution.

Loeb, T. F. 1983. "Trading Costs: The Critical Link Between Investment Information and Results." *Financial Analysts Journal*, May–June, pp. 39–44.

Logue, D. E. and J. R. Lindvall. 1974. "The Behavior of Investment Bankers: An Econometric Investigation." *Journal of Finance*, March, pp. 203–15.

Logue, D. E., and R. J. Rogalski. 1979. "Does It Pay to Shop for Your Bond Underwriter?" *Harvard Business Review*, July–August, pp. 111–17.

Lorie, J. H., P. Dodd, and M. H. Kimpton. 1985. *The Stock Market: Theories and Evidence.* 2nd ed. Homewood, Ill.: Irwin.

Lorie, J. H., and M. T. Hamilton. 1973. *The Stock Market: Theories and Evidence*. Homewood, Ill.: Irwin.

Lunn, J. 1986. "An Empirical Analysis of Process and Product Patenting: A Simultaneous Equation Framework." *Journal of Industrial Economics*, March, pp. 319–28.

Macey, J. R. 1991. *Insider Trading: Economics, Politics, and Policy*. Washington, D.C.: American Enterprise Institute Press.

Mandelker, G., and A. Raviv. 1977. "Investment Banking: An Economic Analysis of Optimal Underwriting Contracts." *Journal of Finance*, June, pp. 683–94.

Mann, H. M. 1975. "The New York Stock Exchange: A Cartel at the End of Its Reign." In *Promoting Competition in Regulated Markets*, ed. A. Phillips. pp. 301–27. Washington, D.C.: Brookings Institution.

Mansfield, E. 1962. "Entry, Gibrat's Law, Innovation and the Growth of Firms." *American Economic Review*, December, pp. 1023–51.

———. 1968. *Industrial Research and Technological Innovation*. New York: Norton.

Mansfield, E., J. Rappoport, J. Schnee, S. Wagner, and M. Hamburger. 1971. *Research and Innovation in the Modern Corporation*. New York: Norton.

Marr, M. W., and A. B. Poulsen. 1988. "Shelf Registration: The Demise of the Regional Broker/Dealer Because of Reduced Underwriting Revenue." Working Paper, Tulane University, December.

Martin, S. 1988. *Industrial Economics: Economic Analysis and Public Policy*. New York: Macmillan.

Mason, E. S. 1939. "Price and Production Policies of Large-Scale Enterprise." *American Economic Review,* supp. 29:61–74.

———. 1949. "The Current Status of the Monopoly Problem in the United States." *Harvard Law Review* 62:1265–85.

Matthews, J. O. 1984. "The Securities Industry: An Industrialization Analysis." Ph.D. diss., Temple University.

Matthews, J. O., and W. Dellva. 1991. "Profitability and Risk in the Securities Brokerage Industry: 1972–1990." Working Paper, Villanova University, pp. 1–25.

Mayer, M. 1980. "Broker-Dealer Firms." In *Abuse on Wall Street: Conflicts of Interest in the Securities Markets,* ed. R. A. Schotland. Westport, Conn.: Quorum Books.

Mayers, D., and C. W. Smith, Jr. 1981. "Contractual Provisions Organizational Structure, and Conflict Control in Insurance Markets." *Journal of Business* 54, no. 3:407–35.

McCauley, R. N., and S. A. Zimmer. 1989. "Explaining International Differences in the Cost of Capital." *Federal Reserve Bank of New York—Quarterly Review,* Summer, pp. 7–28.

———. 1991. "The Cost of Capital for Securities Firms in the United States and Japan." *Federal Reserve Bank of New York—Quarterly Review,* Autumn, pp. 14–27.

Mead, R. H., and K. A. O'Neil. 1986. "The Performance of the Bank's Competitors." In Federal Reserve Bank of New York, *Recent Trends in Commercial Bank Profitability.* New York: Federal Reserve Bank of New York.

Miller, E. 1967. "Background and Structure of the Industry." In *Investment Banking and the New Issues Market,* ed. I. Friend et al., pp. 80–175. New York: World.

Miller, M. H. 1986. "Financial Innovation: The Last Twenty Years and the Next." *Journal of Financial and Quantitative Analysis,* December, pp. 459–71.

Minnerop, H. F., and H. R. Stoll. 1985. "Technological Change in the Back Office: Implications for Structure and Regulation of the Securities Industry." Working Paper No. 85-105, Owen Graduate School, Vanderbilt University, April.

Mitchell, W. E., and R. L. Sorensen. 1986. "Pricing, Price Dispersion, and Information: The Discount Brokerage Industry." *Journal of Economics and Business* 38, no. 4:273–82.

Molinari, S. L., and N. S. Kibler. 1983. "Broker-Dealers' Financial Responsibility Under the Uniform Net Capital Rule—A Case for Liquidity." *Georgetown Law Review,* October, pp. 1–37.

Morris, C. S. 1989a. "Managing Interest Rate Risk with Interest Rate Futures." *Economic Review of the Federal Reserve Bank of Kansas City,* March, pp. 3–20.

———. 1989b. "Managing Stock Market Risk with Stock Index Futures." *Economic Review of the Federal Reserve Bank of Kansas City,* June, pp. 3–16.

Mukhopadhyay, A. 1985. "Technological Progress and Change in Market Concentration in the U.S., 1963–1977." *Southern Economic Journal,* July, pp. 141–49.

National Association of Securities Dealers. *The NASDAQ Securities Fact Book,* various issues.

———. 1985. *Reprint of the Manual.* Washington, D.C.: NASD.

———. 1992a. *1992 Fact Book & Company Directory.* Washington, D.C.: NASD.

———. 1992b. *The NASDAQ Handbook: The Stock Market for the Next 100 Years.* Chicago: Probus.

National Economic Research Associates. 1970. *Commission Costs on the NYSE (1970).* Washington, D.C.: NERA.

Nelson, R. R., and S. G. Winter. 1978. "Forces Generating and Limiting Concentration Under Schumpeterian Competition." *Bell Journal of Economics,* Autumn, pp. 524–48.

———. 1982. "The Schumpeterian Tradeoff Revisited." *American Economic Review* 72, no. 1:114–32.

New York Stock Exchange. *Fact Book,* various issues.

———. 1968. "Economic Effects of Negotiated Commission Rates on the Brokerage Industry, the Market for Corporate Securities, and the Investing Public." A brief submitted to the SEC, August.

———. 1986. *Shareownership 1985.* New York: NYSE.

———. 1990a. *Market Volatility and Investor Confidence,* June 7. New York: NYSE.

———. 1990b. "The USSR/NYSE Seminar: Stock Exchanges and Their Role in Financial Markets." Moscow, October 8–10.

———. 1991a. *Institutional Investor Fact Book 1991,* January. New York: NYSE.

———. 1991b. *Shareownership 1990.* New York: NYSE.

Offer, A. R., and A. Melnick. 1978. "Price Deregulation in the Brokerage Industry: An Empirical Analysis." *Bell Journal of Economic,* Autumn, pp. 633–41.

Organization for Economic Cooperation and Development. 1991. *Accounting Standards Harmonization.* No. 6, *New Financial Instruments.* Paris: OECD.

Panzar, J. C., and R. D. Willig. 1981. "Economies of Scope." *American Economic Review* 71, no. 2:268–73.

Peach, W. N. 1941. *The Securities Affiliates of National Banks. Johns Hopkins University Studies in Historical and Political Science,* vol. 58, no. 3. Baltimore: Johns Hopkins University Press.

Peltzman, S. 1976. "Toward a More General Theory of Regulation." *Journal of Law and Economics,* August, pp. 211–40.

Perez, R. C. 1984. *Inside Investment Banking.* New York: Praeger.

Petruzzi, C., M. DelValle, and S. Judlowe. 1990. "Patent and Copyright Protection for Innovations in Finance." In *The Handbook of Financial Engineering,* ed. C. W. Smith, Jr., and C. W. Smithson, pp. 625–34. New York: Harper Business.

Phillips, A. 1971. *Technology and Market Structure: A Study of the Aircraft Industry.* Lexington, Mass.: Heath.

———. 1978. "The Metamorphosis of Markets: Commercial and Investment Banking." *Journal of Comparative Corporate Law and Securities Regulation,* pp. 227–43.

Phillips, S. M., and J. R. Zecher. 1981. *The SEC and the Public Interest.* Cambridge, Mass.: MIT Press.

Porter, M. E. 1980. *Competitive Strategy: Techniques for Analyzing Industries and Competitors.* New York: Free Press.

Poulsen, A., and M. W. Marr. 1987. "Shelf Registration: An Analysis of Intra-Industry Changes in Underwriting Revenues," Working Paper, Office of the Chief Economist, U.S. Securities and Exchange Commission, Washington, D.C., pp. 1–27.

Primeaux, W. J., and M. C. Smith. 1976. "Price Patterns and the Kinky Demand Curve." *Journal of Law and Economics,* April, pp. 189–200.

Pugel, T. A., and L. J. White. 1985. "An Analysis of the Competitive Effects of Allowing Commercial Bank Affiliates to Underwrite Corporate Securities." In *Deregulating Wall Street: Commercial Bank Penetration of the Corporate Securities Market,* ed. I. Walter. New York: Wiley.

Ranson, R. D., and W. G. Shipman. 1981. "Institutional Buying Power and the Stock Market." *Financial Analysts Journal,* September–October, pp. 62–68.

Reilly, F. K., and D. J. Wright. 1984. "Block Trading and Aggregate Stock Price Volatility." *Financial Analysts Journal,* March–April, pp. 54–60.

Rogowski, R. J., and E. H. Sorensen. 1985. "Deregulation in Investment Banking: Shelf Registrations, Structure, and Performance." *Financial Management,* Spring, pp. 5–15.

Roll, R. 1984. "A Simple Implicit Measure of the Effective Bid-Ask Spread in an Efficient Market." *Journal of Finance* 39, no. 4:1127–39.

Ross, S. 1973. "The Economic Theory of Agency: The Principal's Problem." *American Economic Review* 63:134–39.

Rowen, H. 1976. "The Securities Acts Amendments of 1975: A Legislative History." *Securities Regulation Law Journal,* Winter, pp. 329–46.

Ruder, D. S. 1989. *Concerning the Globalization of the Securities Markets.* Testimony before the Senate Committee on Banking, Housing, and Urban Affairs. 101st Cong., 1st sess., June 15.

Salmanowitz, J. M. 1977. "Broker Investment Recommendations and the Efficient Capital Market Hypothesis: A Proposed Cautionary Legend." *Stanford Law Review,* May, pp. 1077–1114.

Salop, S. 1976. "Information and Market Structure: Information on Monopolistic Competition." *American Economic Review,* May, pp. 240–45.

Saunders, A. 1985. "Securities Activities of Commercial Banks: The Problems of Conflict of Interest." *Business Review—Federal Reserve Bank of Philadelphia,* July–August, pp. 17–27.

Schaefer, J. M., and A. J. Warner. 1977. "Concentration Trends and Competition in the Securities Industry." *Financial Analysts Journal,* November–December, pp. 29–34.

———. 1978. "Rejoinder to West and Tinic." *Financial Analysts Journal,* May–June, pp. 47–49.

Scherer, F. M. 1967. "Research and Development Resource Allocation Under Rivalry." *Quarterly Journal of Economics,* August, pp. 359–94.

———. 1980. *Industrial Market Structure and Economic Performance.* 2nd ed. Chicago: Rand McNally.

Scherer, F. M., and D. Ross. 1990. *Industrial Market Structure and Economic Performance.* 3rd ed. Chicago: Rand McNally.

Schneider, D. W. 1981. "Evolving Proof Standards Under Section 7 and Mergers in Transitional Markets: The Securities Industry Example." *Wisconsin Law Review* 1981, no. 1: 1–105.

Schotland, R. A., ed. 1980. "Introduction." *Abuse on Wall Street: Conflict of Interest in the Securities Markets.* Westport, Conn.: Quorum Books.

Schreiner, J. C., and K. V. Smith. 1980. "The Impact of Mayday on Diversification Costs." *Journal of Portfolio Management,* September, pp. 28–36.

Schwartz, R. A., and D. K. Whitcomb. 1988. *Transactions Costs and Institutional Investor Trading Strategies.* Monograph 1988-2/3. New York: Salomon Brothers Center, New York University.

Schwert, G. W. 1977. "Public Regulation of the National Securities Exchanges: A Test of the Capture Hypothesis." *Bell Journal of Economics,* Spring, pp. 128–50.

———. 1990. "Stock Market Volatility." *Financial Analysts Journal,* May–June, pp. 23–34.

Securities Industry Association. *Fact Book,* various issues.

———. *Securities Industry Yearbook,* various issues.

Securities Investor Protection Corporation. 1992. *Annual Report.* Washington, D.C.: SIPC.

Seligman, J. 1982. *The Transformation of Wall Street: A History of the Securities and Exchange Commission and Modern Corporate Finance.* Boston: Houghton Mifflin.

Sharpe, W. F. 1985. *Investments.* 3rd ed. Englewood Cliffs, N.J.: Prentice-Hall.

Shavell, S. 1979. "Risk Sharing and Incentives in the Principal and Agent Relationship." *Bell Journal of Economics,* Spring, pp. 55–73.

Shearson Hayden Stone. 1978. *Form S-7 Registration Statement,* September 7.

Shepard, L. 1975. *The Securities Brokerage Industry: Nonprice Competition and Noncompetitive Pricing.* Lexington, Mass.: Lexington Books.

Shepherd, W. G. 1972. "The Elements of Market Structure." *Review of Economics and Statistics* 54, no. 1:25–37.

——. 1979. *The Economics of Industrial Organization.* Englewood Cliffs, N.J.: Prentice-Hall.

Shiller, R. J. 1991. "The Significance of the Growth of Institutional Investing." In New York Stock Exchange, *Institutional Investor Fact Book 1991,* January. New York: NYSE.

Silber, W. L. 1979. *Municipal Revenue Bond Costs and Bank Underwriting: A Survey of the Evidence.* Monograph 1979-3. New York: Salomon Brothers Center for the Study of Financial Institutions, New York University.

Smith, C. W. 1977. "Alternative Methods for Raising Capital: Rights versus Underwritten Offerings." *Journal of Financial Economics,* December, pp. 273–307.

——. 1992. "Economics and Ethics: The Case of Salomon Brothers." *Journal of Applied Corporate Finance,* Summer, pp. 23–28.

Smythe, M. K. 1984. "Government Supervised Self-regulation in the Securities Industry and the Antitrust Laws: Suggestions for an Accommodation." *North Carolina Law Review.*

Spence, M. 1983. "Contestable Markets and the Theory of Industry Structure: A Review Article." *Journal of Economic Literature,* September, pp. 981–90.

Starks, L. T. 1987. "Performance Incentive Fees: An Agency Theoretic Approach." *Journal of Financial and Quantitative Analysis,* March, pp. 17–32.

Stevens, J. W. 1979. "The Intersection of the Banking and Securities Industries and Future Deregulation." In *The Deregulation of the Banking and Securities Industries,* ed. L. G. Goldberg and L. J. White. Lexington, Mass.: Lexington Books.

Stigler, G. J. 1947. "The Kinky Oligopoly Demand Curve and Rigid Prices." *Journal of Political Economy,* October, pp. 432–49.

——. 1958. "The Economics of Scale." *Journal of Law and Economics,* October, pp. 54–71.

——. 1964. "Public Regulation of the Securities Markets." *Journal of Business,* April, pp. 117–42.

——. 1968. *The Organization of Industry.* Homewood, Ill.: Irwin.

——. 1971. "The Theory of Economic Regulation." *Bell Journal of Economics and Management Science,* Spring, pp. 3–21.

Stoll, H. R. 1979. *Regulation of the Securities Markets: An Examination of the Effects of Increased Competition.* Monograph 1979-2. New York: Salomon Brothers Center for the Study of Financial Institutional, New York University.

——. 1992. "Debate over the Organization of the Stock Market: Competition or Fragmentation?" Financial Markets Research Center Policy Paper 92-01. Owen Graduate School of Management, Vanderbilt University.

Stone, B. K. 1974. "Systematic Interest-Rate Risk in a Two-Index Model of Returns." *Journal of Financial and Quantitative Analysis,* 9:709–21.

Teece, D. J. 1980. "Economies of Scope and the Scope of the Enterprise." *Journal of Economic Behavior and Organization* 1:223–47.

——. 1982. "Towards an Economic Theory of the Multiproduct Firm." *Journal of Economic Behavior and Organization* 3:39–63.

——. 1987. "Technology Change and the Nature of the Firm." University of California at Berkeley, July.

Telser, L. 1980. "A Theory of Self-enforcing Agreements." *Journal of Business* 53, no. 1: 27–44.

Thurow, L. 1992. *Head to Head: The Coming Economic Battle Among Japan, Europe, and America.* New York: Morrow.

Tinic, S. M., and R. W. West. 1980. "The Securities Industry Under Negotiated Brokerage

Commissions: Changes in the Structure and Performance of New York Stock Exchange Member Firms." *Bell Journal of Economics,* Spring, pp. 29–41.

Tobin, J. 1987a. "On the Efficiency of the Financial System." In J. Tobin, *Policies for Prosperity: Essays in a Keynesian Mode,* pp. 282–96. Cambridge, Mass.: Wheatsheaf Books.

———. 1987b. "The Case for Preserving Regulatory Distinctions." In Federal Reserve Bank of Kansas City, *Restructuring the Financial System,* pp. 167–84. Kansas City, Mo.: Federal Reserve Bank.

Trzyna, P. T. 1992. "Remarks at 1992 Conference and Annual Membership Meeting." International Association of Financial Engineers, December 10, New York.

Tufano, P. 1989. "Financial Innovation and First Mover Advantages: An Empirical Analysis." *Journal of Financial Economics* 25, no. 2:213–40.

U.S. Commodity Futures Trading Commission. 1985. *Annual Report.* Washington, D.C.: CFTC.

U.S. Congress. House. 1963. *Report of Special Study of Securities Markets of the Securities and Exchange Commission.* House Document No. 95. 88th Cong., 1st sess., August.

———. 1971a. *Institutional Investor Study Report of the Securities and Exchange Commission.* House Document No. 92-64. 92nd Cong., 1st sess., March.

———. 1971b. *Study of Unsafe and Unsound Practices of Brokers and Dealers.* House Document No. 92-231. 92nd Cong., 1st sess., March.

U.S. Congress. Office of Technology Assessment. 1990. *Electronic Bulls and Bears: U.S. Securities Markets and Information Technology.* September. Washington, D.C.: Government Printing Office.

U.S. Congress. Senate. Committee on Banking, Housing and Urban Affairs. 1972. *Stock Exchange Commission Rates: Hearings Before the Subcommittee on Securities on S. 3169,* March.

———. 1973. *Securities Industry Study: Report of the Subcommittee on Securities.* 93rd Cong., 1st sess., August.

U.S. Department of Commerce. Bureau of the Census. *Government Finances,* various issues.

U.S. Securities and Exchange Commission. 1936. *Report on the Feasibility and Advisability of the Complete Segregation of the Functions of Dealer and Broker,* June 20. Washington, D.C.: SEC.

———. 1971. *The Financial Condition of Broker-Dealers: A Question of the Adequacy of Capital and Regulatory Safeguards,* June. Washington, D.C.: SEC.

———. 1973. *The Broker-Dealer Community: Historic Trends and Current Financial Structure,* March. Washington, D.C.: SEC.

———. 1974a. *Discussion Paper on Some Aspects of the Capital Markets and the Securities Industry,* October. Washington, D.C.: SEC.

———. 1974b. *Profile of Publicly Owned Registered Broker-Dealers,* December. Washington, D.C.: SEC.

———. 1978. *Staff Report on the Securities Industry in 1977,* May. Washington, D.C.: SEC.

———. 1979. *Staff Report on the Securities Industry in 1978,* July. Washington, D.C.: SEC.

———. 1980a. *Initial Public Offerings of Common Stock: The Role of Regional Broker-Dealers in the Capital Formation Process.* Washington, D.C.: SEC.

———. 1980b. *Staff Report on the Securities Industry in 1979,* September. Washington, D.C.: SEC.

———. 1981a. *Form S-18: A Monitoring Report on the First 18 Months of Its Use,* March. Washington, D.C.: SEC.

———. 1981b. *Staff Report on the Securities Industry in 1980,* September. Washington, D.C.: SEC.

———. 1982a. "Commission Rate Trends, 1975–1981." News release, July 7.

———. 1982b. *Staff Report on the Securities Industry in 1981,* October. Washington, D.C.: SEC.

———. 1985. *The Financial and Regulatory Capital Needs of the Securities Industry,* January. Washington, D.C.: SEC.

———. 1987. *The Use of Repurchase Agreements by Broker-Dealers,* December. Washington, D.C.: SEC.

———. 1988. *The October 1987 Market Break: A Report by the Division of Market Regulation,* February. Washington, D.C.: SEC.

———. 1990. *Broker-Dealer Registration Package,* February. Washington, D.C.: SEC.

———. 1992. *Annual Report.* Washington, D.C.: SEC.

U.S. Small Business Administration. 1977. *Report of the Task Force on Venture and Equity Capital for Small Business,* January. Washington, D.C.: SBA.

Van Horne, J. C. 1985. "The Presidential Address: Of Financial Innovations and Excesses." *Journal of Finance* 40, no. 3:621–31.

Vise, D. A., and S. Coll. 1991. *Eagle on the Street.* New York: Scribner.

Walter, I. 1988. *Global Competition in Financial Services: Market Structure, Protection, and Trade Liberalization.* Cambridge, Mass.: Ballinger.

Walter, I., and R. C. Smith. 1990. *Investment Banking in Europe: Restructuring for the 1990s.* Oxford: Basil Blackwell.

Weimer, D., and A. Vining. 1989. *Policy Analysis, Concepts and Practice.* Englewood Cliffs, N.J.: Prentice-Hall.

Welles, C. 1975. *The Last Days of the Club.* New York: Dutton.

West, R. 1965. "New Issue Concessions on Municipal Bonds: A Case of Monopsony Pricing." *Journal of Business,* April, pp. 135–48.

———. 1966. "More on the Effects of Municipal Bond Monopsony." *Journal of Business,* April, pp. 305–8.

West, R., and S. Tinic. 1971. "Minimum Commission Rates on the New York Stock Exchange Transactions." *Bell Journal of Economics and Management Science,* Autumn, pp. 577–605.

———. 1978. "Concentration Trends and Competition in the Securities Industry: An Alternative Viewpoint." *Financial Analysts Journal,* May–June, pp. 46–56.

Weston, J. F., and T. E. Copeland. 1989. *Managerial Finance.* 8th ed. Chicago: Dryden.

White, L. J. 1991. *The S&L Debacle: Public Policy Lessons for Bank and Thrift Regulation.* New York: Oxford University Press.

Wigmore, B. A. 1990. "The Decline in Credit Quality of New-Issue Junk Bonds." *Financial Analysts Journal,* September–October, pp. 53–62.

Williamson, O. E. 1975. *Markets and Hierarchies.* New York: Free Press.

———. 1990. *Industrial Organization.* Brookfield, Vt.: Elgar.

Willig, R. 1979. "Multiproduct Technology and Market Structure." *American Economic Review,* May, pp. 346–51.

Wright, J. W. 1984. *The American Almanac of Jobs and Salaries.* New York: Avon.

Wright, J. W., and E. J. Dwyer. 1990. *The American Almanac of Jobs and Salaries.* New York: Avon.

Wright, R. W., and G. A. Pauli. 1987. *The Second Wave: Japan's Global Assault on Financial Services.* New York: St. Martin's Press.

Yago, G. 1991. *Junk Bonds: How High Yield Securities Restructured Corporate America.* New York: Oxford University Press.

Zimmer, S. A., and R. N. McCauley. 1991. "Bank Cost of Capital and International Competition." *Federal Reserve Bank of New York—Quarterly Review,* Winter, pp. 33–59.

Zysk, L. G. 1990. "The Private Placement Market." Working Paper, Villanova University, December.

Author Index

Subject Index